LET JUSTICE ROLL DOWN LIKE WATERS

Biblical Justice Homilies throughout the Year

WALTER J. BURGHARDT, S.J.

PAULIST PRESS
New York / Mahwah, N.J.

also by Walter J. Burghardt, S.J.
published by Paulist Press

GRACE ON CRUTCHES
LOVELY IN EYES NOT HIS
PREACHING: THE ART AND THE CRAFT
SEASONS THAT LAUGH OR WEEP
SIR, WE WOULD LIKE TO SEE JESUS
STILL PROCLAIMING YOUR WONDERS
TELL THE NEXT GENERATION
TO CHRIST I LOOK
DARE TO BE CHRIST
WHEN CHRIST MEETS CHRIST
SPEAK THE WORD WITH BOLDNESS
LOVE IS A FLAME OF THE LORD

Cover design by Tim McKeen

Illustrations by Mary K. Burt

Copyright © 1998 by the New York Province of the Society of Jesus

Library of Congress Cataloging-in-Publication Data

Burghardt, Walter J.
    Let justice roll down like waters : biblical justice homilies throughout the year / by Walter J. Burghardt.
        p.   cm.
    Includes bibliographical references and index.
    ISBN 0-8091-3765-8 (alk. paper)
    1. Christianity and justice—Catholic Church—Sermons. 2. Catholic Church—Sermons. 3. Church year sermons. 4. Occasional sermons. 5. Sermons, American. I. Title.
BR115.J8B87   1998
252'.6—dc21   97-37897
                                                                      CIP

Published by Paulist Press
997 Macarthur Boulevard
Mahwah, New Jersey 07430

Printed and bound in the
United States of America

TABLE OF CONTENTS

FEASTS AND MEMORIALS

WEDDING HOMILIES

MEDLEY

PREFACE

A decade ago, Jesuit social scientist Philip Land opened an article on "Justice" in *The New Dictionary of Theology* (Wilmington, Del.: Glazier, 1987, pp. 548–53) with a quotation from the Hebrew prophet Amos: "Let justice roll down like waters" (5:24). Land continued:

> Prior to Vatican II no Roman Catholic treatise on justice would have begun with scripture. It would have taken its start from the definition of justice—*Suum cuique tradere*—to render to each [what is] one's due and proceeded then to analyze in the light of reason the various relations this involves. With Vatican II but especially the 1971 Synod, Justice in the World, justice becomes a call to the Christian from the God of the two Testaments.

A call to the Christian from the God of the two Testaments. In my project Preaching the Just Word, a significant segment of these five-day retreat/workshops focuses on the justice we insist should be stressed in Christian preaching. Not primarily or exclusively ethical justice, giving each person what he or she deserves—important as this is. Rather biblical justice, that is, fidelity to relationships, to responsibilities, that stem from a covenant. What relationships, what responsibilities? (1) To God: Love God above all else. (2) To people: Love each human being like another self, as if we were standing in their shoes. (3) To the earth: Reverence each facet of God's nonhuman creation as a trace of Trinity, a vestige of the God who shaped it.

Biblical fidelity is, very simply, a question of right relationships. Not only what can be demonstrated from philosophy or has been

1

written into law. Even more importantly, what a covenant demands: for the Jewish believer, his/her covenant with Yahweh; for the Christian, our covenant with God cut in the blood of Christ.

Every genuine homily teases out right relationships: to God, to God's people, to God's earth. And not in the first instance what the human mind at its best can devise. Primarily the relationships God has revealed: from Sinai to the Sermon on the Mount, through prophets from Isaiah to Malachi and in the "signs of the times" that intimate divine designs for God's people.

The present collection, the eleventh set of my sermons published by the Paulist Press, is an effort to demonstrate through actual homilies a long-standing conviction of mine: It is impossible to preach a good homily that is not a justice homily in the biblical understanding of justice. Hence my subtitle, *Biblical Justice Homilies throughout the Year.* An encouraging conviction, for we do not have to go through mental contortions to preach God's Word, to preach justice; we can assure the suspicious among our hearers that it is not a debatable philosophy that is being regurgitated from the pulpit; and we can even, if advisable, expunge the provocative word "justice" from our homiletic vocabulary. Still, a conviction for which we must pay a ceaseless price, for God's Word dare not issue trippingly from our tongues; it calls for serious study, continuing contemplation, even a measure of involvement in a world where a reigning sin is injustice, refusal of responsibility.

Walter J. Burghardt, S.J.
January 1, 1997

FROM
ADVENT
TO
ASCENSION

1
THE LORD IS NEAR!*
Advent Vespers, First Sunday (B)

- Philippians 4:1–7

This first evening of Advent I am of two minds, two hearts. I believe I possess Paul's "peace of God, which surpasses all understanding" (Phil 4:7); and I do "rejoice in the Lord" (v. 4), perhaps not "always," still many an enchanted evening. At the same time I am troubled—troubled even though Paul tells me "Don't worry about anything" (v. 6). In point of fact, I am profoundly worried. At peace and worried for the selfsame reason, Paul's declaration that "The Lord is near" (v. 5). To me, the Lord is near in three ways. Two of those ways bring me peace and joy; the third way causes me to worry. I owe you an explanation.

I

First, the Lord is near not only as Paul used that enigmatic Greek adverb *eggys,* not only because, as he saw it, the Parousia is upon us, Christ is close to returning. That return is still a sobering thought for Christians, even if 19 centuries of waiting reinforce for us Paul's later doubts about its imminence.[1] I would rather extend that pregnant adverb beyond its sense in the Philippians text: The Lord is near because the Lord has actually come.

My point is this: An indispensable facet of Advent, of Advent as "coming," is that Christ has already come. In Advent we are not

*This homily is also available on video tape from Vision Video. It aired as part of the "Great Preachers" series on the Odyssey Channel, 74 Trinity Place, New York, NY 10006.

5

play-acting, pretending that the Lord has not yet appeared, retro-jecting ourselves two millennia and waiting with Israel for the Mes-siah to show himself, for Christ to shout "Surprise!" Even in Advent, even before December 25, we think with, we live with, we worship a Presence, a living Lord. The Lord is near because the Son of God has touched our earth in our flesh, and in the touching our planet was changed at its core, could never be the same again.

Early Christian writers expressed this in bold language we tend to discard as exaggeration. For Hilary of Poitiers "the whole of human-ity *(totus homo)* was in Christ Jesus."[2] Conversely, for Cyril of Alexan-dria Christ dwelt in all "through one."[3] For authors like Athanasius, "the world is so truly one whole that when the Word enters into it and becomes one of our race, all things take on a new dignity."[4]

Theologians have spilled oceans of ink deciphering that insight.[5] This evening let me simply say this: A new oneness, a root unity, between humanity and God was conceived in Nazareth and brought to birth in Bethlehem. True, on the first Advent, when Mary spoke her fiat to God through Gabriel, humanity was not yet the Body of Christ, alive with his life, thrilling to his divine touch. But humanity was ready, poised on the edge of divinity. No longer was flesh simply the tinderbox of sin. If it had not yet begun to live with the life of Christ, it all but quivered with his breath. For the flesh that God took is our flesh; in some genuine sense it is my flesh, your flesh, the flesh of every human being born into this world.

So incredibly "near" was God to all of us that first of Advents. Hence my joy each Advent; Christ is near because Christ has come. Hence my peace each Advent; for in Paul's pregnant phrase, "Christ is our peace" (Eph 2:14).[6]

II

But my Advent joy, my Advent peace, is deeper still. Christ is near because Christ is here. *Is* here. The Incarnation is not simply Nazareth, not only Bethlehem. The Incarnation is now. Advent is not B.C., before Christ; Advent is D.C., the District of Columbia. Advent is not so much a preparation for Christ's coming; more real-istically, it is a deeper penetration into a Christ who never left us.

This is not news to a theological union,[7] hardly headlines to the-ologians budding or already blood-bespattered. Intimate to your the-ology, to your spirituality, is a Real Presence, the whole Christ, our old catechism's "body and blood, soul and divinity." It's a ceaseless reality, not disguised in Advent because Jesus is still a-coming. But still a reality to be realized, to be made ever more real, to be recaptured as the sacrament of the Church's unity. I must recover Augustine telling his neophytes that the priest at Communion reveals what they are when he says, "The body of Christ." To which they respond, "Amen"; they subscribe to his statement. And Augustine goes on:

> ...What is that one bread [of which Paul spoke]? "We many are one body" (1 Cor 10:17). Remember, bread is not made of one grain, but of many. When exorcised, you were as if ground in a mill. When baptized, you were as if besprinkled. When you received the fire of the Holy Spirit, you were as if baked. Be what you see, and receive what you are.... Though [the Apostle] did not say what we were to understand of the chalice, his meaning is sufficiently clear.... Recall, my brothers and sisters, how wine is made. Many grapes hang on the cluster, but the juice of [all] the grapes is mingled together in oneness. Thus did the Lord Christ signify us, will that we should belong to him, consecrate on his table the mystery of our peace and unity.[8]

"The mystery of our peace and unity." Really? In actual living? Or has the Eucharist become the mystery of our warfare and disunity? Surely an Advent meditation on my, on our, relationship to a really present Christ.

If the Real Presence of Christ in the Eucharist is all too obvious, take a real presence of which we are all too oblivious. I mean an insight of Ignatius Loyola. You find it in the last meditation of his Spiritual Exercises, his Contemplation on How to Love Like God. He compares Christ to a laborer, ceaselessly working in everything that is. At work in billions of stars, giving them being; not once for all—at each single moment. At work in D.C.'s floral emblem, the American Beauty rose, giving life to its deep-pink and crimson flowers. At work in the grinning dolphin, giving it sight and hearing, taste and touch and smell. At work in you and me, gracing us with intelligence and love, with the freedom of the children of God.

Yes indeed, the Lord is near because Christ is here. Delightfully near. Not only does he dwell with the Father "in unapproachable light" (1 Tim 6:16); he lives in us "body and blood, soul and divinity"; he labors not in us alone but in every single creature of his imaginative shaping. Hence my joy, hence my peace.

III

So then, here I am in Advent, at peace, with profound joy. And still I am troubled. Why? Because the Lord is terribly near, is all around me. I saw him with a tattered coat and paper-thin shoes, huddling over a warm grate on Wisconsin Avenue. I saw him in a Montgomery County wife badly battered by a drunken husband. I saw him dismissed from a job of a quarter century by a downsizing corporation that had blessed its resigning president with a multi-million-dollar bonus. I saw him in an AIDS-afflicted graduate of Georgetown told by Christians that this is God's avenging plague on homosexuals; in a gay youngster who killed himself after writing in his diary, "Why did you do this to me, God? Please don't send me to hell. I'm really not that bad, am I?" I saw him in a teenage girl, unmarried, trying to deal with an unwanted pregnancy. I saw him sleeping on one of America's streets, like a million other youngsters. I saw him in the 2,350 children in adult jails. I saw him in a child with posttraumatic stress syndrome; she had seen her mother raped and murdered. I saw him in a three-year-old with MS, in a preschool girl incestuously abused, in 16 million children hungry in the richest nation on earth. I saw him in a lad blasted by a shotgun for his Reeboks, in an infant killed in his cradle by young thugs just riding by. I saw him in a *Dead Man Walking*,[9] a murderer saved not from execution but for life with God by a nun who cared.

Yes, Christ has come; the Lord is near, terribly near. And I—I am profoundly troubled. Troubled not only because untold thousands will pass by the crucified Christ, pass by on the other side or without a glance; not only because legislators have approved welfare changes that will add a million children to our bread lines. Troubled because I spend most of my hours thinking and talking, writing and preaching about injustice. Not a bad way for a theologian to live; for in 54 five-day retreat/workshops we have listened to the hurts, the joys, and the hopes of men, women, and children in 26 states, in Australia, Jamaica, and Canada. And yet, I have never consciously hugged an HIV-positive, rarely share a meal with the homeless, think about visiting Children's Hospital but just don't get around to it.

And so I stand in your sight something of a schizophrenic. But perhaps that is all to the good. Paul asks the Philippians, asks me through them, to "let [my] requests be made known to God" (Phil 4:6). And so I do.

Dear near Lord: I am genuinely grateful for your Advent peace, for the joy I experience in your coming. But believe me, I am even more grateful because this Advent evening you trouble me. I need a fresh Advent grace. I need to learn from your life on earth, from your first advent, not only how to think but to feel, not only how to preach but to listen, not only how to talk but to touch. I still need to find your face in the features of every crucified human, no matter how inhuman. If I do not, I shall not experience how incredibly near you actually are.

Washington Theological Union
Washington, D.C.
December 1, 1996

2

TO BE JUST IS TO LOVE
First Week of Lent, Year 1, Monday

- Leviticus 19:1–2, 11–18
- Matthew 25:31–46

My focus this evening is the gospel we are ordained to preach. Not an abstract gospel; the gospel of justice. Because this gospel raises innumerable human hackles, is beset with controversy, I shall begin with a contemporary secular conflict, to illustrate how difficult it is to avoid controversy where an issue is serious and affects people. I shall then move into our own Catholic area of controversy signaled by the passages from Leviticus and Matthew. I shall close with some pertinent (or impertinent) observations about you and me, about preaching what is conflictual, controversial.[1]

I

First, a contemporary secular conflict. In today's issue of *Time* magazine, an article under the rubric of Monuments summarizes 50 years of frustration—frustration in efforts to complete a major memorial in Washington to Franklin Delano Roosevelt, the president who "steadied the nation in depression and commanded it in war."[2] Why frustration? Special interests, different emphases, various ways of looking at the same reality, pressure from historians and other experts.

Examples of the tortured progress? A proposed statue of Eleanor Roosevelt showed her in the New Deal period wearing her famous traveling fur piece. Agonizing cries from animal-rights people; happiness only when the project focused on widowed Eleanor, a delegate to the U.N., and by then she was wearing a cloth coat.

More critically, disabled Americans are up in arms. The three proposed sculptures of F.D.R. "have no sign of a wheelchair, leg braces, cane or crutches, all part of F.D.R.'s support system."[3] But this, say some prominent disabled, was central to his very being. Historians do point out that F.D.R. "veiled his disability (only two pictures of him in a wheelchair are among the 125,000 in the Roosevelt library)." Nevertheless, responds the president of the National Organization on Disability, speaking for almost 50 million disabled Americans, we simply must see the wheelchair, because Roosevelt was "the personification of triumph over adversity, and that made him believable when he told the nation they had nothing to fear but fear itself." His deception of the 30s, perhaps necessary for the politics of the time, should not "be perpetuated in a monument intended for the ages."

II

I relate this controversy because it illustrates vividly how good people, with persuasive reasons, can disagree vehemently on issues that initially seem quite simple and straightforward. Which brings me, by a roundabout route, to Leviticus and Matthew. At first glance, the words of the Lord in both passages seem hardly open to misinterpretation, to controversy. But, probe a bit more deeply.

When the most celebrated command in Leviticus states baldly, "you shall love your neighbor as yourself" (Lev 19:18b), can this be misinterpreted, or interpreted differently with good reason? Read the brief, incisive interpretation in *The New Jerome Biblical Commentary:* The passage "proposes self-love as the measure of charity toward a fellow countryman."[4] Can the Lord be serious? Is this a psychological balancing act? As much or as little as each Israelite loves himself or herself, so much or so little love must he and she bestow on their fellow chosen? Or is the self-love in question the love all Israelites *should* have, even if in point of fact not all do?[5] If so, what in the concrete is that love like?[6] Does it include dying for another? If so, under what conditions? On a lighter note, does it take in wise King Solomon, who "clung in love" to "700 princesses and 300 concubines" (1 Kgs 11:2-3)? Do you agree with John McKenzie that "The word 'neighbor' as commonly used [in the Old Testament] does not signify [just] any other Israelite, but rather the Israelites to whom one is 'near,' those with whom one lives and deals habitually"?[7] Then what about the command later on, "you shall love the alien [who resides with you] as yourself" (Lev 19:34)?

Probably out of a biblical-justice prejudice, I tend to agree with scholars such as Jesuit John R. Donahue: At least when Jesus repeats Leviticus, the command to love others as one's self means to act towards them as if we were in their shoes, act as if they were other selves.

Now what of Matthew 25, the "parable" of the Sheep and the Goats? It is often invoked in discussions on faith and justice. Again at first glance, the narrative is clear enough. When the Son of Man returns as king and summons all the nations of the world, the criterion for judgment will be: How did they treat the king (the Son of Man) when he was hungry or thirsty, a stranger or naked, sick or in prison? "As often as you did this to the least of my brothers and sisters, you did it to me" (Mt 25:40).

Simple enough, no? Jesus identifies himself with suffering men and women; any who care for them will be saved, even if not explicitly motivated by Christ. Simple enough till a major debate arose among scholars. For some, "the least" are missionary disciples, who are to announce the teaching of Jesus "to all the nations" (Mt 28:16–20). The parable is a judgment on those pagan nations that reject the proclamation of the missionary disciples.[8] Fortunately, you can still find support for the traditional interpretation, the "universalistic" reading, in competent scholars. Listen to John Meier:

> ...what does it mean to be watchful and ready and faithful? The answer is that to be watchful means to be able to recognize the Son of Man in all those in need; to be ready means to be loving towards the Son of Man in these people; and to be faithful means to translate this love into active service, into concrete deeds of mercy. This is the criterion by which one enters into or is rejected from eternal life. Therefore we are not dealing with supererogatory works, performed to get "extra points." On these works of mercy, which most would not consider their strict duty, hangs their salvation or damnation.[9]

Or you can take a modified version of the "missionary" position. Sufferings such as hunger and thirst, homelessness and nakedness, sickness and imprisonment are the very kinds of things St. Paul mentions as the lot of the missionary. But "What is done positively for them is not to be limited to them." Justice, the parable reveals, "is constituted by acts of loving-kindness and mercy to those is need; the world will be made 'right' or 'just' when the way the least are treated becomes the norm of action."[10]

III

All of which leads to you and me. For this brief adventure into exegesis was not intended to exploit my scholarly bent. These are not just another set of liturgical readings; they are basic to what you and I are all about. And with God's gracious permission, if not by God's explicit design, these are the liturgical readings for the first full day of Preaching the Just Word. These are the actual readings for the day that has focused on biblical justice. A justice that rises above sheer ethical justice—giving to every man, woman, and child what they deserve, what they have a right to demand, because it is written into law or can be proven from philosophy. A justice that is fidelity—faithfulness to relationships, to responsibilities, that stem from a covenant with God or His Christ. Relationships, responsibilities, to all that is: to God above all else, to people whoever and wherever they are, to the earth that nourishes us the while we ravage and ravish it.

Now in preaching the just word, we must be extraordinarily careful. Careful to preach *God's* word. And to preach God's word and not a word of our own making, we have to *struggle* with Scripture and what it actually says to our situations. As with F.D.R.'s memorial, so with the structure we erect, for ourselves and for our people, from the pulpit and outside it. There is ever so much in social justice that is uncertain, debatable, legitimately controverted. The U.S. bishops' pastoral letter on the economy is a case in point. It was praised for proclaiming the gospel and applying it to problems of contemporary society; it was blasted as "excessively concrete and excessively opinionated."[11] Just how specific the Church and the preacher should be is a matter on which good and wise people can and will disagree.

I can understand why many preachers will not touch justice issues with a ten-foot pole—save possibly for abortion. Still, we may not decline the call. It is not an added burden imposed by special-interest Catholics. Justice in its biblical sense is what Judaism and Christianity are all about: fidelity to God, to people, to the earth. Not to preach this is not to preach the gospel.

True, the pulpit is not the forum for solving complex social, economic, or political issues; not the place to pontificate on welfare and the budget, on crime and punishment. Not even on how the gospel of forgiveness applies to Rwanda and Serbia, to the world's refugees, to parents whose daughter has been gang-raped. The meaningful word here is "pontificate." Where issues or applications are not gospel-clear, I do not preach as if I alone am the trumpet of God. Still, controversy need not render me mute. Capital punishment may not be clearly outlawed in God's written Word, but the "signs of the times" may well compel me to address my people on the question, even add my own conviction and its reasons. Not to end all controversy; simply to stimulate the faithful before me to read more widely, think more profoundly, pray more intensely, love as Jesus loved.

More basic than any single issue is a neuralgic pastoral problem: how to persuade our people, in community, to ask three questions: (1) What are the justice issues in our parish? (2) What resources are available for addressing these issues? (3) What in the concrete shall we do?

Beneath all this, what would God love to see in each of us who preach? Fire in the belly. Our people have a right to glimpse in us what we ask of them: that we love the crucified images of Christ as if we were standing in their shoes. That we agonize over those who hunger and thirst, over the naked and the homeless, over the ill and the imprisoned. That we are leaders in a special sense: We sweat blood and shed tears over controversial issues, issues of justice where good men and women disagree, and still we can preach on them with intelligence and love, with passion and compassion—yes, with a readiness to suffer as Jesus did for our fidelity—because we are faithful to responsibilities that stem from our covenant with him ...from our love.

Bon Secours Spiritual Center
Marriottsville, Maryland
March 6, 1995

3
LISTEN TO HIM!
Second Sunday of Lent (A)

- Genesis 12:1–4a
- 2 Timothy 1:8b–10
- Matthew 17:1–9

Good friends in Christ: As I was preparing to preach today's Gospel to you, I had a strange distraction. I was hoping that you would be puzzled by the Gospel: What connection can there possibly be between this Gospel and Lent, between the Jesus of Mount Tabor,[1] face shining like the sun, clothes dazzlingly white, and the Jesus of Calvary's hill, face bloody from the crown of thorns, stripped of his garments for soldiers to gamble over? For some insight into the puzzle, three points. (1) What is Lent all about? (2) What was Jesus' transfiguration all about? (3) What might those reflections be saying to us during this Lent of 1996?

I

First, what is Lent all about? If I go back to my unspent youth, Lent was the downside of Catholic existence. For the forehead, ashes; for the palate, fish; for the face, gloom; for church, the color purple. The stress was on giving up. If sin was not in the picture, then whatever else was sweet, pleasurable, delightful to the senses. Give it up! Why? To express our fellow feeling with Jesus sweating blood in Gethsemane's garden, condemned to a criminal's cross, whipped like a dog, nailed to a tree between two thieves. Our sympathy for a dying Jesus.

With age and theology came deeper understanding, some wisdom. It is not quite true that Lent is for dying, Easter for rising. The whole of Lent is an initiation—a progressively more intense initiation

15

into the paschal mystery. And what is the paschal mystery? The dying/rising of Jesus. Not just his dying; his dying/rising. It is indeed Jesus' journey to Jerusalem, his death march. But a death march that is ceaselessly bringing life. Life through death; in the very dying, rich life. That is why, on September 14, the Church celebrates a significant feast: the *triumph* of the cross. The cross itself is victory.

What sort of dying is it that can bring forth life? Not simply our last earthly breath leading to resurrection. No, all through our earth-bound living, from the baptism that plunges us into Christ, the Christian is dying. Dying to what? To sin and to self. Dying to the sins of our own fashioning and to "the sin of the world," all the weight and burden of human transgression from Adam to Antichrist. Dying to our selves, a self-emptying like Jesus' own—the Jesus who, Paul tells us in an early liturgical hymn,

> though his condition was divine,
> did not regard equality with God
> as something to be exploited for selfish gain,
> but emptied himself,
> taking the condition of a slave,
> taking on the likeness of human beings.
> And being found in human form,
> he lowered himself further still,
> becoming obedient unto death,
> even to death on a cross.

(Phil 2:6–8)

Think of it: Jesus letting go of his yesterdays—letting go of Nazareth and his mother; letting go of his twelve closest friends, from John to Judas; letting go of every burdened man and woman he had touched with his healing; letting go of life itself, his very human living. So we too: letting go of our yesterdays—the pains and the pleasures, the triumphs and the setbacks, so as to live more fully today. Not forgetting them; simply not living in them.

It's our first reading: Abraham, at 75, commanded to leave country and kindred, his father's house, journey to a land he knew not. It too was a kind of dying, refusing to live in the past. For, as the New Testament Letter to the Hebrews tells us, "By faith Abraham obeyed when he was called to set out for a place he was to receive as an inheritance; and he set out, not knowing where he was going" (Heb 11:8).

Not something negative, this dying to sin and self. It is a ceaseless turning to Christ, a day-by-day struggle to reshape ourselves into the image of the Jesus who, John's Gospel tells us, "showed his love for [us] to the very end" (Jn 13:1), to his last dying gasp. It is his life we die into, so that, as Paul exclaimed, "It is no longer I who live, but it is Christ who lives in me" (Gal 2:20).

Such is Christian Lent: by dying to sin and self, living the life of Christ. Not external imitation: wearing Jesus' sandals, speaking his Aramaic. No, Christ within me.

II

Turn now to Jesus' transfiguration. What was it all about? In essence, it is a vision. Peter, James, and John are granted a foretaste of "who he really is and what he will be in God's kingdom."[2] It is a preview of his resurrection. But why do they need this? Because they are journeying with Jesus to Jerusalem. Because not long before this, Matthew tells us, "Jesus began to show his disciples that he must go to Jerusalem and undergo great suffering at the hands of the elders and chief priests and scribes, and be killed.... And Peter took him aside and began to rebuke him, saying, 'God forbid it, Lord! This must never happen to you'" (Mt 16:21–22). Peter was scandalized. Perhaps the other disciples as well.

To give them courage, to lessen the scandal, Peter, James, and John get a preview of Jesus in glory. With him they see Moses, representing the Mosaic law, and Elijah, representing the Hebrew prophets. They are "conversing with him" (Mt 17:3) because he is their fulfillment, he brings the law and the prophets to their high point. The revelation reaches its climax when a bright cloud envelops them, the symbol of God's presence. The disciples do not see God, but they do hear God's powerful voice: "This is my Son, the Beloved." Look at him; see God's unique Son; what you see is what the future holds in store for him and for you.

But there is more, a brief, urgent command, "Listen to him!" Why urgent? Because very soon after the vision, while they are descending from the mountain, the Son they have just seen in glory says to them, "The Son of Man is about to suffer" (v. 12). He is not only God's Son; he is the Suffering Servant, the servant of whom Isaiah predicted:

> He was despised and rejected by others;
> a man of suffering and acquainted with infirmity....
> He was wounded for our transgressions,
> crushed for our iniquities;

upon him was the punishment that made us whole,
and by his bruises we are healed.

(Isa 53:3–5)

"Listen to him," God commands. You have rejoiced to see
God's Son in glory; let that strengthen you when you see God's Servant in suffering.

III

Turn now to...you and me. The next three weeks, the next three
Sundays, you will be mulling over three powerful Gospels—Gospels
that will ask you three probing questions. The Gospels? (1) A thirsty
Jesus and the Samaritan woman at the well: "Give me [water to] drink"
(Jn 4:7). (2) The man born blind: "How were your eyes opened?" (Jn
9:10). (3) Lazarus raised from the dead: "Everyone who lives and
believes in me will never die" (Jn 11:26). The questions? (1) Where do
you thirst? (2) Where are *you* blind? (3) Where are *you* dead?

Three gut-tearing questions. In these three Gospels you will see
three symbols closely associated with Christian baptism: water, sight,
and new life.[3] Symbols—signs that say something more profound
than appears on the surface. You see, Jesus was not primarily interested in a cup of cold water, in 20–20 vision, in a few more years for
Lazarus in Bethany. What Jesus brought to the woman with five husbands and a live-in partner was the water of divine life. The sight
Jesus gave to the blind man was expressed in the healed man's confession, "I do believe, Lord" (Jn 9:38), "perhaps the baptismal confession required in the Johannine Church."[4] Lazarus back from the
grave symbolized what Jesus took our flesh to tell us: "Jesus comes *to
give life that cannot be touched by death,* so that those who believe in
him will never die (11:26)."[5]

But those three Gospels are not today's homily. What today's
Gospel should do for you is what the transfiguration was expected to
do for Peter, James, and John. I mean, give you courage on your
journey to Jerusalem. Courage to face squarely those agonizing questions to come: your thirst, your blindness, the death in your life.

How can Jesus' transfiguration communicate that courage? If
you focus on the words of Jesus' Father from the cloud, "This is my
Son.... Listen to him!" (Mt 17:5). Two imperatives. First, look! See
the paradox. See in the Suffering Servant God's only Son, God not
by poetry but as truly God as is the Father, God taking your flesh and

mine out of love, the most remarkable love in human history, love for you as if only you existed. Make today's second reading your own: God's saving grace "has now been revealed through the appearing of our Savior Christ Jesus, who abolished death and brought life and immortality to light through the gospel" (2 Tim 1:10).

Not only look; listen! Jesus is speaking to you, I assure you. Usually not in a vision—Guadalupe, Lourdes, Fatima. Speaking to you whenever God's Word is proclaimed to you; for the words of Jesus fasting in the wilderness are crucial today: "No one lives on bread alone, but on every word that comes from the mouth of God" (Mt 4:4). Speaking to you in the events TV funnels into your living room: apartheid in South Africa, fratricide in Northern Ireland and peace in Palestine, rape in Rwanda, starvation in the sub-Sahara, refugees watering the ways of the world with their tears. Speaking to you through your own experiences: a newborn baby or a child with Down's syndrome, a wedding or a funeral, diverticula or depression, hostility at home or crisis in the Church, a job you love or a job you've lost—whatever.

Argue with Jesus if you must; challenge God's ways as Job did; face Jesus jaw to jaw; beg God as Jesus did in Gethsemane, "Father, if you are willing, remove this cup from me" (Lk 22:42). But please, listen. Listen as young Samuel did: "Speak, Lord, for your servant is listening" (1 Sam 3:9, 10); not "Speak, Lord, and your servant will think it over." Listen the way Helen Keller, blind, deaf, mute, listened to Annie Sullivan—as if your life depends on it; it does—your eternal life, your life in Christ. Listen, if you can, the way our Lady listened to an angel: "Here am I, the servant of the Lord; let it happen to me as you say" (Lk 1:38).

Very simply, dear friends: As you journey with Jesus to your own Jerusalem, listen to him. It may not be fun, but it will be exciting. In any case, it sure beats giving up M&Ms.

Holy Trinity Church
Washington, D.C.
March 3, 1996

4
PREACH THE JUST WORD WITHOUT FEAR?
Second Week of Easter, Year 1, Monday

- Acts 4:23–31
- John 3:1–8

Three years ago, almost to the day, I preached to Michigan priests on today's passage from Acts.[1] On that occasion I stressed the source of the apostles' boldness, the Holy Spirit who plays so prominent a part in the early chapters of Acts, the Spirit whom Paul presents as an energizer, a Spirit of power, the Spirit of whom he declares, "My speech and my proclamation were not with plausible words of wisdom, but with a demonstration of the Spirit and of power, so that your faith might rest not on human wisdom but on the power of God" (1 Cor 2:4–5).

That homily I do not retract. I still insist that "Preaching the just word is not *in the first instance* a matter of societal competence, economic expertise, political persuasion, of posture and gesture, assonance and resonance, of a heroic style, a rich vocabulary, a presence without peer. In the last analysis, what will turn our people on is the Holy Spirit—the Spirit in us and the Spirit in them."[2]

Consequently, I commend that homily to you, commend rather the Holy Spirit who pours God's love into human hearts (cf. Rom 5:5). But this evening I shall focus on another powerful motivating force, a motive that should rack the heart of every Christian who wants to live the new commandment of Jesus, "Love one another as I have loved you" (Jn 15:12). I shall (1) unload on you some frightening facts about the society that surrounds us, (2) draw some conclusions for your preaching and mine, and (3) end with one pertinent, or impertinent, question.[3]

I

First, some frightening facts. Limited by time, let's stay with our children. Up-to-date statistics. Every day in this land of the free, this richest country on earth, 3 children die from child abuse, 15 from guns, 27 from poverty. Every day 95 babies die before their first birthday, 564 are born to women who had late or no prenatal care, 788 are born at less than 5 pounds, 8 ounces. Each day 1,340 teenagers give birth. Each school day 2,217 teenagers drop out of school. 2,350 children are in adult jails. Every day 2,699 infants are born into poverty, 3,356 are born to unmarried women. Every day 8,189 children are reported abused or neglected, 100,000 are homeless, 135,000 bring guns to school, 1,200,000 latchkey children come home to a house in which there is a gun.[4] If numbers leave you cold, listen to a single voice, eight-year-old Gail:

> In my neighborhood there is a lot of shooting and three people got shot. On the next day when I was going to school I saw a little stream of blood on the ground. One day after school me and my mother had to dodge bullets. I was not scared.
>
> There is a church and a school that I go to in my neighborhood. There are robbers that live in my building, they broke into our house twice. There are rowhouses in my neighborhood and a man got shot, and he was dead. On another day I saw a boy named Zak get shot. By King High School Susan Harris got shot and she died. It was in the newspaper. When me and my mother was going to church we could see the fire from the guns being shot in 4414 building. I was not scared. In my neighborhood there are too many fights. I have never been in a fight before....
>
> I know these are really bad things, but I have some good things in my neighborhood. Like sometimes my neighborhood is peaceful and quiet and there is no shooting. When me and my mother and some friends go to the lake we have a lot of fun....
>
> I believe in God and I know one day we will be in a gooder place than we are now.[5]

II

From such facts, some conclusions for your preaching and mine. First, there is indeed a problem of justice here. Ethical justice, to begin with. Children in the United States are not getting what they deserve, what they have a strict right to claim from their elders, from their elected representatives, from us. No man or woman with a pound of compassion can look at our children—one out of four growing up below the poverty line—and not feel ashamed. No priest with a heart of flesh can mount the pulpit Sunday after Sunday wondering what human tragedy, what inhuman indecency, to preach about.

Justice indeed. But not simply, not primarily, what children can demand from us because they are human persons. Even more crucial, what Christ demands of us because we are Christians. Because, for us, justice is not, in the first instance, a matter of human deserving. The justice that cries out to us from God's inspired Word, from the prophets of old Israel and the prophet that is Jesus, is summed up in one word: fidelity. Fidelity to what? To relationships, to responsibilies that stem from our covenant with Christ, a covenant cut in his blood.

What are those responsibilities? Fidelity to God: Love God above all else, with all our heart and soul, all our mind and strength. Fidelity to our sisters and brothers: Love each human being as another "I," another self, as if we were standing in their shoes. Fidelity to the earth that nourishes us: Cherish each "thing" God has made, has allowed us to make. Treat God's creation with reverence. Mother Teresa summed it up simply, yet profoundly: God does not ask me to be successful, but to be faithful.

When we preach to our people about children, therefore, what we preach with boldness is what children can demand of them not simply because this is what the children deserve, but because this is what Christians must do to remain Christian, to be shaped like Christ, to be faithful, studded with fidelity.

Second conclusion: the prayer of the apostles. "And now, Lord, grant to your servants to speak your word with all boldness" (Acts 4:29). Boldness—in Greek, *parresia*. It's a fascinating word in Scripture. It means not only to speak plainly, openly, concealing nothing, passing over nothing. It means to speak, to act, with courage, with confidence, without fear, especially in the presence of persons of high rank, persons with power.

It is courage in the face of human persons. That is why Paul can write from prison asking the Christians of Ephesus to pray for him, "so that when I speak, [I may] make known the mystery of the gospel with boldness [fearlessly, with freedom]—the gospel for which I am an ambassador in chains" (Eph 6:19-20). A prisoner who speaks in utter freedom.

It is also confidence before God. That is why the Letter to the Hebrews can declare that, because we have a high priest who can sympathize with our weaknesses, who was tempted as we are, we have good reason to "approach the throne of grace with boldness [with joyous confidence], so that we may receive mercy and find grace to help in time of need" (Heb 4:16).

Such, my brothers in Christ, is the grace you and I need these perilous days: to preach the just word with boldness, with confidence, without fear, with a sense of inner freedom. It is not easy. The very word "justice" evokes resentment in the pews. It triggers rough associations: higher taxes to keep lazy folk on welfare; serial rapists escaping capital punishment with the help of bleeding hearts; legal but undeserved affirmative action; immigrants legal and illegal educated and medicated on my hard-earned money. Only God's grace can keep a priest preaching when eyes are angry, lips contemptuous, ears plugged.

III

Third, a question, pertinent perhaps, possibly impertinent. Boldness is not a synonym for brashness, for rashness. For your meditation, and mine as well, would it be brash, rash, or simply Christian boldness to preach what the president of the Children's Defense Fund, Marian Wright Edelman, has written?

> If we are not supporting a child we brought into the world as a father or as a mother with attention, time, love, discipline, money, and the teaching of values....
>
> If we are using and abusing tobacco, alcohol, cocaine, or other drugs while telling our children not to....
>
> If we are spending more time worrying about our children's clothes than about their character....
>
> If we are spending more time on our children's recreation than reading, on their dance steps than their discipline....
>
> If we are more worried about our children's earnings than their honesty...and about their status than their service....
>
> If we think it's someone else's responsibility to teach our children values, respect, good manners, and work and health habits....
>
> If...we believe that the Sermon on the Mount, Ten Commandments, and the Koran pertain only to one day worship but not to Monday through Sunday home, professional, and political life....
>
> If we'd rather talk the talk than walk the walk to the voting booth, school board meetings, political forums, and congregation and community meetings to organize community and political support for our children....
>
> If our children learn racial slurs from us and think that race rather than God's grace determines our sanctity and worth....

If we are not voting and not holding political leaders accountable for voting relative pennies for Head Start and pounds for the defense budget, and for opposing welfare for poor mothers and children while
protecting welfare for rich farmers and corporate executives....

If we think being American is about how much we can get rather than
how much we can give, and that things and not thought, cash and not
character make the person...

Then we are a part of the problem rather than the solution.[6]

My brothers in Christ the priest: Against the fear that is only
human, pray aloud with me the prayer of the apostles: "And now,
Lord, grant to your servants to speak your word with all boldness."

National Shrine of Our Lady of the Snows
Belleville, Illinois
April 24, 1995

5
CHRIST IS ALIVE?
Third Sunday of Easter (A)

- Acts 2:14, 22–33
- 1 Peter 1:17–21
- Luke 24:13–35

Today's Gospel is storyteller Luke at his best. A seemingly chance meeting somewhere between Jerusalem and Emmaus; a short course on the Old Testament; a breaking of bread that Luke sees as Eucharist; a hurried return to Jerusalem to exchange resurrection stories with the Eleven. Almost too much for a single homily. Permit me to focus on two facets of that story. I mean the Emmaus incident as it speaks to our worship and to our belief: specifically, (1) our Eucharistic Christ and (2) our confession that Christ is alive.

I

First, our Catholic worship, our Eucharistic Christ. I mean concretely this community of ours gathered here right now. You see, there are three moments in today's Gospel that foreshadow three stages where Christ is particularly present in our Eucharistic liturgy.

The first moment? Cleopas and his companion starting the seven miles between Jerusalem and Emmaus. Recall the striking words of Jesus, "Where two or three are gathered in my name, I am there among them" (Mt 18:20). The two disciples had indeed come together in Jesus' name. Yes, they were a discouraged duet: "We had hoped..." (Lk 24:21). They thought him dead; and so their chins were drooping, their feet were dragging. Still, they were talking about him; they had loved him, still loved him. And so the Jesus who lived in their hearts appeared before their faces. Even though they did not recognize him, he was there—the risen Christ.

A similar reality transpired as soon as you and I gathered together here. When we sang the gathering song, David Haas's resounding "God Is Alive," Christ our Lord was there—alive. Not only in each of us as individuals; he was there in a special way in the community, in our coming together. "Where two or three [of you] are gathered in my name, I am there among [you]." It would be tragic if we too did not recognize him in our coming together, were not aware of him, did not experience his presence, did not feel him there; if we just sang away the way we sing in the shower. No, in our very gathering God is alive, God is here.

The second moment? Cleopas and his companion listening as the risen Christ "interpreted to them" what "all the Scriptures" said about him (v. 27): the Pentateuch, the prophets—a seven-mile course on the Old Testament and the Messiah. Listening not to an academic lecture but to God's scenario for salvation: life through death. "Was it not necessary that the Christ should suffer these things and [then] enter into his glory?" (v. 26). Little wonder their "hearts were burning" (v. 32). A living Christ, the Son of God, was interpreting the Word of God for them.

A similar reality transpired a few moments ago. Vatican II phrased it simply, yet startlingly: Christ "is present in his word, since it is he himself who speaks when the holy Scriptures are read in the church."[1] Do I believe that? If I do, do I listen the way Cleopas and his fellow disciple listened, the way young Mary listened to God's angel, the way the Samaritan woman listened to Jesus at Jacob's well, the way the blind man listened as Jesus muddied his eyes, the way the crowds listened while their stomachs growled from hunger? When Scripture is proclaimed, God should come alive, for the risen Christ is speaking to us.

The third moment? Jesus "took bread, blessed it, broke it, and gave it to them" (v. 30). Luke shows us the risen Christ doing exactly what he did when he multiplied the loaves, exactly what he did at the Last Supper.[2] "Then," exclaims Luke, "then their eyes were opened, and they recognized him" (v. 31).

A similar reality will transpire not too many minutes from now. The same Christ Jesus, hiding not only his Godhead but his humanity in what looks like bread, feels like bread, tastes like bread, will pillow his head in your hand, on your tongue. The ever-burning question: Do I recognize him? Oh, not abstractly, with some gigantic mind leaps. Do I thrill to the presence of the God-man alive in me? Thrill to an incredible affirmation, "This is my body [and it is] given for you" (Lk 22:19)?

Our gathering; our listening; our eating and drinking. Our God is alive; our Christ is here. One question: How alive am *I*?

II

Second, our belief, our confession that Christ is alive. The two disciples on the road to Emmaus give us insight into a problem that troubles just about every age, each period of Christian history—can trouble you and me. Bear bravely with Burghardt while he sets the problem up.

When Jesus joined the two disciples, walked with them, they did not recognize him. Why not, if they had been his disciples, had walked with him before Calvary? Because in his risen state there was something different about him. Exactly what, we do not know, but a difference in the risen Jesus that made him a stranger in their eyes. Only when he broke the bread "were their eyes opened" (v. 31), opened by God.

They were not the only ones. Remember how Mary Magdalene at the tomb mistook Jesus for the gardener? Why, when she knew him and loved him? Only when Jesus called her by name did she recognize him. Not from his voice; he had already spoken to her, asked her why she was weeping, and his voice had done nothing to reveal him. No, she exclaimed "Teacher!" by a special grace, an illumination from God. Remember how the risen Jesus stood on the beach of the Sea of Tiberias, "but the disciples did not know that it was Jesus" (Jn 21:4)? Only John recognized him, only "that disciple whom Jesus loved." Only John declared, "It is the Lord" (Jn 21:7). Why not Peter and Thomas, Nathanael and James, in the same boat with him, the same distance away? Not glaucoma. To recognize the risen Jesus called for a special grace, a light from above. In the profound expression of St. Thomas Aquinas, the apostles "after the resurrection saw with the eyes of faith the living Christ whose death they knew as an evident fact."[3]

Now for you and me. In preparation for Easter, *Time* magazine's cover stressed "The Search for Jesus."[4] "Some scholars," the cover reads, "are debunking the Gospels. Now traditionalists are fighting back. What are Christians to believe?" Therein lies a disturbing implication. If *scholars* disagree about the historical accounts of Jesus' crucifixion and resurrection, how can the ordinary Christian *believe* Christ was crucified and rose from the dead?

Now biblical scholarship is important. Without it we would be far less knowledgeable about what happened from the lush garden of Eden to the rocky island of Patmos, about the bittersweet history of the Jewish people and the astonishing activities of the early Christians. It is scholarship that has filled libraries with histories of the Jews, with lives of Christ, with thousands of commentaries on the books of the Bible.

And still, no scholar has ever *believed* in Jesus' resurrection because he or she could prove the tomb was actually empty and the disciples had not taken Jesus' body away. On Easter Sunday, neither you nor I cry "Christ is risen" because Catholic scholars have proved the resurrection actually took place. Even if the *Time* article convinces you that history cannot demonstrate for certain that Jesus rose, you do not retreat to a prepared religious dugout where you can mutter in abject defeat, "Well, I believe it anyway."

The science called history cannot give me belief. It can take me to the edge of belief, persuade me that the most sensible reaction to the historical facts is that Jesus actually rose from the dead. But that is not faith, that is not belief. Faith is a gift, a gift only God can give, a gift that enables me to affirm without hesitation, on God's word, that Jesus is God's Son in human flesh, that he actually died for us, that he came to life again, that he is now gloriously alive, the source of every grace by which you and I live his life.

I refuse to apologize for faith, treat it as a foxhole while the bullets of biblical research are flying over my head. Faith is a gift of God, and for all the half century I have reveled in scholarship, a loving faith is the most precious gift God has given me. Most precious because a loving faith means God—Father, Son, and Holy Spirit—deep within me, enlightening my mind, strengthening my will, inflaming my heart. It is with such faith that our hearts too can burn within us if we let the Lord Jesus open the Scriptures to us pilgrims, speak to us as we walk with him. It is with such faith that as we worship here we can recognize the God-man, the risen Jesus, Christ gloriously alive, in the broken Bread, respond to "The body of Christ" with a doubt-shattering "Amen!"

Our gathering; our listening; our eating and drinking. Not only is our *God* alive; you and I are alive. Not by human learning; by God's gracious giving. So then, my sisters and brothers in Christ, when we leave this liturgy, let's leave leaping with laughter. Why? Because our Easter gift is not a springtime egg rolling,[5] not a child's fuzzy bunny, but the grace won on Calvary to sing "God is alive." To sing that and mean it means that *you and I* are alive—alive with the very life of the risen Christ.

So then, the critical question: Am I still on the road to Emmaus, chin drooping, feet dragging, afraid that Jesus may, just possibly, still be dead? Or am I rushing from Emmaus, like Cleopas and his companion, chin up, feet dancing, to tell my little world "The Lord has risen indeed" (v. 34)?[6]

Holy Trinity Church
Washington, D.C.
April 21, 1996

6
YOU ARE A CHOSEN RACE....
Fifth Sunday of Easter (A)

- Acts 6:1–7
- 1 Peter 2:4–9
- John 14:1–12

We Catholics are living in difficult times. Difficult precisely as a church, as a community convinced that Christ is, as today's Gospel insists, the way to the Father because he is the truth and the life (Jn 14:6). Difficult times because so much divides the Catholic community, pits us one against another. Difficult because TV portrays and newspapers headline not what makes us one but what severs us: contraception and Communion in the hand, prochoice and pro-life, male domination and the threat of excommunication in Nebraska. Not what is attractive about us but what scandalizes: priest pedophiles and Catholics clawing one another like cats on a hot tin roof. More humorously, a recent article spoke of the Church as having "more varieties and quirks than a contemporary bagel shop."[1]

In this context I recommend a breathing spell, a Sunday evening time out, a look at the broader, richer picture. And the First Epistle of Peter offers just such a vision. In the midst of Christians harassed by local populations, converts anxious about being aliens and strangers in a hostile world, an inspired writer (who may possibly be the apostle Peter[2]) cries out to them and to us: "You are a chosen race, a royal priesthood,[3] a holy nation, God's own people" (1 Pet 2:9). First, a word on the four titles of honor; second, a word on the broader perspective these titles provide over and above what is so human in our Christian existence; third, the demand these titles lay on all of us, despite our differences.

I

First, the four titles of honor. Here you have four Old Testament titles of Israel that Peter applies to the new household of God, to indicate its unique dignity, four titles that spell out the Christian vocation,

First title: You are "a chosen race." It is a title God gave to Israel through Isaiah: "my chosen people, the people whom I formed for myself so that they might declare my praise" (Isa 43:20–21). The significant word here is "chosen." As with Israel, so with us: The Christian body, the community of all who claim Christ for Savior, is not a community of chance. Basic to Christian existence is a divine election. The Church is a community called; and each of us has been called by God to share the life of that community. You and I are what the New Testament Letter to the Hebrews designates simply as "those who are called" (Heb 9:15), called by God. You and I can apply to ourselves what God said to the early Israelites through the mouth of Moses:

> It was not because you were more numerous than any other people that the Lord set His heart on you and chose you—for you were the fewest of all peoples. It was because the Lord loved you and kept the oath that He swore to your ancestors, that the Lord has brought you out with a mighty hand, and redeemed you from the house of slavery....
>
> (Deut 7:7–8)

Second title: You are "a royal priesthood." The meaning goes back to an earlier verse: "Like living stones, you yourselves are being built[4] into a spiritual house, to be a holy priesthood, to offer spiritual sacrifices acceptable to God through Jesus Christ" (2:5). A holy priesthood. It is an inspired declaration of a Catholic truth all too easily forgotten: All of us are priests. Why? Because all of us are on mission to reconcile the world to God in Christ. Because all of us offer the Church's central act of worship, the Sacrifice of the Mass. Because in that Sacrifice we offer not only Jesus but our very selves. If a small minority are ordained to lead the people in sacrifice, the sacrifice is still "of the people, for the people, by the people." Never forget a momentous monosyllable in the Mass: "we." This bread, O God, this cup *we* offer to you.

Third title: You are "a holy nation." Holy. Not simply or primarily pious, prayerful. Holy means you and I are consecrated to the Lord—as truly as the baby Jesus was consecrated to the Lord in the temple at Jerusalem, "designated as holy to the Lord" (Lk 2:22–23). Oh yes, we are expected to live holily, in a holy manner, but because of an even more basic holiness, because individually and as a community we are set apart for God. For this reason we can say we are a sinful people and still a holy people, for even in our sinfulness we are a people consecrated to God.

Fourth title: You are "God's own people." Literally, the Greek says you are "a people that has become (God's own) possession." How? Peter told us earlier on: "You know that you were ransomed from the futile ways inherited from your ancestors, not with perishable things like silver or gold, but with the precious blood of Christ" (1:18–19). God has bought us with the blood of Christ. Whether we like it or not, we belong to God.

Can you think of a higher calling, a more remarkable existence? A people chosen by God, a people purchased for God's own possession by the blood of God's Son, a sinful people always holy because always consecrated to God, a people that offers to God in sacrifice not only the Christ who died for us but our very selves alive for God: "This is my body [and it is] given for you." Can you think of a higher calling, a more remarkable existence? And it is yours. You are that people.

II

So much for the titles themselves; so much for your calling and mine. Now, what is it that these titles do for us? A single verse from a single New Testament book does not solve our practical problems, will not reconcile our warring factions, will not prove an instant solution to poverty and violence, to abortion and assisted suicide. What that verse should do is put our problems in a broader perspective, help us realize that our church is not just another top-flight club we have joined—the Congressional Country Club, the Elks, the Knights of Columbus, the Daughters of the American Revolution, maybe even the Jesuits!

Admit it: As a church, as a community, we are human, at times touchingly, at times irritatingly, at times scandalously. We believe and we doubt, we hope and we despair, we love sisters and brothers as Jesus did and we tear into one another like the infamous Hatfields and McCoys. It is the human face of the Church, a face that will not disappear till Christ comes again. And yet, it would be tragic if in focusing on the human we forgot that we are part and parcel of something divine. Not divine the way we say it loosely, "My dear, you look simply divine." No, literally divine.

How can this be? Go back to Peter. (1) Our call to be Christians is literally divine because it is *God* who has brought you and me into the Catholic community; God has chosen us. The words of Jesus to his apostles at the Last Supper can be touched to you and me: "You did not choose me; I chose you" (Jn 15:16). Others may have helped: parents, teachers, friends, a priest or sister. But unless God had chosen us, had graced us, none of us would be part of God's "chosen race." (2) Unless God had empowered us, none of us could offer the priestly Sacrifice so central to our worship. (3) Unless God had graced you and me with God's love, from the waters of baptism to the Bread of Life, none of us would be holy with the holiness Peter is praising, part of a community consecrated to the Lord. (4) Only because God's Son, truly God, died for us are we "God's own possession."

III

High-sounding stuff, you say? I agree. But there it is; there the Christian is, in God's own Book. And there is more—more in that single sentence, words that dictate what these titles demand of the Christian. Why this fantastic calling, these remarkable gifts? "In order that you may proclaim the mighty acts of [the God] who called you out of darkness into [God's] marvelous light" (v. 9b). The point is, Christians have not been chosen by God, have not been graced with gifts beyond believing, simply to admire our own beauty—like the classical youth Narcissus, who fell in love with his own reflection in the water of a fountain, pined away in sheer desire, and was changed into the lovely flower that bears his name. Like all of God's gifts, these come with a price tag. They are given...to be given.

Proclaim the mighty acts of God? Yes, bear witness to the gospel. Here words are indeed important. We may resent the Jehovah's Witnesses, shrug off the Pentecostals; but they do bear vocal witness, they do proclaim what they believe. What I preach from a pulpit reaches an infinitesimal number of Americans; what 60 million Catholics preach could transform a country Martin Luther King Jr. once said might be on its way to hell.

Strong words? Too strong? Not when in the world's richest nation one of every four children grows up in inhuman poverty, and the younger you are the poorer you are. Not when each year in the most compassionate of nations 1.5 million unborn are forcibly kept from seeing the light of day. Not when a culture that abhors violence sees a child injured or killed by a gun every 36 seconds, the rate of teenage suicides tripling in 30 years, children preparing not their futures but their funerals. Not when doctors committed to life are allowed by law to take life away, to deal out death, to assist in self-destruction.

How can God's own people preach the mighty acts of God? One answer, highly practical today: by preaching life. Not primarily with our lips; more powerfully by our lives. How? If our world sees that we Catholics respect all life. All human life, of course: life in the womb and life near the tomb, enemy life and life on death row, life on every gold coast and life in rat-infested tenements. Mighty acts of God, for each life, bar none, has been shaped in God's image; and God's image can be disfigured but never totally destroyed. Mighty acts of God, because God's own Son died for each without exception.

Nonhuman life as well—if our world sees that we Catholics reverence the earth that is ceaselessly a "mighty act" of God. I mean the earth that sustains us, the earth without which we would perish, the earth we have for centuries raped and ravaged. I mean the things of God that our Catholic tradition insists bear the trace of God's creating hand, the earth God looked upon at creation's birth and marveled, "It is very good" (Gen 1:31).

People of God's possession, people of God's love: Over 1500 years ago Pope Leo the Great exhorted his people in a Christmas sermon, "Christian, recognize your dignity!"[5] Not your own doing; God's gracious giving. And still it is yours. Live that dignity; recognize that dignity in others. Then you can disagree to your hearts' content—with the courtesy that is characteristic of the Christian, because it is the courtesy of Christ.

Holy Trinity Church
Washington, D.C.
May 5, 1996

7

JESUS' ASCENSION IS NOT A HEAD TRIP
Seventh Week of Easter, Year 2, Monday

- Acts 19:1–8
- John 16:29–33

Between Ascension and Pentecost I find it difficult to preach on the Gospel. Especially John's Gospel. Take today's passage. Five verses, eight sentences, totally without context. And the content? Discouragingly broad. The disciples now find Jesus "speaking plainly," believe he knows everything, believe he "came forth from God." Jesus predicts that they will be scattered, probably each to his own home,[1] will "leave [him] all alone"; but he is never alone, for the Father is always with him. His promises, he insists, promises of the Father's help, have been uttered so that in him they "may find peace." Affliction, suffering, persecution will come, but victory will be theirs because Jesus is the one who conquers.... Spare us, O Lord!

My homiletic salvation? Putting all this in context. So then, three swift questions: (1) What is this all-important context? (2) Why is that context so significant? (3) In light of the context, what might the text be telling *us*? Sounds like a lecture? I hope not; simply fresh insight into a critical Christian reality, into Christ for today, Christ for the people to whom we are privileged to preach,[2] Christ for you and me.

I

First, the context. Not so much the historical context. After all, these words of Jesus were spoken before his crucifixion. I mean the liturgical context. And what is that? Very simply, the Ascension. Celebrated by some last Thursday, by others yesterday, but dominating liturgy and life this week.

35

But once again I had to ask myself: What in reality is Jesus' "ascension"? No difficulty defining it: Ascension is Jesus' return to his Father in glory. But when did that take place? St. Jerome told us 1600 years ago: "The Lord's Day, the day of the Resurrection, the day of Christians...is also called the Lord's Day because on it the Lord ascended as a victor to the Father."[3] It happened the first Easter. Jesus did not have to wait 40 days before he "ascended" to his Father. His ascension is not something distinct from his resurrection. His resurrection *is* his ascension.

Then why the feast? It celebrates Jesus' *final visible* leave-taking from the community of his followers. Only quite late in life did I realize that Jesus did not spend 40 days on earth after his resurrection. Recall how the Gospels speak of his "appearances." He always appears suddenly from somewhere—exactly where, we are never told. And he never "hangs around," always disappears somewhere—exactly where, we are not told. The fact is, he appears from glory. That is why he looks different—from his resurrection on. That is why Mary Magdalene mistook him for a gardener. That is why none of the fishermen save John recognized him on the shore (John by a special grace). Luke did not invent the "ascension" as something distinct from Jesus' resurrection. He simply separated aspects of the paschal mystery to make it more understandable. As Fitzmyer put it in a rare moment of scholarly humor, Luke wanted "to 'eff' the ineffable."[4]

Simply, what happened the first Easter Sunday morning was resurrection/ascension. Jesus' return to life *was* his return to his Father in glory. Forty days later he appeared out of glory to take his final leave from his dearest friends.

II

Which leads into my second point. Why was that final visible leave-taking so important that Luke used apocalyptic stage-props to describe it: a final blessing on the assembly, Jesus lifted up, a cloud taking him out of sight (Lk 24:50–51; Acts 1:9), movement through the heavens or the celestial spheres (Eph 4:10)? Because from that point on, something new, something incomparably rich, would enter Christian living. It is "the holy Spirit of promise" (Eph 1:13), the poured-out promise of the Father, that will empower Jesus' disciples, that will influence the life of each Christian. Jesus still incredibly active, but henceforth through Jesus' Spirit. That is why Paul will speak so emphatically of "varieties of gifts, but the same Spirit": wisdom and knowledge, faith and healing, miracles and prophecy, discernment of spirits and tongues, "all activated by one and the same Spirit" (1 Cor 12:4–11). The Spirit of Jesus.

I am reminded of the day, "the last and greatest day of the festival" of Tabernacles, when Jesus stood up and cried aloud, "If anyone thirst, let him come [to me]; and let him drink who believes in me.[5] As the Scripture says, 'From within him [from within Jesus] shall flow rivers of living water.'" And John adds: "Here [Jesus] was referring to the Spirit which those who came to believe in him were to receive. For there was as yet no Spirit, since Jesus had not been glorified" (Jn 7:37–39).

No, in leaving us, Jesus would not leave us orphans. Here is his promise fulfilled, "When the Paraclete comes..." (Jn 15:26).

III

Which leads to my third point, the final words in today's Gospel. One all-important word: "In the world you [will?] find affliction, but have courage: I have conquered the world" (Jn 16:33). One facet of Christian living no Christian can escape, even with the empowering presence of the Spirit. I mean suffering.[6] In John's Gospel Jesus predicts that his disciples, those who follow him, will suffer. Their suffering will have a double focus. The disciples (1) will be saddened by his death, and (2) after his rising the world will afflict them with persecution. But if their suffering has a double focus, so too has the joy that follows it.[7] Those who follow Jesus (1) will rejoice as they recognize that Jesus has conquered death, and (2) even in their suffering from "the world" they will know a joy no human can take from them.

Here we confront an agonizing contemporary problem. I mean suffering *without* joy. It should impact you and me particularly this week, as we open our eyes to the justice issues, the injustices that afflict the country you love, the people you love. I mean the poverty that drives untold thousands to despair and crime, the joblessness that wracks homes and families, the difficulties that agonize Asians and Africans, Middle Easterners and Latin Americans, Filipinos and so many others in feeling welcome here. I mean the scores of injustices you yourselves have recorded this afternoon, the injustices that now inflame the walls of your conference room. I mean the men, the women, perhaps especially the children who do not have the peace Jesus promised, who somehow cannot live Jesus' "Do not let your hearts be troubled" (Jn 14:27), do not experience the joy Jesus promised his followers "no one will take" from them (Jn 16:22).

How do we preach resurrection joy to such as these, still experiencing their varied calvaries? Not primarily by promising them a heaven to come: "Have courage, it will soon be over." Jesus left his peace here on earth; Jesus promised a joy in the midst of anguish. I can mouth the pertinent theology: Jesus' ascension is our ascension; it was the whole Body of Christ that the glorified Jesus presented to his Father. True of course, wondrously true. But for our people Jesus' ascension is not a head trip; somehow it has to touch them where they live, how they live.

But how? I have no push-button answer. This I do suggest. Our people are more likely to sense the peace of Christ if they see their preachers obviously living the gift Jesus gave his followers before he died: "'Peace' is my farewell to you. My 'peace' is my gift to you, and I do not give it to you as the world gives it" (Jn 14:27). That peace is not an end to warfare, even to psychological tension; it is not "a sentimental feeling of well-being."[8] Jesus' peace is God's own life brimming within us—even when, especially when life on earth is gross, inhuman, unjust, unlivable. Christ's gift of peace is the same as Christ's gift of joy: his grace, his life coursing through us like another blood stream.

How do I, this preacher of God's gospel, come across to my people? Like the easygoing, comfortable, unchallenging pastor Milo O'Shea and Jack Lemmon portrayed on stage and screen?[9] Or like the crucified, compassionate, challenging Christ, brimful of God's own life, believing against all odds, hoping against hope, loving even the unlovable? This week between the glorification of Jesus and the gift of the Spirit, a burning question: Is Jesus *my* peace? Is Jesus *my* joy?

Manoir d'Youville
Ile St. Bernard, Châteauguay
Quebec, Canada
May 20, 1996

ORDINARY
TIME

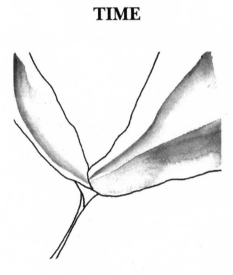

8

AMAZING GRACE:
APOSTLES THEN AND NOW
Third Sunday of the Year (A)

- Isaiah 8:23—9:3
- 1 Corinthians 1:10–13, 17
- Matthew 4:12–23

"Follow me, and I will make you fishers of men and women" (Mt 4:19). The call of Christ. Over the centuries today's Gospel has lifted the hearts of the faithful; today it threatens to divide the Catholic body. Let me begin with a recent experience, go back to today's Gospel, and return to today with its privileges and its problems.

I

First, a recent experience. Just before Christmas I was entranced by a TV special. It was a stunning presentation of the Kennedy Center's Honors, the 25th year—honors for five remarkable artists. There was playwright Neil Simon, whose swift succession of hit comedies and musicals—remember *Barefoot in the Park?*—gave such joy to so many, whose *Odd Couple* still illumines human relationships. There was ballet artist Jacques d'Amboise, who through dance taught all manner of children, children as different as night and day, taught them to believe in themselves, had them dance their way to self-respect. There was B. B. King, "king of the blues," who grew up in a harsh Mississippi and took the blues on the road, gospel music too—a 20-year trip, 200 singles, five million miles. There was Marilyn Horne, whose song was the driving force of her life, who made an evening of music an affair of the heart, whose voice echoed life and love, laughter and tragedy.

But, to my mind most moving of all, there was Sidney Poitier. Here was a man whose face over fifty years changed the face of film itself. Here was incredible integrity that became a symbol of what the black could achieve in a white man's Hollywood. Here was a person of dignity stunned by the strict separation of black and white, for he saw himself not as a colored man but as a man. Here was an actor who gave new insight into the black in *The Blackboard Jungle, Edge of the City, A Raisin in the Sun, Porgy and Bess, Lilies of the Field,* and *Cry, the Beloved Country.* Here was a black whose response to a redneck sheriff in *In the Heat of the Night* still rings down the decades, "You can call me Mr. Tibbs." I found it utterly appropriate that his portion of the honors ended with a heart-stopping rendition of... "Amazing Grace." The tears in Mr. Poitier's eyes were characteristically real.

Why all this from a pulpit? Because each of those five amazing artists responded to a call, to an amazing grace. I don't yet know to what extent they saw their lives as calls from God; I would not be surprised to learn that King and Horne and Poitier sensed it. I do know that God calls in surprising ways, and that the ultimate judgment here is a declaration of Jesus, "By their fruits you will know them" (Mt 7:16). And I praise them from a pulpit today because they recall an earlier call, the first call from Jesus to be apostles, to be disciples, to follow a star.[1]

II

So then, to Matthew's Gospel. Did Peter and Andrew, James and John actually leave their nets "immediately" and follow Jesus (Mt 4:20, 22)? Not at all impossible; not when we read a bit later that a would-be disciple who wanted time to go and bury his father was told by Jesus, "Follow me, and let the dead bury their own dead" (Mt 8:21–22). Matthew may well be suggesting the powerful attraction of Jesus, may well be hinting at the demands made by a gospel call: no delay, leave all else now. On the other hand, it is still possible that Matthew is compressing a longer story, possible that there may have been time for a growth in attraction. We find hints of this in John's Gospel. Remember how Andrew and John spent a day with Jesus, how Andrew then brought his brother Peter to him? Remember how Philip followed immediately and then tried to persuade Nathanael to come along? Remember Nathanael's reaction? "Can anything good come out of Nazareth?" (Jn 1:46).

But if we are not sure how quickly each of the Twelve responded to Jesus, one element in their vocation is clear as crystal. Like Mary of Nazareth before the angel Gabriel, so the Twelve before

Jesus: None of them received a script, not one was given a scenario, detailing what apostleship would bring in its train. It was only gradually, only through harsh experience, that they would learn the cost of discipleship. What cost? Each day of your life, be ready for a cross. When invited to a dinner, always take the lowest place. Though disciples of God's Son, you are not to be served but to serve. When slapped on one cheek, turn the other to the slapper. When you love, love especially the sinner and the outcast, the oppressed and the powerless. If hurt, forgive—not seven times but seventy times seven, without limit. Loyal though you twelve claim to be, one of you will sell his Master for silver, another will deny to a servant girl that he ever knew Jesus. And all save one will refuse to stand beneath his cross. When you (John) grow old, you will die a death you do not want.

Nothing of this at the beginning. Why, Sidney Poitier had a better sense of the red-necked racism and the subtle snobbery he would encounter in Hollywood. For Peter and the rest, nothing but a grace—an extraordinary grace—grace to say yes to a most extraordinary man. Grace to leave a profitable job—fishing, for example, or collecting taxes—and follow this strange, attractive teacher wherever he might lead.

Grace indeed. Not some vague, gossamer, ghostly trail of smoke. Simply the power, the dynamism, that flowed out of God-in-flesh. It is a striking example of what John would write two generations later: "From his fulness we have all received, grace upon grace" (Jn 1:16). Amazing grace.

III

Finally, let's return to today, to ourselves, to our privileges and our problems. Here we discover two facets to our calling. On the one hand, "Follow me." It is our call to be disciples. On the other hand, "I will make you fishers of men and women." It is our call to be apostles.

Disciples. "Follow me." Our original call sounded in your baptism and mine. It reminds me of Belgian Cardinal Léon-Joseph Suenens' striking declaration: The greatest day in the life of a pope is not his coronation but his baptism, the day of his mission "to live the Christian life in obedience to the gospel."[2] Such is God's summons to every Christian. This is Christian discipleship at its most basic, discipleship no genuine Christian dare avoid—rich or poor, old or young. male or female, ordained or lay. To live as Jesus lived. Oh not to walk in sandals, talk in Aramaic, have no home wherein to rest your head. Rather to walk in the footsteps of the Jesus who declared to his disciples, "My food is to do the will of Him who sent me and to complete His work" (Jn 4:34).

Three powerful monosyllables: Do God's will. It sounds so dull, so prosaic. And yet it is the stuff of Christian living. It is Christ's call to fidelity. Fidelity to responsibilities that stem from our covenant with God in Christ. What responsibilities? Three. (1) Love God above all else, with your whole heart and mind, all your soul and strength. (2) Love each human person, each sister and brother, like another "I," because each is shaped, as you are, in God's likeness. (3) Reverence God's nonhuman creation, earth and sea and sky and all that is in them, because each bears God's imprint, each carries a trace of the Lord who fashioned it, each reveals to me the grandeur of God, hints to me what God must be like. Because, in St. Paul's inspired, mystery-laden vision, "the whole of creation has been groaning in labor pains, groaning to be set free from its bondage to decay, to obtain the freedom of the glory of the children of God" (Rom 8:20–22).

Disciples indeed, we who follow in Jesus' footsteps. But more than disciples. After "Follow me" Jesus added, "And I will make you fishers of men and women." Apostles. Literal translation: men and women "sent." Sent to do what? To "complete God's work." And what is that? For the lay Christian Vatican II put it powerfully:

> The redemptive work of Christ has for essential purpose the salvation of men and women; and still it involves as well the renewal of the whole temporal order. Consequently, the Church's mission is not only to bring to men and women the message of Christ and his grace, but also to penetrate and perfect the temporal sphere with the spirit of the gospel. In carrying out this mission of the Church, the laity therefore exercise their apostolate in the world as well as in the Church, in the temporal order as well as in the spiritual. These areas, though distinct, are so intimately linked in the single plan of God that our very God intends, in Christ, to take up the whole world again and make of it a new creation, initially here on earth, consummately on the last day. In both areas the lay person, at once believer and citizen, should be guided ceaselessly by one and the same Christian conscience.[3]

The mission of Christians is a twin mission: to link every man, woman, and child to God, *and* to shape this earthly city into a city of justice, of peace, of love. Each of you shares in that mission; for the root mission that sends a Christian to sanctify the Church and reshape the world is not ordination, not a vow ceremony, not a special adult commissioning. You were sent on mission, anointed as apostles, the moment you were baptized—you and I and every Christian without exception.

As with the original apostles, as with Sidney Poitier, so with you and me. Our Lord Jesus rarely if ever sends us forth with a script, a scenario, "This Is Your Life." The ways apostleship takes us, the highs and lows, the joys and sorrows, the Tabors and Gethsemanes—these are not scotch-taped to our baptismal fonts. Only gradually, at times through harsh experience, will we realize what Protestant martyr Dietrich Bonhoeffer called "the cost of discipleship." We can be sure of two realities only: (1) The Holy Spirit will ceaselessly surprise us; (2) however startling or even crucifying the surprise, God will always be there.

As I cruise our country with my project Preaching the Just Word, I am agonizingly aware that many of our believing, hoping, and loving women Catholics are convinced that their call as disciples and apostles can only be justly recognized and implemented by way of ordained priesthood. I struggle with that issue day in and day out, struggle with the theological arguments pro and con, struggle with every Vatican document, struggle with the personal angst of dear female friends—and some enemies. But as we struggle, with Rome and perhaps with one another, as we think and pray, agonize and argue, I submit that we must continue to give our highest priority to the mission itself: to America's children (one out of four) who are living in some kind of hell, to the elderly rummaging for food in garbage cans, to the AIDS-afflicted crying to us for compassion instead of condemnation, to African Americans for whom God still pleads "Let my people go," to abandoned mothers weeping like Rachel over their hungry children.

And please, please pray for your homilist now returned to you. Pray for him wisdom when theological and pastoral problems sear his soul. Pray for him courage when he knows what is right but finds it difficult to do. Pray for him, above all, love for the crucified Christs he touches each day.

As Peter said to Jesus on the mount of transfiguration, "It is good to be here" (Mk 9:5).

Holy Trinity Church
Washington, D.C.
January 21, 1996

9

WITH HIS OWN BLOOD
Third Week, Year 1, Monday

- Hebrews 9:15, 24–28
- Mark 3:22–30

In this section of the Letter to the Hebrews (chapters eight to ten) there is a central concept and there is a preponderant person. The central concept? Sacrifice. The preponderant person? Jesus. Let me begin with Jesus and his sacrifice, move on to ourselves and our sacrifice, and end specifically with sacrifice and Preaching the Just Word.[1]

I

First, the sacrifice of Jesus.[2] The author of the letter sends us literally sky-high. You remember how the high priest within Jewish worship had the right of access to the Holy of Holies. Why? Because he bore with him the blood of the animals that were sacrificed. Similarly, Jesus' life offered in sacrifice gave him the right of access to the heavenly sanctuary. A verse that precedes today's reading declares, "he entered once for all into the Holy Place, not with the blood of goats and calves, but with his own blood, thus obtaining eternal redemption" (v. 12).

The point is, Jesus' sacrifice was not simply completed with his death on the cross, as if when he "bowed his head and gave up his spirit" (Jn 19:30), he wrote finis, end, to his sacrifice. No. An essential part of the sacrifice was Jesus' entrance into heaven. Jesus' sacrifice began on earth but is completed in heaven. And there, in fact, it never actually ends. Recall that breath-taking phrase, "thus obtaining eternal redemption." The redemption is eternal because it is based

46

on an eternally acceptable sacrifice of Jesus. Jesus' priesthood is eternal not in the sense that it had no beginning, but in the sense that it will never end. In contrast to the transitory, passing priesthood of the Old Testament, annually repeated on the Day of Atonement, Jesus' sacrifice is a single sacrifice that is consummated in heaven, where it continues eternally.

Here, in Jesus' sacrifice, is the basis on which he is mediator of the new covenant. Through that sacrifice he has brought deliverance, redemption, from the sins committed under the old covenant. Atonement has been made and the new covenant has been inaugurated. Jesus "entered into heaven itself, now to appear in the presence of God on our behalf" (v. 24). Not for some magnificent moment; for ever.

And the author concludes: "Christ, having been offered once to bear the sins of many,[3] will appear a second time, not to deal with sin, but to save those who are eagerly waiting for him" (v. 28). The Parousia will bring complete and final salvation. The First Coming focused on sin; the Second Coming will focus on life eternal.

II

Turn now to ourselves, to our sacrifice—the sacrifice of all Christians. Here bear patiently with me for a small measure of scholarship that has intrigued me for half a century.

In the mid-40s, when I was doing graduate work in patristics at the Catholic University of America, my favorite professor was an exile from Nazi Germany, Johannes Quasten. Expert in the Fathers, in early liturgy, and in Christian archeology, Quasten took great delight in developing an early Christian understanding of Romans 12:1: "I appeal to you, brothers and sisters, by the mercies of God, to present your bodies as a living sacrifice, holy and acceptable to God, which is your spiritual worship." A living sacrifice, our spiritual worship. As some early Christians understood the text, the Christian sacrifice, our worship, is the Supper conjoined with the cross. In that text the Greek word translated "spiritual" is *logikos*. As these early interpreters stressed it, the sacrifice that is translated as "spiritual" is a play on the adjective. *Logikos* (remember "logical"?) has to do with our *logos* (small l), the most profound aspect of the human person, our spiritual side; but *logikos* as an adjective also refers to the Logos (capital L), the Word of God, specifically the Word made flesh. And so they concluded that the sacrifice which is the Eucharist is *logikos* in two ways intimately linked. It is the sacrifice of the Logos (capital L), the Word made flesh; and it is at the same time the sacrifice, the offering, of what is most precious in our person, the deepest part of our existence. What some spiritual writers speak of as the large host and the small host simultaneously on the paten at Mass. "We offer...."[4]

I am not about to spill blood for this interpretation of Romans 12:1. I do believe, however, that those early theologians were gifted with an insight that should carry over into our time, into our lives, into our ministry. Our central act of worship is the Eucharist, which re-enacts the Supper room and the hill called Calvary. That Eucharist is central not only because bread and wine are transfigured into Christ's body and blood; not only because we receive on hand and tongue our very God incarnate. All true. But the Eucharist is more than a single act, more than a church worship. It should carry over into the life of every priest, every deacon, every Christian. Our lives are eucharistic to the extent that they are living examples of the words of consecration, "This is my body given for you."

But this is possible only if God's Logos and our logos are one in sacrifice, one in the cross taken up day after day. In principle, your life, my life, the Christian life is a consecrated life. Consecrated not only in the sense of being sacred, but even more importantly in the sense that it is dedicated especially to the crucified images of Christ. Because all Christians can echo the programmatic sentence in which Jesus in his home synagogue summed up his mission, his purpose in taking our flesh: "The Spirit of the Lord is upon me, because [the Lord] has anointed me to bring good news to the poor, has sent me to proclaim release to the captives and recovery of sight to the blind, to send the oppressed away relieved" (Lk 4:18).

III

This leads neatly into my third point: Preaching the Just Word. We who are committed to preaching justice are commissioned to a harrowing apostolate, if only because the oppressions of our time are so many and so inhuman. Not an abstraction called poverty, but one of every four children hungry in the richest nation on earth, lusting in vain for a 99-cent McBurger. Not a racist remark here and there, but a whole people still feeling themselves second-class citizens in "the land of the free," African Americans of whom the Lord still pleads with us, "Let my people go!" Not a savage Schwarzenegger celluloid, but the brutal reality of children from California to the District of Columbia gunning other children down for a pair of Reeboks. Not just a First Lady called "a bitch" by a Congressman, but four million women abused by their spouses each year, 43 percent of single mothers below the poverty line, females earning half to three fourths of what men earn, women crying aloud that their voices and their experience have for all too long gone unheard not only in government and industry, in home and school, but in the churches and religious life.[5]

The list is long and devastating. You experience much of it from day to day. And the effort to literally do "justice" to it can lead to discouragement, despondency, depression, perhaps despair. This morning you learned that the justice which drives us is not primarily ethical justice, giving to every man, woman, and child what each strictly deserves. That in itself is a heart-rending vocation that divides even our Catholic congregations. But your task and mine transcends ethical justice. What you and I must preach is primarily biblical justice. I mean fidelity to relationships, to responsibilities that stem from a covenant cut in the blood of Christ, responsibilities to God, to people, to the earth. From one perspective, awesome, for the task is so vast; from another, consoling, for it links your vocation to a worship that is, shall we now say, *logikos*. The just word we preach is a word that stems from the Logos, the living Word of God who still carries our flesh; and the just word is a word that should be forced from our own logos, the deepest reality that is you and I, the preacher stimulated by the Spirit of Christ deep within us, the Spirit who alone can change hearts and minds—yes, your heart and mine.

And remember, inexpressibly powerful for preaching the just word is the Eucharist. For at the altar the Logos of God joins with our own logos in an incomparably effective offering to God's children, "This is my body (and it is) given for you." Given in sacrifice for the crucified images of Christ. That word, "my body for you," is what sends us from church to world, from altar to people, from Christ crucified on Calvary to the images of Christ crucified on the highways and byways of the earth. That word, "my body for you," Christ's body and mine, is what raises social work to Christian apostolate, to Christian sacrifice. Like the work of Christ, with the work of Christ, your word and mine has to do with redemption, eternal redemption.

In a sense, we too enter a holy of holies: God's good earth and God's good people. And we enter it not with the blood of goats and calves, but with our own blood. For that is what it takes to change a culture. Such indeed is Christian sacrifice, and it makes bloody demands not only on our life style but on our preaching. For this reason I presume to end with a pertinent piece of advice tendered many years ago by a prince of sports writers, "Red" Smith. Someone asked him, "Red, how do you manage to put out such consistently splendid columns day after day, week after week?" His reply? "Easy. I simply sit at my typewriter till beads of blood appear on my forehead."

Beads of blood. And this for a perishable crown.

San Damiano Retreat House
Danville, California
January 23, 1995

10
WILL IT BE CHABLIS OR ZINFANDEL?
Sixth Sunday of the Year (A)

- Sirach 15:15–20
- 1 Corinthians 2:6–10
- Matthew 5:17–37

This evening I simply must share with you a cartoon. It was sent by a friend. It pictures two characters, a patient and his doctor. The patient is halfway back in his chair, his mouth wide open. The doctor, his depressor on the patient's tongue, is staring into the man's mouth. His diagnosis? "I see your problem, Reverend. You have a three-point sermon lodged in your larynx."

Yes, an accurate diagnosis: I have another three-point homily lodged in my larynx. This time I want to begin in Jerusalem with Ben Sira, move on to Corinth with St. Paul, end in Washington with you and me.

I

Our journey begins in Jerusalem with a book and its author.[1] The book is titled *The Wisdom of Ben Sira*. Ben Sira spent his life studying the law, the prophets, other segments of God's revelation; he was a respected scribe and teacher; he ran an academy for young Jewish men; he traveled much, came in contact with other cultures and wisdom traditions. About the year 180 before Christ he committed to writing the essence of the wisdom he had imparted by word of mouth. Why did he write? To show how superior the Jewish way of life was to the Greek, that genuine worship was to be found primarily in Jerusalem, not in Athens. The book itself is a compilation of this teacher's class notes!

The bit of wisdom that Ben Sira confronts us with in today's extract is basic. You are free men and women, he tells the Jews of Jerusalem. You can choose to do good, you can choose to do evil. So, if you stray into sin, don't blame it on God, "God made me do it." When the Lord created you, He created you with free choice. "If you will, you can keep the commandments, and to act faithfully is a matter of your own choice" (Sir 15:15).[2]

But what, for Ben Sira, is this choice between good and evil? When you come right down to it, what is good and what is evil? Now comes a sentence to scotch-tape to your refrigerator: "Before [you] are life and death, and whichever [you] choose will be given to [you]" (15:17). But what is life, and what is death? Listen to Moses in Deuteronomy, the law Ben Sira knew by heart: "I have set before you life and death, blessing and curse; therefore choose life, that you and your descendants may live." How? "By loving the Lord your God, obeying His voice, and cleaving to Him; for that means life to you..." (Deut 30:20). "But if your heart turns away, and you will not hear, but are drawn away to worship other gods and serve them, I declare to you this day that you shall perish" (v. 17).

To choose life is to choose love; to live is to love God, a love shown by obedience: Walk in God's ways, obey God's voice. To choose death is to choose other gods; to be dead is to worship idols, anything and everything that is not the one true God.

II

So much for the wisdom of Ben Sira. Move now more than two centuries ahead, turn to what you heard from St. Paul: "Among the mature we impart wisdom, although it is not a wisdom of this age.... We impart a secret and hidden wisdom of God...what the heart of no man or woman has conceived...[what] God has revealed to us through the Spirit" (1 Cor 2:7, 9–10). A wisdom the good and loving heart of wise old Ben Sira could not imagine. The wisdom Paul imparts is...God's own Son saving us by dying for us. God's wisdom is Christ; God's wisdom is Calvary; God's wisdom is a cross.

Here Paul has an intoxicatingly imaginative idea. "None of the rulers of this age understood this [wisdom of God]; for if they had, they would not have crucified the Lord of glory" (v. 8). If the men in power had known that God's plan for our salvation was to be "achieved through the humiliating death of Jesus, they would have tried to frustrate it by letting him live."[3]

In Paul's inspired vision, choosing life instead of death means, paradoxically, choosing life *through* death—life through the death of Christ. But not in some objective fashion: I living here in America, Christ dying there in Jerusalem. Christ's cross is here, erected over history, over my history. For the Christian, as Paul put it, "living is Christ" (Phil 1:21), living like Christ, playing my part in the saving work Christ began in his short life. Paul expressed it powerfully when he wrote these lines to the Christians of Colossae, a rather insignificant town in Asia Minor: "I am now rejoicing in my sufferings for your sake, and in my flesh I am completing what is lacking in Christ's afflictions for the sake of his body...the Church" (Col 1:24).

Paul did not invent that theology. It goes back to Jesus' own words of wisdom, "Whoever does not take up the cross and follow me is not worthy of me" (Mt 10:38). It is not a summons to unrelieved sadness, to a Christian masochism, pleasure in being abused, "Hit me again, I like it." On the contrary. This is Christian realism. Realism because it recognizes that, for all its joys, its delights, its occasional ecstasies, human living is not one long picnic, an endless merry-go-round, Barnum & Bailey. It's tough. Life is tough; even love is a tough love. But the realism is Christian...if. If Christians see it, joy and sorrow, as their sharing in the cross of Christ that even now redeems the world. Redeems the world through us. Through God's mysterious grace, what you and I do, especially what you and I suffer, touches another life, and that in turn touches another, until who knows where the grace stops or in what far place and time my suffering will be felt. Our lives are linked, far more intimately than we suspect.

III

This moves us to the District of Columbia. In today's liturgy it moves us to part of Jesus' Sermon on the Mount. To meditate on that "sermon" is to gather concrete ideas on how to choose life—life in Christ. You may argue till doomsday on which are commands and which are counsels; beyond debate is that all reflect life in Christ.

I must confess, I find Jesus ceaselessly embarrassing; I suspect most Catholics do. It's relatively easy for us not to murder; but how keep justified anger within bounds for Jesus' sake and still not repress it neurotically for psychology's sake? Adultery, thank God, is not in my catalogue of personal sins, but what of Jesus' "I say to you, everyone who looks at a woman with lust has already committed adultery with her in his heart" (Mt 5:28)? I have never demanded "an eye for an eye" (Mt 5:38),[4] but do I follow Jesus in not resisting evil when I still proclaim some wars just, when I've rarely if ever turned the other cheek, when I simply do not give to everyone who begs from me? It may surprise you that I have enemies, some who denounce me as dangerous to your orthodox health; but can I say in all honesty that I love them? At times I wonder as I wander.

Let me close with a story, a choice for life, for love of God, for obedience to God, that is very practical.[5] (It may say different things to different worshipers among you; frankly, I hope it does.) The story was told by a man who had been assisting at Mass with his wife during the summer of 1994 in the Castro, the gay district of San Francisco. As he tells it, the priest presiding was slender of frame, balding in skull, thin of voice, half-reading from notes, but he had captured his congregation. He took a Gospel story familiar to us all and made it live in Northern California. The kernel of his story:

> A man had a vineyard in the Napa Valley that had just been attacked by fungus. So, he went to his son and said: "Chablis, will you help me in the vineyard?" Chablis answered: "Yes, of course." But Chablis, distracted by friends, got in his red sports car, drove down to San Francisco and was never heard from again.
>
> The man then went to his other son. "Zinfandel, will you help me in the vineyard?" Zinfandel replied: "No, I'm busy." But Zinfandel walked away, and had *second thoughts*. [Long pause.] He returned and worked the vineyard.
>
> "God is in our second thoughts," the frail priest explained. "Not in the temptations that propel us to what is wrong. No, God is in those brief moments before we decide or act, those moments when we catch ourselves considering things; those moments we call...*second thoughts*. So, at the Safeway store as you look over the wine aisle this week, ask yourself: When the temptations swirl about me, will it be Chablis or...Zinfandel?"

Holy Trinity Church
Washington, D.C.
February 11, 1996

11
FOR YOUR LENTEN PENANCE, LET GO!
Eighth Week, Year 1, Monday

- Sirach 17:19-24
- Mark 10:17-27

Last week, in the East Texas town of Beaumont, you Gonzaga Jesuits had me worried. In odd hours during our Preaching the Just Word retreat/workshop for the priests of the Diocese of Tyler, I had time to mull over what I might say to you this evening.[1] But for hours I was mightily puzzled. What frustrated me was the Gospel reading.

An entrancing Gospel, this conversation between Jesus and a rich young man whom he "looked at with love" (Mk 10:21), a young man who walked away from Jesus with sadness in his heart because he possessed so much, could not dream of giving up what he owned. But what might this scene have to say to a score of Jesuits who (1) have not only kept the commandments from your youth, but (2) have vowed away all you possess, can call nothing your own, and (3) follow Jesus already as your one and only master?

A puzzle indeed; but once again the God of good homilies came through—gifted me unexpectedly with a powerful parable. So then, let me (1) repeat the parable for you, (2) permit the parable to speak to you and me, and (3) suggest the pertinence of all this to the Lent that is almost upon us.

I

First, the parable. It is a Jewish story, a typically powerful parable, especially in its unexpected ending. It runs like this:

> Once upon a time, two families came to a rabbi wanting him to settle a dispute about the boundaries of their land. He listened to

55

the members of one family as they recounted how they had received this land as their inheritance from their ancestors and how it had been in their family for generations. They had maps and papers to prove it. Then the rabbi listened to the other family. Its members described how they had lived on the land for years, working it and harvesting it. They claimed that they knew the land intimately and that it was their land. They didn't have the papers to prove it, but they had the calluses and sore backs and the harvest and the produce of the land.

The rabbi looked at them both and backed away from between them. They turned on him and said, "Decide, rabbi, who owns this land." But the rabbi knelt down on the land and put his ear to the ground, listening. Finally he stood up and looked at both families. He said: "I had to listen to both of you, but I had to listen also to the land, the center of this dispute, and the land has spoken. It has told me this: 'Neither one of you owns the land you stand on. It is the land that owns you.'"[2]

II

Thus the parable. Now let's point the parable at ourselves. As so often with parables, this one stands us on our heads, forces us to see things from God's vantage point. With my vow of poverty, I may call nothing my very own. Not the works of the Church Fathers that thrilled me for decades and still line my office shelves. Not the T-shirt on my back and the Reeboks on my feet. Not the Lasagna I had for dinner. Not my room on the second floor—its desk and chairs, its bed and hangings. Not the Crest toothpaste or the Gillette shaving cream in my medicine cabinet. Not the bills in my wallet. I own nothing.

Now let me stand on my head and look at the problem from God's point of view. Not what do I own, but what owns me? Spiritual writers used to insist that there is a peril in possessing almost anything—a child with a Raggedy Ann doll, a Donald Trump with his megabuildings, a Marcos or a Noriega with his limitless power. The peril? What they possess can possess them; the master becomes a slave, imprisoned by his possessions.

Technically, abstractly, I may not "own" anything; my solemn word attests to that. But do God's very gifts own me, possess me, enslave me, so that unwittingly they are gods to me, my idols? My skill with words, the power to turn an audience on, the standing ovation—has the master turned slave? Is it still the kingdom of God that I serve, the reign of Jesus, or have I shaped a golden calf out of my God-given gifts?

Ignatius Loyola continues to warn me: Never underestimate the power of the Evil One to turn the gift of God into an enslaving chain. And so cleverly that I still pride myself on being in command, on having no motivation other than the greater glory of God! But Ignatius also knew that to possess nothing as my own is to possess an incredible freedom—the freedom expressed so powerfully in the prayer that for Jesuits says it all, the prayer a paralyzed Pedro Arrupe spoke mutely, through another's lips, in his final message to the Society of Jesus back in 1983:

> Take, O Lord, and receive all my liberty, my memory, my understanding, my whole will, all I have and all I possess. You gave them to me; to you, Lord, I return it [all]. It is all yours; dispose of it entirely as you will. Give me your love and your grace; this is enough for me.

III

This leads quite naturally into my third point: the pertinence of all this to the Lent that is all but upon us. As I grew up, there was a sharp dividing line between Lent and Easter. Lent meant that we lived again in memory the dying of Jesus, so that on Easter we might relive his rising. Six weeks of suffering for him and sadness for us, then all of a sudden he and we were alive again. Today tragedy, tomorrow triumph; Lent dying, Easter rising.

Nonsense, say our better liturgists. Neither in Lent's liturgy nor in Lenten living dare we pretend that Jesus is not yet risen, that we have to wait for Easter to see his resurrection, to live it, to enjoy it. This is to stress the history at the expense of the mystery. There is indeed a history: Jesus did move from a desert to a garden to a cross to a rock from which he rose. And in Lent we try to relive that movement. But not as if Jesus is not yet risen. Even in Lent you and I are *risen* Christians.

The point is this: The whole of Lent is a progressively more intense initiation into the paschal mystery. And what is the paschal mystery? Not a dying or a rising Christ. A duality, the twin reality of Jesus dying/rising. The paschal mystery is *one* mystery: life in and through death.

Still, we cannot pretend the other way either. Simply because we have risen with Christ in baptism, we cannot make believe that Lent does not really exist. Risen we are, but not yet *fully* risen. "We ourselves," St. Paul agonizes, "we who have the first fruits of the Spirit, groan inside ourselves as we wait for...the redemption of our bodies" (Rom 8:23). That is why our laughter is not yet full-throated; that is why it is often through tears that we smile; that is why we still have to pray, "Father...remove this cup from me" (Lk 22:42).

Precisely here we rejoin our parable. Lent is for remembering, for reproducing. We must ceaselessly reproduce the journey of Jesus to Jerusalem, not only symbolically and liturgically but in our flesh and bones and in the wrenching of our spirit. For here is our dying not simply to sin but to self. Where nothing I have possesses me, owns me. It's letting go of where I've been, letting go of yesterday, of the past that is so much part of me. Not forgetting the past; simply refusing to live there, as if somewhere back there I can pinpoint the acme of my existence.

No, good friends. Whether it's turning 21, 40, or 65; whether its losing my health or my hair, my looks or my lustiness, a person I love or a possession I particularly prize; whether it's a change of life, of pace, or of function; whether it's as fleeting as applause or as abiding as grace—I have to move on. Wherever I've been, I dare not live there. Whatever the "land" that owns me, I have to let go. Essential to my Christian journey is the journeying of Christ. Paul put it pungently: He "did not treat like a miser's booty his right to be like God, but emptied himself of it" (Phil 1:6–7). When he breathed his last, he had given us everything he had to give. His pierced hands were empty.

For your Lenten penance, dear brothers in Christ, let go!

Our Lady's Chapel
Gonzaga College High School
February 27, 1995

12

INVITE THE POOR, THE CRIPPLED?
Ninth Week, Year 1, Monday

- Tobit 1:3; 2:1–8
- Mark 12:1–12

Today's liturgy confronts us with an intriguing book. Protestants classify Tobit among the Apocrypha; we Catholics receive it within the biblical canon. We don't know who wrote it, where he wrote it, exactly when he wrote it. It has been described as a "fascinating amalgam of *Arabian Nights* romance, kindly Jewish piety, and sound moral teaching."[1] Its principal value? "[T]he picture it gives of Jewish culture and religious life in an age not too remote, either in time or temper, from that of the New Testament."[2] Its immediate pertinence for you and me as we plunge into this retreat/workshop?[3] A justice issue. Three short reflections: (1) Tobit and his son Tobiah; (2) biblical justice; (3) you and I.

I

First, mull over Tobit and his son Tobiah. Tobit was a man who loved God and loved his fellow Jews. When he was still a young man, his tribe and other tribes used to sacrifice to Baal. Tobit alone went often to Jerusalem for the feasts, gave generously of his produce to the priests and to the needy. Carried away captive to Nineveh, he alone refused the food of the Gentiles. "I performed many acts of charity to my brethren. I would give my bread to the hungry and my clothing to the naked; and if I saw any one of my people dead and thrown out behind the wall of Nineveh, I would bury him" (Tob 1:16–17). For such forbidden burying, for such defiance toward the king, Tobit paid a costly price.

One of the men of Nineveh went and informed the king about me, that I was burying [those executed]; so I hid myself. When I learned that I was being searched for, to be put to death, I left home in fear. Then all my property was confiscated and nothing was left to me except my wife Anna and my son Tobiah.

(Tob 1:19–20)

You have just heard how, back in Nineveh with a new king more favorably disposed to him and a splendid Pentecost dinner set before him, Tobit said to his son, "Go and bring whatever poor man of our brethren you may find who is mindful of the Lord, and I will wait for you" (2:2). Tobit has rubbed off on Tobiah. But before Tobiah can discover a poor man to share their table, he comes back and says, "Father, one of our own people has been strangled [presumably executed] and thrown into the market place" (2:3). Tobit's reaction? Before tasting a mouthful of the delectable dinner, he springs up, leaves his house, removes the dead body to a place of shelter, and when the sun has set he digs a grave and buries it. No matter that his neighbors laugh at him, jeer at him: "[Hey, look at good old Tobit!] He is no longer afraid that he will be put to death for doing this; he once ran away, and here he is burying the dead again!" (2:8).

Tobit's reward? He falls asleep, fresh droppings of sparrows fall into his open eyes, and he turns blind. Unable to work, poverty is his lot. And he prays: "It is better for me to die than to live, because I have heard false reproaches, and great is the sorrow within me. Command that I now be released from my distress to go to the eternal abode; do not turn your face away from me" (3:6).

II

Turn now from the bare facts; turn to the significance of Tobit's life. In a momentous monosyllable, his life is a *just* life. He is the just man whom the Prior Testament praises, the just man of whom the Psalmist sings. And who is just in God's own Book? The man or woman who is faithful. Faithful to what? To relationships, to responsibilities, that stem from a covenant with God. What relationships, what responsibilities? Tobit heard three responsibilities no true Israelite should breach: to God, to sisters and brothers, to the earth.

God above all. For the first commandment was etched on Tobit's heart: "Hear, O Israel: The Lord is our God, the Lord alone.

You shall love the Lord your God with all your heart, and with all your soul, and with all your might" (Deut 6:4–5). This was the God to whom Tobit prayed, "Righteous are you, O Lord; all your deeds and all your ways are mercy and truth, and you render true and righteous judgment for ever. Remember me and look favorably upon me" (Tob 3:2–3a). And his just counsel to Tobiah: "Do not be afraid, my son, because we have become poor. You have great wealth if you fear God and refrain from every sin and do what is pleasing in His sight" (4:21).

Not only God; Tobit's neighbor, his fellow Israelites. He knew the covenant, relished and lived its terribly difficult commandment, "You shall not take vengeance or bear any grudge against the sons of your own people, but you shall love your neighbor as yourself" (Lev 19:18). He did indeed: fed the hungry, clothed the naked, buried the dead at the risk of his life and possessions. Not only Tobit's neighbor: "The stranger who sojourns with you shall be to you as the native among you; for you were strangers in the land of Egypt" (Lev 19:34).

Responsibility, believe it, not only to rational creatures, creatures able to think and to love. Responsibility to the earth as well, to the land without which the Jew is only half a Jew, the earth a creating God entrusted to man and woman not for despotic abuse but for reverential care (Gen 1:28).

III

Third point: How does just Tobit touch you and me? Pressed by time, I simply suggest one connection. It will hardly pose a threat to our life—only to our life style.

You and I are indeed ordained to *preach* the biblical word, the just word. Vatican II insisted that proclamation of the gospel is a priest's "primary obligation."[4] But words are not the be-all and the end-all of our ministry. The Letter of James is uncompromising: "What good is it, my brothers and sisters, if you say you have faith but do not have works? Can faith save you? If a brother or sister is naked and lacks daily food, and one of you says to them, "Go in peace; keep warm and eat your fill," and yet you do not supply their bodily needs, what is the good of that? So faith by itself, if it has no works, is dead" (Jas 2:14–17). And the First Letter of John applies to us too: "Little children, let us love, not in word or speech, but in truth and action" (1 Jn 3:18).

Go a giant step further. Tobit's way of life, his celebration of Pentecost, his dinner, recalls to my mind the startling counsel of Jesus to a leader of the Pharisees who had invited him to dinner:

> When you are going to give a luncheon or a dinner, do not call your friends, or even your brothers, your relatives, your rich neighbors, lest they only invite you in return and so you are repaid. Rather, when you are going to give a banquet, invite the poor, the crippled, the lame, and the blind. Then you will be blessed, for they cannot repay you; you will be repaid at the resurrection of the just.

> (Lk 14:12–14)

Invite the poor to your table? The crippled? The lame? The blind? Tobit did. Jesus did. I don't recall ever doing so.... Do you?

St. Joseph Center
Greensburg, Pa.
June 5, 1995

13

BLESSED IF YOU HUNGER AND THIRST FOR...WHAT?
Tenth Week, Year 2, Monday

- 1 Kings 17:1–6
- Matthew 5:1–12

As the years move inexorably on, each year swifter than its predecessor, I find the Beatitudes making more and more sense. Not simply the sheer exegesis—what they meant when Jesus uttered them. With that, what they say now—how they touch my day-to-day Jesuit existence. In the context of this retreat/workshop,[1] permit me to focus on one beatitude—a beatitude that can bring to our religious life and to our specific apostolates a contemporary urgency, blood-and-guts challenges.

The beatitude begins "Blessed are those who hunger and thirst." For what? Translations vary. Is it "for righteousness"? Is it "for holiness"? Is it "for justice"? Nuances indeed; still, each of those words—righteousness, holiness, justice—each declares or implies right relationship: to God. to people, to earth. Relationships that stem from our covenant with God. Blessed are you if you love God above all else; blessed if you see in every human person another self; blessed if you reverence the earth on which you tread so lightly or so heavily.

Let's settle for the word "justice." Let me dwell on it in a singular way: as it touches the objects that focus our vows of religion. What objects? In a famous Woodstock College conference almost 50 years ago, John Courtney Murray declared: By the three vows I risk not becoming a man, am in danger of declining "the encounter with three elemental forces...encounter with the earth, with woman, and with [our] own spirit."[2] A word on each. Not quite as my dear deceased friend approached the "three elemental forces." More from a personal perspective influenced by the Just Word.

I

First, encounter with the earth. I am not interested in defining religious poverty, in distinguishing between serious sins, venial violations, and positive or negative imperfections. I am concerned about a critical facet of biblical justice: our relation to created reality, to everything that is not God or the human person, to the "things" that in the Catholic tradition are, each and all, traces of God, vestiges of divinity. No accusations here; I speak immediately of myself.

Here the heart of the matter is what St. John Chrysostom called "those ice-cold words." He meant, and I mean, "mine and thine." They have insidiously invaded my Jesuit life, my relationship to things. Ice-cold words.

Mine and thine. The 12 collections of my homilies (what a Jesuit wag called "never an unpublished homily"), those books are mine, purchased with intellectual torment, emotional anguish, a hiatal hernia and all too frequent diarrhea. Keep that copyright! I sense it in my personal library, now roughly a thousand tomes. My personal library. Oh yes, I loan any book requested. But notice, I *loan* it. It's mine. My personal computer; my room. And of course, Preaching the Just Word: my project. I designed it; I preside over it. Superiors, take care before you send me to Murray-Weigel[3] without it! *Theological Studies* was my journal for 23 years; I nursed it through dark nights and sunny days. To play on Jesus' declaration about his own life, no one took *TS* from me; I gave it up of my own free will.

Little things? I admit it. But these little things are symbolic of a poison that infects our society, secular and religious: having rather than being. It contradicts the declaration of Vatican II, "A person is more precious for what he or she is than for what he or she has."[4] It recalls John Paul II setting side by side with the anguish and miseries of underdevelopment a contemporary superdevelopment that

> makes people slaves of "possession" and of immediate gratification, with no other horizon than the multiplication or continual replacement of the things already owned with others still better. This is the so-called civilization of "consumption" or "consumerism," which involves so much "throwing-away" and "waste".... To "have" objects and goods does not in itself perfect the human subject, unless it contributes to the maturing and enrichment of that subject's "being," that is to say unless it contributes to the realization of the human vocation as such.[5]

II

Second, encounter with woman. I mean a refusal to enter the world of Eve. Here I am not concerned with chastity, the risk of a premature senility (sex is dead), remaining the proverbial bachelor, "crotchety, unstable, petulant, and self-enclosed."[6] Here the risk is a reality that the 34th General Congregation of Jesuits expressed with unexpected honesty:

> ...we Jesuits first ask for the grace of conversion. We have been part of a civil and ecclesial tradition that has offended against women. And, like many men, we have a tendency to convince ourselves that there is no problem. However unwittingly, we have often been complicit in a form of clericalism which has reinforced male domination with an ostensibly divine sanction. By making this declaration we wish to react personally and collectively, and do what we can to change this regrettable situation.[7]

That confession lays a heavy burden on the mind, heart, and lips of all of us called to proclaim the Just Word. Before I dare to preach on women, I must realize, must confess, that I have been an intimate part of a culture that took women seriously only as wives and mothers, all too often regarded them more as sexual objects than as persons, failed to recognize their singular intelligence, gave little thought to the extent and depth of feminine spirituality. In consequence, I must listen to women not only when they offer polite suggestions on greater equality, but as they rage against what they see as injustice within the churches. I must give ear not only to a loyally Christian feminism, but even to radical feminists who are convinced that in attitude and action on women the Catholic Church is beyond redemption.

I find it fascinating that John Paul II discovers in Genesis God's desire for human equality frustrated. It is not that sin has "destroyed" our likeness to God; still, it has "obscured" our identity, "diminished" the relationship of man and woman, their ability to reflect God each in his or her own way.[8] One effect is declared in Genesis 3:16: "Your desire shall be for your husband, and he shall rule over you." Patriarchy, the structural domination of men over women, reveals vividly humanity's ruptured relationship, "the disturbance and loss of the stability of that fundamental equality which the man and the woman possess in 'the unity of the two.'"[9]

My brothers, the encounter with woman is not simply, perhaps not primarily, a challenge to chastity, the risk of a sexual relationship.

It is a challenge to our justice, the risk of equality between man and woman.

III

Third, encounter with our own spirit and its power of choice. Murray called it "the most bruising encounter of all."[10] It is the risk in obedience. What risk? A wrong relationship to God. The risk in being other-directed, with our choices made for us, refusing ultimate responsibility for them. We risk "an end both to aspiration and conflict"; we can spare ourselves "the lonely agony of the desert struggle."[11]

No, the justice that is fidelity to God does not lay the responsibility on another, whether God or a human person. Remember Adam refusing responsibility? "The woman you gave me, she gave me fruit" (Gen 3:12). *She* did it! Remember Eve? "The serpent tricked me" (v. 13). The serpent did it! The danger stems from the classical notion of the authority-freedom relationship, magisterially summarized by Murray:

> Those who hold office make the decisions, doctrinal and pastoral. The faithful in the ranks submit to the decisions and execute the orders.... To obey is to do the will of the superior; that is the essence of obedience. And the perfection of obedience is to make the will of the superior one's own will. In both instances the motive is the vision of God in the superior....[12]

Much there that is commendable: a vivid awareness of God, of the charism that accompanies authority. But Vatican II recognized two fresh signs of the times: (1) a growing consciousness among men and women of their dignity as persons, a dignity that demands of them that they "should act on their own judgment, enjoying and making use of a responsible freedom, not driven by coercion but motivated by a sense of duty"; (2) a growing consciousness of community, of each person's responsibility to participate fully in community and to contribute actively to community.[13]

Two conclusions here—one for us, one for our people. (1) I dare not shift the blame for my failures on others, divine or human, God ("She did it") or a superior in God's place ("he did it"). To be human, the judgment must be mine. I dare not spare myself "the lonely agony of the desert struggle." (2) Our people must be allowed "a responsible freedom." Why? Listen to our good friend, imaginative Bill O'Malley:

> We can no longer depend on the comforting simplism of "The Church Teaching" and "The Church Taught"; there are too many Ph.D.'s out in the pews now. The magisterium and the People of God are now like Henry Higgins and Eliza Doolittle at the end of "Pygmalion." He had found a tatterdemalion flower girl and turned her into a lady. But once the metamorphosis took place, neither Higgins nor Eliza knew quite what to do about the new relationship. He was no longer the all-knowing teacher, and she no longer the biddable pupil. Not only does the official church have an obligation to listen more to the people, but the people have the intimidating obligation to speak up.[14]

Things, woman, God: three relationships that stem from our covenant with God in Christ. Relationships intimate to our humanity; intimate to being a deacon, a brother, a priest; intimate to a Jesuit or diocesan commitment. Relationships that spell biblical justice. Relationships that mimic God's own fidelity to God's promises. Yes indeed, "blessed are [we if] we hunger and thirst for" such fidelity.

St. Ignatius Retreat House
Manhasset, New York
June 10, 1996

14
IT'S NOT MY PROBLEM!
Twelfth Sunday of the Year (A)

- Jeremiah 20:7–13
- Romans 5:15b–19
- Matthew 10:16–33

I would not be surprised if today's Gospel puzzled you.[1] All of a sudden, seemingly out of nowhere, Jesus warns his disciples in stern syllables: You will suffer at the hands of fellow Jews and secular authority; within families brother will betray brother, a father his child, children will rise against parents and have them put to death; in preaching you must proclaim Jesus' message fearlessly, unafraid of those who can kill only the body, never the soul. It's the problem of passages without a context. It reminds me of a teacher in my seminary days who was enslaved to his typed page; he simply read from it, word after word. At the sound of the bell ending class he would obediently stop speaking, even in the middle of a sentence; next day he would resume lecturing...from the middle of that sentence, exactly where he had left off.

Today's Gospel makes complete sense only in a context, only if we remember where we left off last Sunday. So then, not daring to trust your memories, let me begin there, link the two Gospel passages; then I shall move from first-century Palestine to 20th-century America; and I shall close with the usual blunt question, "So what?"

I

Last Sunday's Gospel had for overture Jesus' experience of his people. What did Jesus see as he gazed on his fellow Jews? Listen to Matthew: "When he saw the crowds, he had compassion for them, because they were harassed and helpless, like sheep without a shepherd" (9:36). What Jesus called "the lost sheep of the house of Israel" (10:6). Not one group within Israel; the whole of Israel.[2] The ordinary Jews crowding in on Jesus looked despondent, dejected. Why? Because they lacked true leaders—leaders who could prepare the people for the restored Israel the prophets had promised. This description of a people "harassed and helpless" was even more appropriate when Matthew was writing his Gospel—after the events of the year 70, when the Romans crushed a Jewish revolt, left much of Jerusalem in ruins, burned the Temple to the ground, left only the Temple's western wall, now the Wailing Wall, still standing.

The "harassed and helpless" before his eyes move Jesus to think of a mission, his first mission: to Israel.[3] "Go nowhere among the Gentiles, and enter no town of the Samaritans, but go rather to the lost sheep of the house of Israel" (Mt 10:5-6). Why? Because he himself is actually Israel's shepherd. He knows God's declaration through the prophet Micah: "But you, O Bethlehem of Ephrathah, who are one of the little clans of Judah, from you shall come forth for me one who is to rule in Israel, whose origin is from of old, from ancient days" (Mic 5:2).

But Jesus will not, perhaps cannot, shepherd Israel alone. "The harvest is plentiful," he says, "but the laborers are few" (Mt 9:37). And so he chooses 12 special associates, apostles who will share his power, help to bring about a restored Israel, a people more faithful to its God, living its covenant confidently, joyfully, no longer "harassed and helpless." These are Jesus' missionaries, sent by him to proclaim that "The kingdom of heaven has come near"; they are to "cure the sick, raise the dead, cleanse the lepers, cast out demons" (Mt 10:7-8).

The problem? "The laborers are few." In Jesus' own lifetime, primarily 12 apostles; some help from 72 disciples and a few totally devoted women. Therefore what? "Therefore ask the Lord of the harvest to send out laborers into his harvest" (9:38). Therefore pray. Not in desperation. Pray because only God can actually, effectively send men and women to work the harvest.

It is in this context that in today's Gospel Jesus warns his laborers, those who are his disciples. To be a disciple of Jesus is to follow in his footsteps. Therefore those who labor for Christ can be sure of one thing: They will suffer. "You will be hated by all because of my name" (Mt 10:22). And not only physical suffering. They will endure the agony of seeing the dark side of the Gospel, its tragic results. Families will be ruptured within; betrayal will tear parents and children apart, will sever siblings. Only those who endure to the end will be saved.

II

Move now from the first century to the twentieth. In our time too "the harvest is plentiful, the laborers few." Let me explain.

Less than two weeks ago, on the Op-Ed page of the *New York Times,* a column appeared under the title "Nike's Pyramid Scheme."[4] The author claimed that "More than a third of Nike's products are manufactured in Indonesia, a human rights backwater where the minimum wage was deliberately set below the subsistence level in order to attract foreign investment," where "It took four years of sometimes violent struggle" to raise the minimum wage to $2.20 a day. He uncovered the chief executive's salary: $864,583; his bonus in fiscal 1995: $787,500; his stock: $4.5 *billion.* He reported that Nike pays the world's greatest basketball player $20 million a year "to help create the demand for its products."

Please understand me. This is not a tirade against Nike's Indonesian wage scale, Philip Knight's earnings, Michael Jordan's pay check. The economic factors are too complex to be unfolded, much less blasted, in a homily; I am still struggling to grasp them. What I do grasp, and gulp at, is Mr. Jordan's original reaction to the situation. He "said, in essence, that it wasn't his problem. It is up to Nike, he said, 'to do what they can to make sure everything is correctly done.' He added: 'I don't know the complete situation. Why should I? I'm trying to do my job. Hopefully, Nike will do the right thing.'"

I am aware that Mr. Jordan has more recently announced that he will sit down with Nike executives to discuss the Indonesian issues. I am pleased, if not filled with hope, especially when Nike is moving into Vietnam, where the minimum wage is less than half of Indonesia's: $30 a month. In any event, my quarrel is not with any individual; it is much broader. Why is it that those in our culture who labor to bring about the kingdom of God are few? One potent reason: Uncounted Christians keep saying "It's not my problem!" Massacre of Serbs in Bosnia, Jewish-Palestinian hatred in the Middle East, Protestant-Catholic conflicts in Northern Ireland, one of every four U.S. children growing up in poverty, the income gap between richest and poorest the widest since World War II,[5] more African Americans in custody than in college, the AIDS-afflicted increasing by leaps and bounds, murderers on death row, land mines in Cambodia—these and so many more, millions mutter, are not my problems. Issues become my problems when they touch me, affect my job, my wages, my family: illegal immigration, affirmative action, welfare programs, violence on my street, increase in taxes. I cannot solve the world's problems. Even Jesus did not do that, could not. Did not, could not, solve the leadership problem in Palestine, rescued only a small number of the lost sheep. And look what happened to him: crucified between two thieves. Little wonder that the effective laborers are few. It's not my problem.

III

From all this my third point surges: So what? We Christians—all of us who confess Christ as Savior and Lord—belong to a community that claims our God had in mind from the beginning a single human family, each person an image of divinity, each bound to every other as children of the same God. We believe our Jesus shaped us into a single body, the Body of Christ, wherein, despite all our divisions, no one can say to any other "I have no need of you" (1 Cor 12:21), wherein our parish is not the District of Columbia or Upperville but the world. We profess a biblical justice that goes beyond what people strictly deserve, a justice that means fidelity to relationships stemming from our covenant cut in the blood of Christ, a covenant that demands of us that we not only love God above all else but love every sister and brother, especially the hungry and thirsty, the naked and the stranger, the ill and the imprisoned, as if we were standing in their shoes, love them as Christ loved and loves us.

For us there are no strangers. If an ancient pagan poet could say "Nothing that is human is foreign to me," each Christian has to confess "No person of God's shaping is a stranger to me." The 8000 Serbs massacred in Bosnia were my sisters and brothers. The women and children crafting our $140 sneakers in Indonesia are our own kin in Christ, young and aging for whom he poured out his blood. The HIV-positives call out mutely to the rest of us for at least the compassion of our Christ. Indelibly imprinted in my memory are words a very young homosexual, Bobby Griffin, wrote in his diary: "Why did you do this to me, God? Am I going to hell? That's the gnawing question that's always drilling little holes in the back of my mind. Please don't send me to hell. I'm really not that bad, am I?...Life is so cruel and unfair."[6] Bobby killed himself.

Not our problems? The words stick in my throat. I know, the further issue, the burning question, is, what can we do about it in the concrete? First, think globally. True, neither you nor I can save the world; only God can do that. Still, a primary need is to recognize the needs of that world, our world. In the context of those needs, think, judge, act. This past year I have been challenged to the core, challenged to think, judge, and act, by the response of the Jesuits' 34th General Congregation to the contemporary challenge from women:

> In response, we Jesuits first ask for the grace of conversion. We have been part of a civil and ecclesial tradition that has offended against women. And, like many men, we have a tendency to convince ourselves that there is no problem. However unwittingly, we have often been complicit in a form of clericalism which has reinforced male domination with an ostensibly divine sanction. By making this declaration we wish to react personally and collectively, and do what we can to change this regrettable situation.[7]

No need to act alone; little *use* acting alone. Your parish is a community, with gifts of nature and of grace that blow the mind. Harness those gifts, those charisms. Skills of all sorts, yes; economic and political power, of course; the energy of "the bold and the beautiful"; but also the pain and tears of the bedridden, the loneliness of the elderly forgotten, "completing in [their] flesh," as Paul insists, "what is lacking in Christ's afflictions for the sake of his body, the Church" (Col 1:24). All of this in the power of the Spirit, the Holy Spirit we call Power—the Greek *dynamis* that comes to mean dynamite. In the power of that Spirit one crucified convict and 12 ordinary men fired a revolution heard round the world. The age of miracles is not over. The proof? An electrician in Poland, a nun in Calcutta, a prisoner in South Africa. Walesa, Teresa, Mandela—the irresistible power in solidarity, in commitment, in suffering.

Yes, it will involve suffering—the suffering Jesus predicted. Not likely execution or assassination, like my six Jesuit brothers and their two lay helpers murdered by the military in El Salvador; probably not like our African American sisters and brothers watching in sorrow as their churches crumble to ashes in the hatred of arsonists. For us the price may be economic, a change in life style; it may be profoundly personal, cradling an AIDS infant in my arms; it may mean the scorn of friends, family tensions, like the relatives of Jesus who said he was "out of his mind" (Mk 3:21).

A final thought. Some years ago a sympathetic non-Catholic

said to one of our Catholic brethren, "You know, if you Catholics could get your act together, you'd be dangerous." Let me change two words and add one: "If we *Christians* could get *our* act together, we'd be *doubly* dangerous."

Trinity Episcopal Church
Upperville, Virginia
June 23, 1996

15
ON A CATHOLIC TIGHTROPE
Twelfth Week, Year 1, Monday

- Genesis 12:1–9
- Matthew 7:1–5

Three weeks ago, in Washington, D.C., I had already sketched in rough outline the heart of this evening's homily. Its springboard would be Abraham, our father in faith—Abraham who at 75 rose up in response to God's word and ventured forth to a land alien to him, to a future he knew not. In this context I would speak of your priesthood and mine: my launching out at 75 to a future far from clear, to dioceses and even countries alien to me; your own call from God, a year ago or 50, to priestly service only dimly foreseen, to proclamation of a biblical justice never hinted at in homiletics.[1]

Last Saturday, at one in the morning, that homily hit the vertical file. Jet lag had murdered sleep. Within 48 hours I had flown from Washington, D.C., to Oklahoma City, preached on the feast of St. Aloysius Gonzaga, delivered two addresses to a workshop on evangelization, flown to Los Angeles to make contact with Father Raymond Kemp,[2] boarded Qantas 100 with him for a 15-hour flight to Melbourne, checked in at the Jesuit Provincial residence, slept for six hours, enjoyed a sleepy dinner with the community, bedded down at nine—and at one I was wide awake. I wandered into the community room, picked up the London *Tablet* for May 27, hit upon an agonizing article by the head of religious education at Notre Dame High School in Norwich,[3] and the original homily was doomed. Let me (1) sum up the article and (2) touch it to you and me.

I

First, the article. One morning in March of this year the sports hall at Notre Dame High School was filled with students attending a Mass of their own free will. The occasion? A memorial service for a pupil killed in a road accident on his way to school. The bidding prayers came from the hearts and lips of Michael's friends. One 13-year-old stood by the altar and began: "God, why have you taken Michael away from me? He was my friend and he made me laugh...." Students and faculty wept. The writer, Clare Richards, went on:

> I wept for Michael and his grieving family listening to these prayers, but I wept too for something else. The honesty, direct-ness and simplicity of our pupils was reflected in that prayer. It said what people actually felt. It had the spontaneity of a psalm. And it was totally unlike the lame and anodyne prayers we churn out week by week. An adult would have written: "Dear Lord, take Michael into your heavenly kingdom and give strength to his family...."[4]

Clare Richards wept too because "the 'official' Church has lost its spontaneity, and worse, it usually ignores the honesty and fresh-ness of children's faith."[5]

> The young are just as much the Church as the Pope, the bish-ops, the priests, the nuns, and the sacristan. The truth is they do not feel it, and, with ever-growing evidence, they do not really think that it matters too much. Catholic RE teachers stand in the firing line by representing the establishment, with all its emphasis on rules and toeing the party line. It can be a painful and thankless task.[6]

Clare Richards sometimes wonders why she comes home from school so exhausted. Age? Paperwork? Perhaps. "But deeper down I suspect it is the result of trying all day to walk a tightrope."[7] Asked to write a book on Roman Catholic Christianity, she agonized: Whom was she writing it for? For the pupils, of course. "But I had to keep looking over my shoulder at what the authorities would accept."[8]

It angers her that church leaders can hand out the "official line" in public "only to admit in private that they agree with the rest of us. And if they do speak out, as Bishop Gaillot of Evreux recently did, they get shot down."[9]

Richards tells of a parish council meeting where proposals were made for ways of getting the young people "to join us here. What about us going out to join them where they are?"[10]

And I will tell you where they are. They are critical of those who hand out the party line as absolutes. They are disgusted by hypocrisy. They have no time for insincerity. And they do not go in for large institutions. But they do respond to the Gospel. Straight. They like Jesus....

You can see why I feel uncomfortable. I am entrusted by Catholic governors to support the party line. I even had to get the imprimatur for my book to ensure it was acceptable to Catholic schools. I was not ready to fall completely off the tightrope on the pupils' side. I took the teacher's safety precaution of sitting on the rope. Educationalists say I have to do that anyway. But Michael's friend deserves better. I ask his forgiveness if I have been less honest than he in sharing my faith.[11]

II

But how does Clare Richards' dilemma relate to you and me? Not indeed in every detail. Specifically in that we too must do something of a balancing act on a tightrope. Actually two tightropes. On the one hand, between the demands of authority and the needs of our people; on the other hand, between the demands of justice and the enslavements of our people. A word on each.

First, authority versus needs. As priests, we are not Lone Rangers. We represent an institution. Not my charism to define ultimately, even to declare officially, what the Catholic Church believes, how Catholics must live, how they are to worship. And yet beliefs, morality, worship are not disembodied entities floating about in outer space. It is always a living, throbbing, unrepeatable person— this man, this woman—who is struggling to believe, working through a moral crisis, straining to change a lifetime of traditional ritual. And when doubt and dissatisfaction, tension and distrust reach irrepressible proportions, it is not the pope who answers the pastoral telephone; it is the parish priest.

And what if the parish priest shares the struggle of his people? What if he is himself unsure of contraception or in vitro fertilization, of priestly celibacy or women's ordination? How follow Cardinal Hume's "No Catholic is free to dissent from what is taught" in *Evangelium vitae*[12] and avoid the charge of hypocrisy, of insincerity? How follow moralist Richard McCormick's argument that the encyclical is perfectly correct on principles but incorrect in certain applications[13] and avoid the censure of authority? How far can you carry Vatican II's declaration that "all the faithful, clerical and lay, possess a lawful freedom of inquiry and of thought, and the freedom to express their minds humbly and courageously about those matters in which they enjoy competence"?[14]

Not as abstract conundrums do I propose these questions; I have suffered aplenty from my reaction to *Humanae vitae*—ironically, not from pope or local bishop, usually from peers in priesthood. But I have no push-button answer to such questions; answers will come, if they come at all, from profound prayer and ceaseless study, from agonizing discernment and courage even to crucifixion.

Second, the tension between the demands of justice and the enslavements of our people—of your people. What are they ? I did not fly from the United States with a hatful of answers for the continent of Australia. Still, four days have raised a hatful of questions—questions that should sear the soul, torment the mind, of every priest. I am told that in a developed world that exalts the equality of the sexes the macho male is still a fixture in Australia. Are Catholic males immune? I am told that racism, if not rampant, continues to confront the Asian and the Aboriginal. The incident on Qantas 461 from Sydney to Melbourne, where an attendant asked a white lady if she wanted to move away from three Aboriginal artists (with whom she was actually traveling)—was this exceptional or typical? Why the discrimination in housing and employment among ethnic populations, unfair interest charges and wage structures? Is the materialism and consumerism that John Paul II assailed, the endless lust for more and more, the constant replacement of the old with the new, the attendant waste—is this now a mark of your culture, even your Catholic culture? Is the spousal abuse that is slowly seeping into the headlines a sacrilege that rouses your rage? How have your people reacted to the gay and the lesbian—not only the morality of their actions but the undeniable dignity of their humanity? And why the increase in drug addiction, in teenage suicides?

These are simply examples that relate to justice—enslavements heard almost in passing. Your own experience is far more pertinent. Our concern in this retreat/workshop is not only to identify the enslavements but how to preach thereon; our courage too, or lack thereof. Here what is utterly indispensable is how we understand the justice we are ordained to preach. Not simply, or even primarily, ethical justice: Give to each man, woman, and child what each deserves, because it can be proven from philosophy or has been written into law. Rather, biblical justice: fidelity to right relationships, to responsibilities, that stem from our covenant with God cut in the blood of Christ. What relations, what responsibilities? (1) To God: Love the

Lord your God above all else, with all your heart and mind, all your soul and strength. (2) To people: Love every human as brother or sister; love each like another self, whatever the color or class, the accent or smell. (3) To the earth: Love the things of God, the earth on which you dance; respect God's every creation; realize that the Genesis command is not to subdue, to subjugate, but to handle with care, with reverence. In terms of this morning's biblical presentation, liberation from Australia's enslavements, your own Egypts, your people's Pharaohs.

Dear brothers in the priesthood of Christ: This week should be an increasingly intense initiation into the Just Word, the kind of fidelity God expects of us and of our people. Not only intellectual, a head trip. Rather, a conversion of the whole person, heart as well as mind, passions as well as convictions. Fire in the belly. So fiery a flame that when you preach, when you spell out responsibilities that stem from a cross on Calvary, icy hearts will defrost, prejudices will fall apart, and under the all-conquering grace of God your people may increasingly become free, the single Body of Christ, the community wherein, as St. Paul put it, no one, absolutely no one, can say to any other, "I have no need of you" (1 Cor 12:21).

Corpus Christi College
Melbourne, Australia
June 26, 1995

16
WHY, GOD, WHY?
Thirteenth Week, Year 1, Monday

- Genesis 18:16–33
- Matthew 8:18–22

You know, our God ceaselessly surprises me, at times delights me. This morning, as we probed God's Word,[1] we discovered what it means for us to be just. Not merely to give to another what that other deserves, can claim as a genuine right. More importantly, to be just is to be faithful. Faithful to relationships, to responsibilities, especially as these stem from a covenant with God. We are just to the extent that we love God above all else, treat every child of God like another self, and handle God's good earth with reverence.

And now, this evening, God's written Word just proclaimed surprises us with an even more fundamental question: When is *God* just? More pungently still, *is* God just? Is God in right relationship? Two settings, two points: (1) the city that was Sodom; (2) the world that is ours.

I

First, the city that was Sodom. More specifically, Abraham bargaining with God (Gen 18:16–33). Most of my adult life I've misunderstood the story. I thought Abraham was interceding for Sodom, bargaining for God's mercy on that corrupt city. Not at all. Abraham is engaged in a learning process. He wants to find out if Yahweh is really, actually, genuinely just. Does God distinguish between the righteous and the wicked? Or are all Sodom's citizens in the same divine destructive net? Abraham's method? He dares to bargain with God.[2]

Notice the intriguing way the story unfolds. It begins with a divine soliloquy. Yahweh asks Himself, "Shall I hide from Abraham what I am about to do?" (v. 17)—my plans for him and his descendants. Why the question? Because "in the ancient Near East, a servant of the god or king was also a friend, privy to his master's plans."[3] So, Yahweh's answer: Since Abraham's people will be great among the nations, the servant (Abraham) will now be gifted with knowledge of God's plan. Besides, since Abraham will have to charge his people to "keep the way of the Lord by doing what is right and just" (v. 19), it is only fitting that the founder of such a people should now see God doing what is right and just in Sodom. And what is that? Punishing sinners only. God announces His plan and the dialogue follows.

Abraham's opening question is blunt indeed, the heart of the problem: "Will you indeed sweep away the righteous with the wicked?" (v. 23). Then he goes through the numbers game. Suppose I find 50 righteous, 45, 40, 30, 20—finally, only ten righteous in the whole city. Whatever the number, however small, "Far be it from you to slay the righteous with the wicked, so that the righteous fare as the wicked! Far be that from you! Shall not the Judge of all the earth do what is just?" (v. 25). The Lord God agrees; only the sinners will be destroyed; Lot, his wife, their two daughters will be brought outside the city before its destruction (cf. chap. 19). And the dialogue partners depart, each his own way. God has been revealed as just—the Creator God in right relationship with God's creatures.

II

So much for the city that was Sodom; but what of the world that is ours? Last week, just about this time, I was preaching to some 34 priests here. In a similar liturgical context, I retold a story I had read in the London *Tablet*. A memorial Mass was celebrated in Norwich for a teenage student killed in a road accident on his way to school. The bidding prayers came from the hearts and lips of Michael's friends. One 13-year-old stood by the altar and began: "God, why have you taken Michael away from me? He was my friend and he made me laugh...."[4]

"Why?" Perhaps the most agonizing three-letter question in the English language. A question hurled directly at a supposedly just God, a God invariably faithful to divine promises, a God by definition in right relationship to the creatures shaped in God's image and likeness. This is the God of whom the Psalmist sang:

The Lord is merciful and gracious,
    slow to anger and abounding in steadfast love....
[The Lord] does not deal with us according to our sins,
    nor repay us according to our iniquities.
For as the heavens are high above the earth,
    so great is His steadfast love toward those who fear Him....
For [the Lord] knows how we were made,
    remembers that we are dust.

(Ps 103:8–14)

If so, then why? Why the senseless murders from the infants in Jesus' own Bethlehem to the hundreds of children killed by gunfire in my own Washington back yard? Why the innocents born with Down's syndrome, encephalitic, drug-addicted? Why the Holocaust that destroyed six million Jews at the whim of a Nazi butcher? Why the bestial rapes in Bosnia and the endless starvation in the sub-Sahara? Why the drunken driver who wiped out a whole family in a split second? Why the cancer that took my father and only brother within three weeks of each other? Why, why, and why?

For most of my four-score years I struggled with that mystifying monosyllable. I looked to the ancient Israelites as they focused now on the sins of their ancestors, now on their individual sins, now on the sins of the nation. I was heartened on hearing the Psalmist, "When the righteous cry for help, the Lord hears, and rescues them from all their troubles" (Ps 34:17); disheartened to read, "I say to God, my rock, 'Why have you forgotten me?'" (Ps 42:9). At long last I resonated to dear old Job. You remember how Job kept protesting his innocence; he could prove he had done nothing to merit what he suffered. You remember how he found human searching inadequate, experienced peace only when God "answered Job out of the whirlwind" (Job 38:1), appeared to him—not to answer Job's questions, only to demand his trust. Trust in a God never unfaithful to divine promises, in right relationship to Job, even on his dunghill.

A disciple of Christ, one who boasted with Paul only in following Christ crucified, I ransacked the New Testament for an intellectually satisfying answer. I have discovered more than enough to nourish a spiritual life in union with Christ: "We suffer with [Christ] so that we may also be glorified with him" (Rom 8:17). Especially Paul's profound declaration, "I am now rejoicing in my sufferings for your sake, and in my flesh I am completing what is lacking in Christ's afflictions for the sake of his body, that is, the Church" (Col 1:24). Still, the Gospels and Paul are not a solution to the problem of evil—no answer to a crib death, no answer to 55 million dead in

World War II. No answer to every why. No answer to heartrending questions about the justice of an omnipotent God, God's own declared fidelity to the children of God.

And yet, by God, God must be faithful, whatever the appearances to the contrary. The proof? A cross outside Jerusalem. Each human being from the first Adam to the last Antichrist can declare with Paul, "The Son of God loved me and gave himself for me" (Gal 2:20). A God who gave an only Son to crucifixion out of love for me—out of love for every human—how can this God be somehow out of sync with the images of His Son? How can such a God not care any more?

I have ceased to argue it. With Mary beneath the cross, argument is sterile. Here, in the flesh of God, here is the justice of God. "This is my body...given for you" (Lk 22:19).

Corpus Christi College
Melbourne, Australia
July 3, 1995

17
FREEDOM FROM, FREEDOM FOR
Sixteenth Week, Year 1, Monday

- Exodus 14:5–18
- Matthew 12:38–42

That remarkable Protestant theologian Dietrich Bonhoeffer, martyr to Nazi madness, helped mightily to popularize an important distinction: "free from" and "free for." I am free from God's nonhuman creation, he declared, to the extent that I am not dominated by the world, am not the world's prisoner through technology, exercise reverential dominion over the earth as a gift from God and not a matter of my own grasping. But "there is no 'being-free-from' without 'being-free-for.' There is no dominion without serving God.... God, our brother, and the earth belong together.... Only where God and man's brother come to man can man find the way back to the earth."[1] Being free from nonhuman creation in reverential rule over it, and being free for God and our sisters and brothers—here, for Bonhoeffer, is the image of God in the first human God created.[2]

I find Bonhoeffer's distinction an exciting way to look at the Exodus. That escape from Egypt, that flight from Pharaoh, was an event extraordinarily rich for a theology of liberation—liberation from evil and liberation from unjust social structures. But there is a problem here. The Exodus as liberation, "freedom from," can hide from us the fuller reality of God's intervention, "freedom for." So then, three stages to the movement of my thought: (1) the Hebrew Exodus as freedom from; (2) the Hebrew Exodus as freedom for; (3) what this might say about our own exodus, the Christian exodus, yours and mine.[3]

I

First, the Hebrew Exodus as freedom from, as liberation. Let your imagination loose, relive the background. Picture the Hebrew people enslaved in Egypt. See the taskmasters oppressing them with forced labor. But recall what Exodus emphasizes: "the more they were oppressed, the more they multiplied and spread, so that the Egyptians came to dread the Israelites" (Exod 1:11–12). Pharaoh's reaction? Not only intolerable labor but genocide. He said to the Hebrew midwives, "If [the newborn] is a boy, kill him" (v. 16). The Hebrew response? The midwives revolted. They "feared God; they did not do as the king of Egypt commanded them, but they let the boys live" (v. 17). God's response? "So God dealt well with the midwives; and the people multiplied and became very strong" (v. 20). This revolt of the midwives "is an important paradigm of resistance to oppression."[4] Their no to Pharaoh let God's promise to Abraham continue and it prepared for the rescue of Moses from death.

The next step in freedom from? Liberation of the liberator. Moses had to suffer the same fate as the people. When Pharaoh heard that Moses had killed an Egyptian, "he sought to kill Moses" (2:15). And so the man destined by God to free God's people was forced to flee from Pharaoh, forced to settle in Midian, forced to live as an alien in an alien land. But liberation is at root an act of God. So God appears to Moses in a flame of fire out of a bush. "Come, I will send you to Pharaoh to bring my people...out of Egypt" (3:10). Moses protests, "Who am I" to confront Pharaoh, to lead the Israelites out of Egypt's oppression? God's reply? "I will be with you..." (3:11–12). Moses will be a prophet, one who speaks for God and for a people without a voice. But it is God who will free the people from Pharaoh. It is the Lord who speaks to Pharaoh by the mouth of Moses: "Let my people go..." (5:1).

Even the ten plagues, nature itself turning against Egypt, did not deter Pharaoh. He was determined not only to enslave the Israelites. The ultimate question was: Who would be their "god," Pharaoh or the God of their fathers? For Pharaoh, the most outrageous demand must have been not simply "Let my people go" but "Let my people go, so that they may worship me" (9:1). Worship someone other than Pharaoh. And so, when the Israelites walked on dry ground through the Red Sea, they had been liberated not only from servile oppression but from an alien god.

II

Still, Israel's journey was not sheer liberation. It was a journey from liberation to freedom. Or, in Bonhoeffer's terms, "freedom from" to "freedom for." For what? The challenge of Sinai: to be transformed from a herd of "wretched fugitives" into a responsible people, to adopt a way of life that is not license, not freedom from regulation, but a "bondage in freedom," freely chosen obligations.[5] A way of life that does not reproduce the very evils that have been overthrown, the attitudes of the oppressors, Egypt's way of governing. In brief, "a contrast society."[6]

How was this to be done? By a covenant, a formal agreement between Yahweh and Israel. A covenant that "reveals a God who wishes people to live in a community combining worship and obedience to him with care for neighbor, a God who remains faithful even when people break the covenant."[7]

It is in the context of the covenant that biblical justice is most evident, fidelity to the demands of a relationship. A fidelity expected of God as well as of the people. It is in the law codes of Israel that the covenant demands on the people are revealed. And this especially in their concern for the powerless in the community. "You shall not wrong or oppress a resident alien, for you were aliens in the land of Egypt. You shall not abuse any widow or orphan" (Exod 22:21–22).

We Christians have a long-lasting tendency to see in Israel's laws a nitpicking, oppressive effort to limit the freedom of God's people. In point of fact, Israel's code of laws had for purpose a community not ruled by power and greed, a family of God where the treatment of the marginal was the touchstone of right relationship to God. The Torah is "faith coming to expression in communal forms and structures."[8] Here is the contrast society in living color.

III

Finally, what is it that the Exodus from Egypt and the covenant on Sinai might say to you and me? If you haven't already guessed it, it has to do with freedom from and freedom for. St. Paul has told us bluntly what we have been freed from: from sin, from death, from self.

From sin. If you have died with Christ, he told the Christians of Rome, you are no longer slaves to sin: "Sin will have no dominion over you, since you are not under law but under grace" (Rom 7:14; see vv. 6–7). Oh yes, we can still sin, still do; but not because Sin has the power to tyrannize over us, not because we cannot help ourselves.

We sin freely, and with God's grace we are empowered to say no to sin freely.

From death. "The law of the Spirit of life in Christ Jesus has set you free from the law of sin and of death" (Rom 8:2). The death that stems from sin, the death that means separation from the God who is Life, this death will not be ours as long as God's Spirit dwells in us. And even the death that ends mortal life has been transfigured: We rise unto life without end.

From self. From my whole person when ruled by sin. I mean Paul's *sôma,* the body of sin and of death. I mean the self Paul spoke of so agonizingly: "I do not do the good I want, but the evil I do not want is what I do" (Rom 7:19). "We know that our old self was crucified with [Jesus], so that the body of sin might be destroyed, and we might no longer be enslaved to sin" (Rom 6:6). From this we have been freed. "Who will rescue me from this body of death? Thanks be to God! [It is done] through Jesus Christ our Lord" (Rom 7:24).

A formidable triad, this sin and death and self from which we have been liberated. But liberated for what? To be a people, a single family, in harmony with Jesus' prayer at the Last Supper for all who believe, "that they may all be one. As you, Father, are in me and I am in you, may they also be one in us, so that the world may believe that you have sent me" (Jn 17:21). For we too have a covenant, a pact with God cut in the blood of Christ. "This is my body ...given for you.... This cup that is poured out for you is the new covenant in my blood" (Lk 22:19–20). Even, at times like ours, liberated to be a contrast society, Paul's "new creation" (2 Cor 5:17), in revolt against the Pharaohs of our time, the ways of thinking and living that threaten to enslave us.

What enslavements? A greed, a consumerist society, a social structure, a ceaseless lusting for more and more that has widened the gap between the haves and the have-nots. We need a host of Catholics like Dorothy Day who

> could not go to Communion and be insensitive to the reality that someone was hungry; she could not enjoy the warmth of Eucharistic consolation and know that she had a blanket while her brothers and sisters did not; she could not "go to the altar of God" and be aware that someone was sleeping over a grate on the sidewalk.[9]

It is not a wallowing in guilt; it is a realistic recognition that, to some extent, just about all of us have been affected by a culture that esteems having over being, judges God's images by the clothes they wear and the homes they inhabit, wants more prisons and HIV units but "not in my back yard," clamors 80 percent for the gas chamber, a life for a life.

What enslavements? A society that has transmuted the creative individualism that long distinguished our history into a rugged individualism that prizes the private "me" over the communal "we." A society where the elderly are terribly lonely and the young are at terrible risk. The children. As I mull over the 12,000 battered bodies and shriveled souls that swarm each year into Covenant House at Times Square, as I agonize over the million youngsters who sleep on America's streets each night, as I weep over 25 percent of our children growing up in hopeless poverty, there echoes in my ears Elizabeth Barrett Browning's "The Cry of the Children":

> Do ye hear the children weeping, O my brothers,
>   Ere the sorrow comes with years?
> They are leaning their young heads against their mothers,
>   And *that* cannot stop their tears.
> The young lambs are bleating in the meadows,
>   The young birds are chirping in the nest,
> The young fawns are playing with the shadows,
>   The young flowers are blowing toward the west—
> But the young, young children, O my brothers,
>   They are weeping bitterly!
> They are weeping in the playtime of the others,
>   In the country of the free.[10]

Good brothers and sisters in Christ: For all the agonies that afflict our common ministry today—ceaseless demands, unreal expectations, rare appreciation, low morale, pedophilia—you and I are uncommonly blessed. Not only have we been freed from Sin's demonic dominion, from death's horrifying hopelessness, from the tyranny of a shackled self. We have been freed for a breathtaking role in the divine dream for the freedom of God's people. All of us are privileged to murmur with the risen Christ, "This is my body [and it is] given for you," for your freedom. Day after day, we are privileged to proclaim boldly and to shape slowly God's vision of justice: a community where each sees in every other—the child and the aging, rich and poor, whatever their color or smell or accent—an image of Christ, a sister or brother, another self, each struggling in some way to live a human existence.

True, a whole culture seems arrayed against us—a culture we share, a culture with all the attractive power of its politics and its pornography. its music and its movies, its guns and its games, its young and restless, its bold and beautiful. We have only one advantage: our Gospel, our Good News, what Paul called "the power of God for salvation" (Rom 1:16). If it is to be a struggle of power, we need not be afraid—unless we mistake the power as our own. It is not our personal power that draws people to love God above all else, to love others as other selves, to touch God's earth with reverence. It is the power of God.

Do you really believe that? Do you believe Paul when he says to you, "Consider your own call, brothers and sisters.... God chose what is foolish in the world to shame the wise; God chose what is weak in the world to shame the strong; God chose what is low and despised in the world...so that no one might boast in the presence of God" (1 Cor 1:27–29)? If you don't believe that, kneel before the cross: "We proclaim Christ...crucified" (v. 23).

Christ the King Seminary
East Aurora, N.Y.
July 24, 1995

18

LITTLE ONES, LEADERS,
AND GOD'S WORD
Twenty-sixth Week, Year 1, Monday

- Exodus 23:20–24
- Matthew 18:1–5, 10

Today's Gospel is entirely appropriate for today's feast, for a memorial of Guardian Angels. But in its original context, it was not angels that were the centerpiece; the angels are there because of the children. And even the children are not there for their own sake. A real child is set before the disciples as a symbol for humility—"not because children are naturally humble, but because they are dependent."[1] And the "little ones" for whom the child stands, who believe in Jesus, who are not to be scandalized, are not other little children; the "little ones" are minor community members, those who are led, those who are small not in age but "in esteem, importance, influence, power."[2] Today's Gospel is a lesson in Christian leadership.

So then, three rubrics frame my discourse: (1) little ones, (2) leaders, (3) you and I.

I

First, little ones. When the disciples asked Jesus, "Who is the greatest in the kingdom of heaven?" (Lk 18:1), the question was not out of place, inappropriate. Not in first-century Judaism, where social status was taken with utmost seriousness.[3] How does Jesus respond? He challenges cultural assumptions about social status. The child he sets in the midst of his disciples is an example of a social nobody. "The child had no status and no social importance. Jesus challenges his followers not to think in terms of social hierarchies."[4] Be willing to become a social nobody. And Matthew, concerned for

89

life *within* the Christian community, is particularly concerned for his "little ones." Do you remember that touching passage where Matthew's Jesus says, "Whoever gives a cup of cold water to one of these little ones" (Mt 10:42) will not go unrewarded? No distinguished status within the community, not in the power structure, modest personal gifts, perhaps little or no education—these "little ones" called for special pastoral care.

As in the Gospel, as in Matthew's community, so in our Church, in our diocese, in our parish. We too have our "little ones," the powerless, those without influence, "the members of the body that" Paul says "seem to be weaker" (1 Cor 12:22). They cover much ground. Not only the poor and the disabled. "Little ones" are the laity, especially women and teenagers. "Little ones" in some places are African Americans and Hispanics, in some parishes permanent deacons. "Little ones" are the drug-addicted and the AIDS-afflicted.

I am not carrying the banner for a democratic church. But even in a hierarchical church it is still true that in God's eyes we are not greater or less because we exercise power or are powerless. Before all else, I yearn for all Catholics to realize that by baptism we are all equally sons and daughters of God, all equally members of the Body of Christ, all called to be perfect as our "heavenly Father is perfect" (Mt 5:48). For more than two decades I have been haunted by a powerful sentence in Cardinal Suenens' book *Coresponsibility in the Church:* The greatest day in the life of a pope is not his coronation but his baptism, the day of his mission "to live the Christian life in obedience to the gospel."[5]

In these "little ones" I discover an intriguing paradox. On the one hand, they can have an influence far beyond their insignificant social and ecclesiastical status. For by their sufferings, by their generous sharing in Christ's own cross, by their Mary-like "lowliness" (Lk 1:48), they "complete what is lacking in Christ's afflictions for the sake of his body, the Church" (Col 1:24). They are hardly powerless— at least before God. On the other hand, it is fairly easy to forget them; only rarely do they make the headlines, only rarely grace the diocesan newspaper; they are not the lectors, the Eucharistic ministers; they live in the Church's shadow.

II

All of this leads quite naturally into my second point: our leaders. A leader, Andrew Greeley wrote somewhere, is not someone in a position of power—a Duvalier, a Noriega, a Marcos; a leader is someone who can move the minds and hearts of men and women.

Within Catholicism those who by their very office are expected to exercise leadership are primarily the pope and the bishops. A homily is not the place to argue the respective competencies of Catholic bishops as leaders in the Greeley mold. But I cannot help recalling the lovable pastoral style of John XXIII and the warm intelligence of Apostolic Delegate Jean Jadot; I remember and treasure the intelligent graciousness of Detroit's Cardinal Dearden and the pastoral gentleness of Baltimore's Cardinal Shehan, the courage-under-fire of Seattle's Archbishop Hunthausen and the grace-under-fire of Chicago's Cardinal Bernardin, the soft-spoken love of Erie's retired Bishop Murphy.

But within Catholicism, fortunately, it is not only popes and bishops who are Greeley-type leaders. We have been blessed with a Cesar Chavez, a Jack Egan, a Mother Teresa, a Dorothy Day, a John Courtney Murray. What I find intriguing is that men and women like these moved hearts and minds in different ways. For example, Chavez by his sacrificial courage in the face of powerful agricultural opposition; Egan by his lifelong passion for justice; Mother Teresa by a fascinating wedding of holiness and inflexibility; Dorothy Day by living and eating with the poor in rat-infested hovels; Murray by employing his rich gifts of mind and tongue in the service of what he called "civilized conversation."

And you know, these and so many others felt very much at home with the "little ones." Not only those like Day and Chavez, who lived with the poor and marginalized. I mean John XXIII as apostolic legate to Turkey signing 800 baptismal certificates for Jewish children trying to escape from Germany to Palestine; John as pope with his arm around a prisoner and admitting, "You know, I have a cousin in jail." I mean Archbishop Jadot struggling to learn what American Catholicism is really like, speaking always from knowledge and with compassion, proposing to Rome as bishops men with pastoral gifts, paying a price in Rome for his unusual *modus operandi*. I mean the graciousness of Murray to high and low; for, as his Jewish secretary put it, all you had to be was a human being and he respected you, even loved you.

III

All of which leads to you and me. Priests and permanent deacons are expected to be leaders. Not commanders-in-chief; simply men who can move minds and hearts. The pastoral tasks that touch minds and hearts are many and demanding—from the way we celebrate the Eucharist, through the way we administer a parish, to the way we oil the dying to life beyond. But for our purposes this week,[6] I shall focus on one of our most important pastoral privileges, in some ways the most neglected. I mean preaching God's Word.

Not an option; an obligation. An obligation that goes back to St. Paul's set of questions to the Christians of Rome: "'Everyone who calls on the name of the Lord shall be saved.' But how are they to call on one in whom they have not believed? And how are they to believe in one of whom they have never heard? And how are they to hear without someone to proclaim him? And how are they to proclaim him unless they are sent?... So faith comes from what is heard, and what is heard comes through the word of Christ" (Rom 10:13-17).

Is there anything we do that consistently, day after day, week after week, has more potential for moving minds and hearts? You may answer, "The Eucharist, stupid!" Yes, but the homily is an integral part of the Eucharistic liturgy. Not only that. You know by now that the liturgical forms and texts have been rather rigidly fixed through the centuries for all peoples, all ages, all conditions. What we do in the homily is transport the age-old symbols to this time, this place, this people. What the rite expresses in a common way, in a general way, the homily personalizes. It not only comments on the mystery in the light of the liturgical texts; it draws the faithful into the mystery, helps them unite their life to the mystery.[7] Life not as "an empty framework of existence, a kind of general and anonymous spiritual life," not "what remains of man's life after everything that really interests him has been eliminated," but "life as filled or crossed by all kinds of events, great or small, a life that is committed to the conditions and tasks of every day."[8] The homily is the bond between the liturgy of the Word and the liturgy of the bread and cup; yes, the bond between Christ's Eucharist and our people's lives.

Our people's lives—especially our Lord's "little ones." Yes, such is the wonder of our words, and such is the cross that overshadows our words. You know, despite our homiletic deficiencies, most of our people still share our Eucharist with hope—hope that a word will issue from our lips that makes some sense out of the week just past, sheds a glimmer of light on a cancer, the unexpected death of a dear one, unemployment, hunger, despair, a blue funk, or just the joylessness that accompanies so much of everyday living.

Move minds and hearts with words? Why not? John Denver and Amy Grant do it day after day, sell millions of albums with words. Why not you and I? Only if there is no fire in our bellies. Only if we fail to realize that it is God who gives the increase, God who, the story of Balaam's beast demonstrates, can open the mouth of an ass (Num 22:28).

Do you want to be a leader? Preach. Preach as Jesus preached— aware of God's presence within you and all around you; aware of a believing, hoping, loving people before you, Christ's "little ones" thirsting for God's word from your lips; consumed, as Jesus was, by a fire in the belly that will not let you rest till you have shared the "good news"—the good news that alone makes sense out of your ordination. God's words on your lips—it can change lives, transform minds and hearts. Including...yours and mine.

Mission Point Resort
Mackinac Island, Michigan
October 2, 1995

19

LEST SHE FINALLY WEAR ME OUT
Twenty-ninth Sunday of the Year (C)

- Exodus 17:8–13
- 2 Timothy 3:14—4:2
- Luke 18:1–8

Today's Gospel is a short-story masterpiece, another Oscar for Jesus. Two strong characters fill the four verses: a corrupt judge "who neither feared God nor had respect for people" (Lk 18:2), and a widow whose rights he refuses, a woman powerless without a male in a patriarchal society, unable to obtain justice. But this widow will not play her traditional role, will not lie down and be walked over. What does she do? In Jesus' words, she "kept coming to him," kept "bothering" him (vv. 3, 5). She makes a nuisance of herself.

How? Use your imagination. Not only does she confront the judge constantly in court; she buttonholes him on the street, interrupts his supper, packs his mailbox with endless notes, perhaps tosses midnight stones at his bedroom window. And the judge gives in. Not because he has changed his mind, is convinced of her rights. No, for the first time he is afraid: She will wear him out, give him no rest. Afraid of a powerless woman, a persevering woman, a relentless woman, an unjust judge does what is just.

Today I ask you to revamp that story. No longer a single judge uncaring of people; rather, 535 legislators with enormous power. No longer a single widow; rather, the most vulnerable of humans, millions of children in poverty, without a powerful lobby to represent them. In this new story, this real-life story, let a disciple of Jesus (1) describe the children, (2) sketch the peril, and (3) suggest what you and I can do as their voices.

I

First, the children.[1] In the richest country on earth, almost 16 million grow up in poverty. The younger children are, the poorer they are: One in every four children under six is poor, 27 percent of children under three. One poor child out of two lives in extreme poverty, in families whose incomes fall below half the federal poverty line.

Not a genteel, graceful poverty; not the dignified poverty of Jesus, Mary, and Joseph. This is the poverty that batters the body and crushes the spirit. This is the poverty that makes for death; for low-income children are two times more likely than others to die from birth defects, four times more likely to die from fires, five times more likely to die from infectious diseases and parasites, six times more likely to die from other diseases. This is the poverty that makes for disease and illness; for this brand of poverty stunts growth, destroys the body's iron, facilitates asthma and chronic diarrhea, child abuse and drug addiction. This is the poverty that afflicts intelligence; for it slows the mind, affects test scores, lowers attention span, increases school dropouts. This is the poverty that leads to violence, to crime, to senseless killing for a Reebok. This is the poverty that breaks up families, makes our streets concrete jungles, crowds our jails with juvenile delinquents.

I am not excusing, absolving of blame, every youngster addicted to coke or crack, every lad who steals or mugs, rapes or kills. I *am* saying that millions of our young have little or no chance of living a human existence, much less a Christian existence, because a grim, merciless, unforgiving poverty grinds them into an inhuman dust, most from the moment they escape from their mother's womb.

II

Second, the peril. Not the peril precisely in the poverty of our children; rather, the peril from the powerful, from 535 legislators who will decide how the poor are to manage their lives, how poor children are to live. As a Special Report of the Children's Defense Fund put it, "The lives of millions of children will be thrown into jeopardy if Congress proceeds with its plans to shred the safety net protecting children and families from destitution."[2] I look at my own limited area. As the CDF sees it, in the year 2000, children in the District of Columbia, Maryland, and Virginia would be facing budget cuts in six programs: school lunch subsidies, $18.1 million; Aid to

Families with Dependent Children, $97.1 million; food stamps, $205.6 million; Supplementary Security Income for disabled children, $114.9 million; child-care subsidies, $24.2 million; food subsidies for children in day-care and Head Start programs, $39.7 million.[3] Roughly $500 million in basic welfare benefits.

Multiply those figures across the country, and the sum total is mind-boggling, devastating. The new approach to budget cutting "threatens to rip a $40 billion hole in the federal safety net guarding" the survival of our children.[4] Forty billion dollars.

These are not cold statistics. These are babies without milk, abused children without safe homes, disabled children without appropriate beds, destitute children without shelter or heat, spastic children unable to afford speech therapy.

This is six-year-old Alison Higginbotham.[5] With a rare disorder called infantile spasms, Alison must be supervised constantly, wears diapers, cannot speak, cannot feed herself, cannot walk any distance. To meet her special needs—expensive shoes, a special bed, a ramp for her wheel chair, transportation for speech therapy—her father and mother receive about $395 a month in Supplemental Security Income, about $4800 a year. With that Alison is guaranteed loving care at home—the love that heals even if it cannot cure. Without it the state and federal governments would pay $60,000 a year for institutional care.

III

Third, what has all this to do with you and me, with the Catholic vision of life? Let's begin with a basic reality that underlies genuine Christian living. I mean the biblical understanding of justice. Pervading the Prior Testament and the New, pulsing through the Hebrew prophets and the prophet Jesus, is a sense of justice that transcends, goes far beyond, what any man, woman, or child strictly deserves, what they have merited, have earned, can claim as a rigorous right. Biblical justice is fidelity—fidelity to relationships and responsibilities that stem from a covenant with God, with Jesus.

What relationships, what responsibilities? To God, to people, to the earth. For a Jew or a Christian to be just means, in the first instance, to love God above all else, to love God with my whole heart and mind, all my soul and strength. It means, second, the commandment Jesus said was "like" loving God: I must love every sister and brother like another self, as if I were standing in their shoes. It means, third, that I reverence the earth that nourishes me, respect it as God's gift, refuse to ravage it, to rape it, to simply make it serve my every selfish need.

It is the second commandment of the law and the gospel that must trigger our reaction to budget cuts that target our children. Alison Higginbotham is not a statistic. Alison is my sister; she is a second self. In a genuine sense, what happens to her happens to me. Even more profoundly, what I do for her I do to Jesus. "Truly I tell you, just as you did it to one of the least of my brothers and sisters, you did it to me" (Mt 25:40). It is truly Jesus with infantile spasms, Jesus who cannot feed himself, Jesus who cannot walk, needs a wheel chair and a special ramp. And the reverse is frightening: "I was sick and you did not take care of me." "When was it we saw you sick and did not take care of you?" "Truly I tell you, just as you did not do it to one of the least of these, you did not do it to me" (vv. 43–45). "Depart from me..." (v. 41).

Am I crossing the line into politics? I suspect so. But the day we separate politics from morality will be a dark day for America. I may well be deaf to certain significant details of the projected welfare reform. But what I hear with startling clarity is a reasonable, unavoidable economic question: How do we balance a national budget run wild? What I do not hear is a corresponding human question: How do we save our children?

I have no push-button solutions to complex social, political, and economic issues. I realize that some welfare recipients are lazy, that others cheat. Granting all this, I still beg our legislators: Don't punish the children for the sins of their parents! Don't make it American law that if a woman on welfare has another child, within wedlock or outside it, *the child* must go hungry. If you must balance the budget, don't do it by slashing funds for school lunches, by cutting foster care for abused or neglected children. Don't enable our national defense by disabling the weakest of our little ones.

A moment ago I said "*I* beg our legislators.... " Alone, I have no power; rarely does a solitary citizen change the face of Washington. The answer is people power. When hundreds of thousands marched on Washington in the 60s, marched for equal rights, Washington listened: Congress, a Supreme Court, a President. They had pricked the conscience of half the nation. Whites and blacks had pledged their lives, were willing to be whipped by the Klan, bitten by sheriffs' dogs, and gunned down by rednecks for their sisters and brothers. Blood shed in Selma and Birmingham reached the steps of our Capitol.

Today 16 million children living in poverty cannot march on Washington. Their cries are weak whimperings. They have no voice but ours. But our voices, for the most part, are raised for guns against crime, for death sentences against murderers, for term limits in office, for tobacco rights, for tax breaks. Thousands of trained lobbyists crowd the corridors of Congress. But I hear no outcry in those marble halls, "Save our children! End child poverty! Help the crippled to walk, the blind to see, the deaf to hear, the living dead to rise from their tombs!"

We ordinary folk are powerful people; the proof is the millions spent on political campaigns. What miracles might be wrought if each adult, each family, across the country were to wire our representatives, were to demand that their highest priority be not to balance the budget but to protect our children! But to do that, we have to believe. Believe that this country's endangered species is not the whooping crane in Texas but America's children, the children in our parishes, the children on our street. Sixteen million of them!

In odd moments of musing, I imagine a Congress divided not on party lines but in a way more representative of our people. I mean a slim majority composed of men and women living precariously on the upper edge of the poverty line, each with an afflicted child in need of constant care too expensive for the family salary. I mean a fat majority impregnated with the wisdom of Scripture: Isaiah's "Is not this the fast that I choose: to share your bread with the hungry, and bring the homeless poor into your house; when you see the naked, to cover them, and not to hide yourself from your own flesh?" (Isa 58:6–7). And Jesus' "The Spirit of the Lord is upon me, because [the Lord] has anointed me to bring good news to the poor, has sent me to proclaim release for prisoners and sight for the blind, to send the down trodden away relieved" (Lk 4:18). How different the debates would be, how compassionate the perspectives!

A final word. Today's Gospel ends with a sobering question from Jesus: "When the Son of Man comes, will he find that faith on the earth?" (Lk 18:7–8). What faith? Confidence in the power of Jesus to change the human condition. In our situation, the power of Jesus to touch the hearts of our legislators. How? Not only because we persist in prayer. Just as importantly because, like the unrelenting widow, we make nuisances of ourselves. Because we refuse to be silent when our children are imperiled. Because with our faith in the Son of God, we can wear out the more powerful. With our faith in the Son of God....

Children's Defense Fund Sunday
October 22, 1995

20

ON A NATION WHERE...
LORD, HAVE MERCY
Twenty-ninth Sunday of the Year (A)

- Isaiah 45:1, 4-6
- 1 Thessalonians 1:1-5b
- Matthew 22:15-21

At first glance, today's Gospel says nothing even remotely touching the defense of children. Some disciples of the Pharisees try an early version of entrapment. They will ask Jesus a question—the kind of question that will make him look bad no matter what answer he gives. "Is it lawful to pay taxes to the emperor, or not?" (Mt 22:17). If he says it is lawful, he acknowledges a foreign pagan sovereignty over Israel, risks offending the nationalistic parties. If he says it is not lawful, he can be reported as disloyal to the empire, risks encouraging rebellion against Roman rule.

We know, and marvel at, the answer Jesus gave. He does not encourage rebellion. He simply accepts the state as it is, the lesser of two evils. The worse evil would be anarchy. As a rabbinic aphorism had it, "Pray for the peace of the ruling power, since but for fear of it men would have swallowed up each other alive."[1] Jesus advocated nonviolent social change (see Mt 5:38-48).

True, but in the middle of the story there is a sentence I have passed over through most of my preaching existence (a half century); it seemed so harmless. And yet, in point of fact, it is uncommonly significant for all who labor for justice, Jesus' vision of justice. The entrappers open with a compliment intended to catch Jesus off guard: "Teacher, we know that you are sincere, and teach the way of God truthfully, and court no man's favor; for you are not impressed (not influenced) by the position people hold" (v. 16).[2] Let me mull over that sentence (1) as it applied to Jesus, (2) as the early Christians lived it, and (3) as it touches the threat to children in 1996.

I

First, Jesus himself. Indeed he was not impressed, not influenced, by the position people held, by their power or their possessions. To grasp what this means, go back a bit, to the Jewish background of Jesus, to the Israelite conception of justice. What did justice mean? Fidelity to relationships that stemmed from their covenant with Yahweh: Love God above all else, love every sister and brother like another self, touch the earth with reverence. Focus for a moment on that second relationship—justice among the Jews, within their community, their common identity as members of the covenant community. It was shown in a special way by the relationship between rich and poor.

You see, except for legal contexts, justice was not *equal* treatment; justice was *appropriate* treatment—treatment that would tend to equalize the relationship and provide access to resources. Examples are vivid. When grain, grapes, or olives were harvested, the reaper was not to return to pick up what was missed the first time. These "leftovers" had to go to the poor, to the widow and orphan, to the resident alien. As for interest on loans, "If you lend money to my people, to the poor among you, you shall not deal with them as a creditor, you shall not exact interest from them" (Exod 22:25). A cloak taken in pledge from a poor person must be returned before nightfall; "for that is his only covering, it is his mantle for his body; in what else shall he sleep?" (Exod 22:26–27).

Such was the tradition Jesus inherited, the tradition he confirmed when he proclaimed his program in the synagogue at Nazareth: "The Spirit of the Lord is upon me, for the Lord has anointed me, sent me to preach good news to the poor, to proclaim release for prisoners and sight for the blind, to send the downtrodden away relieved" (Lk 4:18). Not special favor for people in positions of power. Not even equal treatment for all; appropriate treatment. The way kings in Israel were expected to act, representatives of God, acting as God would act toward the impoverished and the downtrodden, not because these were necessarily holier than the well-to-do, simply because they were in greater need.

Such was the way Jesus acted. Not equal treatment; appropriate treatment. Different strokes for different folks. Different for toll collector Zacchaeus and the woman bleeding for 12 years; different for the Samaritan woman with five husbands and the woman caught in adultery; different for the uncaring rich man and poor Lazarus begging at his gate; different for the Pharisees he castigated and the children he took in his arms; different for Peter erupting against Jesus' prediction of his passion and the bedeviled man erupting from the tombs.

Jesus' justice? Make all relationships right; deal with each man, woman, and child in the way appropriate to each—fit, proper, suitable.

II

Move now to the early Christians. Typical, I think, is the Letter of James—actually a sermon. A sermon toward the end of the first century. A sermon on how Christians ought to live. Listen to his strong indictment.

> My brothers and sisters: Do you with your acts of favoritism really believe in our glorious Lord Jesus Christ? For if a person with gold rings and in fine clothes comes into your assembly, and if a poor person in dirty clothes also comes in, and if you take notice of the one wearing the fine clothes and say, "Have a seat here, please," while to the one who is poor you say, "Stand there," or, "Sit at my feet," have you not made distinctions among yourselves, and become judges with evil thoughts? Listen, my beloved brothers and sisters: Has not God chosen the poor in the world to be rich in faith and to be heirs of the kingdom that He has promised to those who love Him? But you have dishonored the poor. Is it not the rich who oppress you? Is it not they who drag you into court? Is it not they who blaspheme the excellent name that was invoked over you?
>
> You do well if you really fulfill the royal law according to the Scripture, "You shall love your neighbor as yourself." But if you show partiality, you commit sin and are convicted by the law as transgressors.
>
> (Jas 2:1–9)

No partiality indeed. But then, isn't "James" advocating equal treatment for all? Listen as James continues a bit later: "What good is it, my brothers and sisters, if someone says he has faith but does not have works? Can faith save him? If a brother or sister is naked and lacks daily food, and one of you says to them, 'Go in peace, keep warm and eat your fill, and yet you do not supply their bodily needs, what is the good of that?' (2:14–16). Again, as with the Hebrew tradition, as with Jesus, partiality only in the sense that *appropriate* treatment demands a bias in favor of the more needy. Not the greedy, only the needy.

III

Move now to today. I mean the threat to children in 1996. Late in 1995, Marian Wright Edelman, president of the Children's Defense Fund, wrote an open letter to President Clinton.[3] She called for his opposition to Senate and House welfare and Medicaid block grants, "which will make more children poor and sick." She argued against destroying "the 60-year-old safety net for children, women and poor families," declared it "wrong to leave millions of voteless, voiceless children to the vagaries of 50 state bureaucracies and politics."

Precisely here is a particularly urgent need for the vision of the ancient Jew, the vision of Jesus: not equal treatment— appropriate treatment. It is now an accepted American aphorism that "The younger you are, the poorer you are." For the most vulnerable of our people, what does appropriate treatment demand? Not a bias for a balanced budget; rather, a preference for the poor, an option for the oppressed, a choice for children. Let this be not so much a litany of devastating statistics as a cry from the heart, a nation's prayer for forgiveness.

- On a nation that is the world's richest, yet allows one of every four children to grow up in inhuman poverty, hungry for the mountains of food we waste each day...Lord, have mercy.
- On a nation with one of the most innovative and advanced health-care systems in the world, yet 40,000 little ones each year do not reach birthday number one, and African American infants die at twice the rate of whites...Lord, have mercy.
- On a nation where insurance gets household dogs dialysis, pacemakers, and kidney transplants, gets cats hip replacements, cataract surgery, and cancer treatment,[4] while almost ten million children are without health insurance...Lord, have mercy.
- On a nation that trumpets our love for children and family values, yet every 26 seconds a child runs away from home, every 47 seconds a child is abused or neglected, every 67 seconds a teenager has a baby, every 7 minutes a boy or girl is arrested for drug abuse, every night a million youngsters sleep on our streets...Lord, have mercy.
- On a nation that abhors violence, yet every 36 minutes a child is injured or killed by a gun, the rate of teenage suicides has tripled in 30 years, and children are preparing not their futures but their funerals...Lord, have mercy.
- On a nation bent on balancing its budget by cutting children's food stamps, school lunches, Medicaid health coverage, Aid to Families with Dependent Children, Supplemental

Security Income, federal child-care subsidies, Head Start, and remedial education...Lord, have mercy.

I recall that, not long before his death, Martin Luther King Jr. wrote to his mother to share with her the title of his next sermon. The title? "Why America May Go to Hell." I am not a pessimist by nature or from experience; I retain an extraordinary reliance on the power of God's grace. Still, one frightful fear refuses to forsake me: When one out of every four children I see is living in some sort of hell, how rosy does the year 2001 look?...How Christian?

Children's Defense Fund Sunday
October 20, 1996

21
ALL ELSE IS...GREED
Twenty-ninth Week, Year 2, Monday

- Ephesians 2:1–10
- Luke 12:13–21

For Christians concerned for biblical justice,[1] today's Gospel is a striking example of biblical injustice. For if biblical justice is fidelity—fidelity to relationships that stem from a covenant, then biblical injustice is infidelity—infidelity to such relationships. And the parable of the Rich Fool runs the gamut of these unfaithful relationships. So then, three precious cameos: (1) today's Gospel, (2) today's greed, (3) today's preacher.

I

First, today's Gospel. Skim through the rich farmer's infidelities. He is *faithless to the earth,* irresponsible to the land that brought forth so plentifully, yielded crops in such abundance that he had no place to store them. Why faithless, why irresponsible? Because we dare not interpret the Genesis command to "subdue and have dominion" (Gen 1:28) as if God has given us unrestricted power to do with the earth whatever we will. The mandate given humankind is not exploitation but reverential care. What God gave the rich farmer was not despotism but stewardship. And a steward is one who manages what is someone else's. A steward cares, is concerned, agonizes. Stewards may not plunder, may not waste, can be called to account for their stewardship. The rich fool had not pondered a sobering sentence from the Psalmist, "The earth is the Lord's, and all that is in it" (Ps 24:1). Or a powerful pronouncement of the Lord in Leviticus: "The land is mine; with me you are but aliens and tenants" (Lev 25:23).

The rich farmer was *faithless to his sisters and brothers,* irresponsible where Israelites and aliens were concerned, had no regard for the poor, for the widow and the orphan. All he could think about was his isolated self. Recall his address—to whom? Only one dialogue partner: himself. "Self *(psychē),* you have ample goods laid up for years to come. Take it easy, eat, drink, be merry" (Lk 12:19). Unaware that the Lord intended the earth for all, for each and every human, had in mind a habitat for humanity. Unaware that the earth, material reality, is given us to be shared, given us to be given.

The rich farmer was *faithless to his God,* irresponsible where his Creator was concerned. Oh yes, he thought of God, but too late; thought of God only when God spoke to him. Not till God announced, "You fool! This very night that self of yours *(pyschē)* is being demanded back from you" (v. 20). In the Greek verb for demanding back, the farmer's "self" is a loan; and now the loan is being called in—the "self" that for the rich farmer took the place of God. Little wonder that Jesus ends the parable with the succinct warning, "So it is with anyone who piles up treasure for himself and is not rich with God" (v. 21). A poignant phrase, isn't it: "rich with God"? It is the parable in a nutshell. Handle what you have as God's steward, share what you have with images of God less fortunate than you, and real riches will be yours: You will be rich in God's eyes.

Not surprisingly, the rich farmer was ultimately faithless in another direction: *faithless to his own self,* that self he had told to relax, to eat and drink, to enjoy life to the full.

II

Turn now from today's Gospel to today's greed. Yes, greed. For the Gospel parable has for prologue a warning of Jesus: "Take care! Be on your guard against every form of greed" (Lk 12:15). Is there greed in our dear land today? Listen to Lee Atwater, the architect of presidential politics who almost singlehandedly turned the Bush campaign around in 1988. Dying of a brain tumor at 40, this gifted man made this poignant confession:

> The '80s were about acquiring—acquiring wealth, power, prestige. I know. I acquired more wealth, power and prestige than most. But you can acquire all you want and still feel empty.... It took a deadly illness to put me eye to eye with that truth, but it is a truth that the country, caught up in its ruthless ambitions and moral decay, can learn on my dime. I don't know who will lead us

through the '90s, but they must be made to speak to this spiritual vacuum at the heart of American society, this tumor of the soul.[2]

This is not to claim that all of American society is greedy, has fallen victim to what Luke's Greek word for greed means literally: a lusting for more and more. Still, my own experience and TV's incredibly successful commercials lead me to resonate to John Paul II when he deplores a "civilization of 'consumption' or 'consumerism,'" which "makes people slaves of 'possession' and immediate gratification, with no other horizon than the multiplication or continual replacement of the things already owned with others still better."[3] And some protagonists of the free market have confessed frankly that, for capitalism to work, greed is indispensable.

Sadly, the greedy increase the needy. A recent report by an official who resigned from the present Administration sends chills down my spine. Though "the poverty rate for the elderly is now lower than the rate for society as a whole," "the rate for children—about one child in five—remains notoriously higher." And it would be higher still, were it not for government benefits. And yet, the program most drastically cut in the welfare bill approved by Congress and signed by the President is...food stamps. This despite the fact that food stamps "now help sustain one American in 10...fully half of the recipients are children, [and] families with children receive 80 percent of food stamp benefits."[4]

Yes, by the law of averages, some folks on welfare are greedy; but not the children. The children are simply needy, and our society has decided to look the other way. The children have no lobby, and government sees no urgency in their poverty. Meanwhile Congress gives the Pentagon $12 billion more than the Pentagon requested! How many of our 14.6 million children growing up poor, hungry, indecently housed could $12 billion nourish in mind, spirit, and flesh?

III

Today's Gospel and today's greed, how do they touch today's preacher? In two ways: our words and our life. On December 7, 1965 an ecumenical council declared that priests "have as primary duty the proclamation of the gospel of God to all."[5] And what is that gospel? Jesus expressed part of it pithily and pungently in the Nazareth synagogue: "The Spirit of the Lord is upon me, for [the Lord] has anointed me; He has sent me to preach good news to the poor, to proclaim release for prisoners and sight for the blind, to send the downtrodden away relieved, to proclaim the Lord's year of favor" (Lk 4:18–19).

Still, for all the power in that early statement, it expresses only part of Jesus' gospel of justice, only part of the gospel we are called to proclaim.[6] The examples Jesus gave are just that—examples. Powerful examples of the fidelity to relationships we are privileged to preach. Relationships that stem from a covenant. For us, not only the covenants in the Hebrew Testament, but specifically the covenant cut in the blood of Christ. Concretely, I must preach to my people a relationship to God that involves loving God with all their heart and mind, all their soul and strength. I must preach a relationship to people where our faithful see in each man, woman, and child an image of God, treat each like another self, love each as Jesus loved and loves us, even at times unto crucifixion. I must preach a relationship to "things," to all nonhuman created reality, that calls from our Catholic congregations reverence and care, because the earth and all it brings forth are traces of a Trinity.

In a word, to preach God's vision of justice I must preach the single community our imaginative God still has in mind: a community in which the Creator and all creation live in a harmony that sin cannot substantially corrupt, an interdependence of man, woman, and nature that is an essential facet of salvation's story.

But words are not enough. My words have to express what I live. The homily is not disembodied words; the homily is I. Recall Paul: "What is required of stewards is that they be found faithful" (1 Cor 4:2). Fidelity. Do I love God above all else? Do I love every sister and brother as Jesus loves me? Do I touch the things of earth with the reverence God asked of humankind at its birthing? Important questions for effective preaching, for Christian living within my parish. Shivering questions because my own salvation is inseparably linked to those three questions. To say yes to those questions is to be rich in God's eyes. All else, my brothers and sisters, all else is...greed.

Jesuit Spirituality Center
Grand Coteau, Louisiana
October 21, 1996

22
DO I HEAR THE CHILDREN CRYING?
Thirty-first Sunday of the Year (A)

- Malachi 1:14b–2:2b, 8–10
- 1 Thessalonians 2:7b–9, 13
- Matthew 23:1–12

In preparing this homily, I was tempted to preach on today's Gospel. It is a powerful Gospel. Against the scribes and Pharisees, the language of Matthew's Jesus is surprisingly strong. They are hypocrites, blind guides, snakes, a brood of vipers. Therefore do what they say, but don't do as they do! The principle is indeed precious, worth preaching. Still, the first reading, a passage from the prophet Malachi, offers even richer material for Christian living. It forces us to focus on a crucial fact we tend to forget in everyday practice. Listen to Malachi again (2:10):

> Have we not all one and the same Father?
> Has not the one God created us?
> Why, then, are we faithless to one another,
> violating the covenant of our ancestors?

To grasp the significance of Malachi's questions, we have to ask three questions of our own: (1) What lies behind Malachi's words? (2) How do these Old Testament sentences affect New Testament Christians? (3) What practical meaning might they have for you and me today?

I

What lies behind Malachi's words?[1] He was denouncing abuses—very specific abuses. He could not remain silent when he saw before him priests who were ignorant, self-indulgent, grasping and greedy, offering in sacrifice animals that were blind or lame. "Try presenting that to your governor—will he be pleased?" (Mal 1:8). He had to protest when he saw Jewish men divorcing their wives and marrying attractive foreign girls. "To the wife of your youth you have been faithless, though she is your companion and your wife by covenant. Did not the one God make her?" (2:14–15). He had to shout aloud against "those who oppress the hired workers in their wages, the widow and the orphan, those who thrust aside the alien" (3:5), abuse the stranger, the immigrant. For these and other violations of the covenant Malachi cried, "Take heed to yourselves and do not be faithless" (2:16).

Faithless, unfaithful—there's the crucial accusation. God's covenants, God's pacts with the Israelites, focused on fidelity: God would be unfailingly true to God's promises, and God's people promised to live according to God's law, live the commandments that summed up their obligations, their responsibilities. What responsibilities? Remember how God freed the Israelites from Egypt, from slavery under Pharaoh? It was not simply freedom-from; it was freedom-for. Freedom to shape a new kind of society, different from the despotic Egypt they had escaped. A society in which all Israelites would (1) love one God above all else; (2) love every human person like another self, especially the powerless like the widow and the orphan, love each as if they were standing in his or her shoes; (3) handle "things," all that God has created, with reverence, as gifts of God, to be shared liberally rather than clutched possessively.

As he looked on his people in the light of Israel's covenant, Malachi wept.

II

But how do Malachi's protests, Malachi's tears, touch New Testament Christians? One basic way. Christians too have a covenant with God—a covenant cut in the blood of Christ. What does this mean in the concrete? On broad lines, it means what Belgian Cardinal Léon-Joseph Suenens declared: The greatest day in the life of a pope is not his coronation but his baptism, the day of his mission "to live the Christian life in obedience to the gospel."[2]

To live the Christian life in obedience to the gospel. Such is our common vocation, not only the pope's but yours and mine, our privilege and our burden. And what is the Christian life? In a single syllable, love. Oh, not the parody of love TV too often portrays—the one-night stand, "days of wine and roses," pleasure without pain. A tough love. The love St. Paul described: "Love is patient, kind, not envious or boastful, not arrogant or rude; does not insist on its own way, is not irritable or resentful, rejoices [only] in the truth; bears all things, believes all things, hopes all things, endures all things" (1 Cor 13:4–7). Such is the love Jesus summed up in a compelling command, "Love one another as I have loved you" (Jn 14:12). Not an invitation; a command.

As Jesus has loved us. And how has Jesus loved us? He was born for us, he lived his whole life for us, he died for us. It sounds so simple, slips so facilely from my lips. And yet our whole effort to "live the Christian life" flows from Jesus' love for us. Out of love for us God's own Son took our flesh, was born as we are born; he grew up in a backwater town much as we grow up; when he preached God's kingdom, his relatives shouted he was mad. For love of us he was pinned to a cross, experienced such fearful agony that he murmured to his Father, "My God, my God, why have you forsaken me?" (Mk 15:34).

Such is the love our covenant with God in Christ demands of us. Not always the cruel dying, though that too we find today in Bosnia and Rwanda. Always the fidelity that calls for sacrificial living: loving God above all the attractions of a pleasure-mad society; loving even the least attractive of our sisters and brothers as images of Christ; handling simply everything we see and hear, all we touch and taste and smell, with reverence, as a gift of God, a trace of our triune God.

III

Finally, bring this down to earth, to practical everyday living. Remember our covenant: fidelity to relationships, to responsibilities. Pressured by time, I offer one example: our nation's children. In my own back yard, Washington, D.C.,

> for the sixth consecutive year the District's rates are among the highest for child mortality, violent deaths among teenagers, child abuse and neglect, out-of-wedlock births among teens. low-birth-weight babies, juvenile arrests, and children who live in poverty and in need of medical care....[And] the rate of HIV infection among D.C. adolescents also is the highest in the nation.[3]

Children are "grossed out" from having witnessed loved ones and others assaulted, raped, and murdered. Ten- and twelve-year-olds have gonorrhea; eight-year-old girls are sold into prostitution; four-year-olds are given marijuana and alcohol by parents, at times as a joke, at times to sedate them. Thirteen-year-old boys sell drugs to buy shoes and clothing for their siblings.

And in all this chaos politicians and financial authorities have drastically reduced, even withdrawn, funding for critical programs that could relieve and correct these maladies. Listen to a child-services administrator, psychiatrist, and pediatrician:

> Members of Congress decry conditions in the District while they slash its budget. I wonder if those who wield power from the White House, as well as those who aspire to assume that authority, really hear the cries of our desperate children. Neglect, arrogance, politics, false promises and—dare I say it?— apparent racism only have added nails to the coffins that bury D.C. kids, the majority of whom are African American.

Do *I* hear the children crying? Not only the healthy newborn but the infant HIV-positive, the three-year old with MS, the preschool girl incestuously abused, the school-age youngster malnourished.

I turn from the District of Columbia to the Commonwealth of Kentucky. What do I find?[4] One in four children is growing up below the poverty line; in every county in 1990[5] children's poverty exceeded that of the general population. And poverty rates are even higher for young families: Last year one third of all families with children whose parents were under 30 lived below the poverty level. For younger single-mother families the poverty rate was 70.7 percent. The number of reports for child abuse and neglect has increased almost twofold in ten years: 37,911 in 1994. From 1992 to 1994, more than one in four births was to an unmarried woman; and your Jefferson County posted rates above the state average. In the context of current welfare reform, your Catholic Charities submits a doleful prediction:

> The loss of federal funding raises very real questions about whether the current safety net programs will still be in place to catch children in need. Or, will the Kentucky General Assembly repeal or weaken guaranteed assistance for poor, hungry, ill, disabled, abused, or neglected children? The likely answer is that hundreds and thousands of Kentucky children will suffer harm under these new public policies.

A homily is not the place to solve complex social issues—especially if the homilist comes to you from Washington! A homily *is* the place to ask, Do Kentuckians hear the children crying? If so, how do they respond? With ethical justice: Give the children what their parents can prove they themselves deserve? Or with biblical justice: No helpless child of God should go hungry in the richest nation on earth, no sick child should lack medical care with our incomparable resources, no disabled children should go without a wheel chair or an education because they have no lobby to plead their cause before the General Assembly?

I do not come with solutions—believe me! I dare not criticize any single one of you; your presence here proclaims your fidelity to "our Father." I can only beg you, literally for Christ's sake, to listen to the cries of Kentucky's children, your children; come together to share those cries with intelligence and compassion; pray for light to see and strength to act. For if Kentucky lets one child in four grow up in some kind of hell, Malachi will still ask his 2,500-year-old question:

> Have we not all one and the same Father?
> Has not the one God created us?
> Why, then, are we faithless to one another,
>   violating the covenant of our ancestors?

Cathedral of the Assumption
Louisville, Kentucky
November 2–3, 1996

23
GUEST LIST FOR A PARTY
Thirty-first Week, Year 2, Monday

- Philippians 2:1–4
- Luke 14:12–14

Today's liturgy links two intriguing readings: a tough Gospel of Jesus and an encouraging epistle of Paul. Let's take the Gospel first, then listen to Paul; for if Jesus' is the story, Paul's is the theology. We can close with a glance at ourselves.

I

For me, today's Gospel is an eye-opener, and it makes me gulp. Here is Jesus at dinner on a Sabbath in the home of a prominent Pharisee. Enjoying himself, I'm sure, in the company of distinguished guests—lawyers and Pharisees.[1] As always, a gracious guest, even when he disagrees with a host. A fascinating conversationalist this Jesus, whatever the topic—religious, political, social. Suddenly the honored guest turns to his host with a strong suggestion. When you are planning a party, here is a guest list that will knock your peers "out of their socks." Don't follow your time-honored social conventions. Don't send invitations to your friends; don't invite even your brothers, your relatives, your rich neighbors. Such invitations anticipate a return: They will have to invite *you* to lunch or dinner; not to do so would be gross, insensitive, discourteous. (I wonder whether Jesus whispered this to his host or said it aloud for all the guests to hear. Probably out loud.)

Well then, whom to invite?[2] Note here Jesus' striking parallel. The types you do not invite are four: friends, brothers, relatives, rich neighbors. The types you do invite are likewise four: the poor, the crippled, the lame, the blind. Four affluent types, able to return in kind; four unfortunate types, unable to return in kind.

Why a guest list of the disadvantaged alone? Because it is a test of real love. "Real love never reckons with recompense";[3] real love doesn't look for a reward. In this instance there is indeed a recompense, utterly unexpected. But it doesn't come from the unfortunates; they cannot reciprocate. The poor don't have the cash; the crippled, the lame, and the blind are hindered by their handicaps. The recompense comes from God. Ultimately and definitively, God rewards such love at the resurrection. Then it is that such generous lovers will stand with "the upright" (Lk 14:14), repaid with God's very self, days without end.

II

Happily, today's passage from Paul undergirds the guest list of Jesus with some profound pastoral theology. Crucial to Paul's argument is *koinōnia,* fellowship in the Spirit, sharing in the Holy Spirit. What characterizes life "in Christ" (that incredibly pregnant Pauline phrase) is our common participation in the gift of the Spirit. "In the one Spirit we were all baptized into one body—Jews or Greeks, slaves or free—and we were all made to drink of one Spirit" (1 Cor 12:13). With this as basis, Paul tells the Christians of Philippi that his joy will be complete if they have the same mindset, if they share the same love, if in humility they see others as better than themselves, if a practical concern for others rather than concern for self is the driving force of their lives. And all this on the model of Christ's own self-emptying, Christ's own obedience unto death.

Hence a Christian's guest list. Not my own interests; only what is best for the other. Not those who can further my interests; only a love that moves out from self-interest to what will serve the less fortunate.

III

That much said, what of us?[4] You see, today's Gospel story is not primarily about lunch or dinner, not a Christian "Ann Landers" on how a host can win blue chips for heaven. What confronts us here is the second great commandment of the law and the gospel: "You shall love your neighbor as yourself" (Lev 19:18; Mt 22:39), like another self—the love Jesus said is "like" loving God. In the abstract, where the "neighbor" has no face, the command to love someone like another self is attractive, has a poetic ring about it. But in the concrete, where the "neighbor" is every sister and brother, has flesh and blood, is terribly unattractive or wields despotic power, the command is a fearful one. And still, Jesus insisted on it: "Love your enemies and pray for those who persecute you, so that you may be children of your Father in heaven.... If you love [only] those who love you,...do not even the tax collectors do the same?" (Mt. 5:44–46).

But this evening let me focus swiftly on one group only, the unfortunates who correspond to the poor and the crippled, the lame and the blind in today's Gospel. This past weekend I preached in your cathedral.[5] I told the congregations what I had found in the Commonwealth of Kentucky: one in four children growing up below the poverty line; poverty rates even higher for young families; for younger single-mother families the poverty rate 70.7 percent; reports of child abuse and neglect increasing twofold in ten years; from 1992 to 1994, more than one in four births to an unmarried woman, and your Jefferson County with rates above the state average. And, in the context of current welfare reform, the doleful prediction of your Catholic Charities: Very likely thousands upon thousands of Kentucky children "will suffer harm under these new public policies."[6]

I asked then, as I ask now, do Kentuckians hear the children crying? Do you?

More broadly, this very afternoon you have cluttered the walls of this conference room with injustices around the world and within your parishes: racism, prejudice against immigrants, scapegoating the poor, domestic violence, unemployment, homelessness, inequality in the Church, consumerism, the NIMBY (Not in my back yard) syndrome, xenophobia, and a hundred more.

Where do you go from here? As prophets, to protest, as Malachi did yesterday, "Have we not all one and the same Father? Has not the one God created us? Why, then, are we faithless to one another, violating the covenant of our ancestors?" (Mal 2:10). Still, not enough by half. As prophets in parishes, you must gather your people together to discuss three urgent questions: (1) What are the major injustices within this specific parish? (2) What resources do you have to combat these injustices? (3) Concretely, what shall you do?

A final thought. I said earlier that our Gospel passage is not primarily about a luncheon or a dinner. Not primarily. Still, the meal is not insignificant, not without pertinence for biblical justice in action. The text: "When you give a banquet, invite the poor and the crippled, the lame and the blind" (Lk 14:13). I've never done that. Have you?

Catherine Spalding Conference
& Retreat Center
Nazareth, Kentucky
November 4, 1996

24

THE FAITH THAT DOES JUSTICE
Thirty-second Week, Year 2, Monday

- Titus 1:1–9
- Luke 17:1–6

After a full day devoted to justice and injustice—justice in God's Book and injustice in God's world[1]—it may seem awkward to confront a Gospel that culminates in faith: "Increase our faith" (Lk 17:5). Wouldn't it be a more fitting coincidence, were Jesus to say "Increase our justice"?

In point of fact, Jesus does precisely that. To make sense out of so strange a statement, we must ask three questions: (1) What is Gospel faith all about? (2) What is it that links faith to justice? (3) How does all this touch not only you and me but your people and my people?

I

First, what is Gospel faith, specifically the faith Jesus is constantly demanding, ceaselessly admiring? It is not purely and simply an act of my intellect alone, a head trip, a yes to truths God has revealed through Jesus. The almost total emphasis within Catholicism on the intellectual quality of faith "was developed in the intellectualistic theology of the medieval period, and the controversies aroused by the Reformation teaching on faith as an act of confidence."[2] A yes of the mind is indeed important; faith has a content. But even more important for New Testament faith is a yes to Jesus himself, accepting Jesus as actually being what he claims to be. "The faith of the Gospels, like the OT faith,...is trust and confidence" arising from "an acceptance of a person and his claims."[3]

117

It's Abraham called by God to leave his country, his kin, his father's house (Gen 12:1), and setting out "not knowing where he was going" (Heb 12:8), simply trusting in the God who was calling; Abraham willing to sacrifice his only son, not knowing how God's promise of "a great nation" (Gen 12:2) from his loins would be fulfilled, simply trusting in God to make good on a divine promise.

It's Mary of Nazareth saying yes to God's messenger, not knowing how God's Son would be born of her, simply trusting the God who promised that the Holy Spirit would overshadow her. That is why her kinswoman Elizabeth could say, "Blessed is she who *believed* that there would be a fulfilment of what was spoken to her by the Lord" (Lk 1:45).

It's Jesus himself descending into death's darkness not with proof of resurrection, not with experience of resurrection, only with trust in his Father's love: "Into your hands I entrust my spirit" (Lk 23:46). Entrust...surrender with confidence.

It's Paul in prison expressing to the Christians of Philippi "my eager expectation and hope...that by my speaking with all boldness Christ will be exalted now as always in my body, whether by life or by death" (Phil 1:20).

Such is the faith Jesus promised would move mountains (Mt 17:20; 21:21; Mk 11:23).

II

But such faith, such trust, such confident acceptance of Jesus, what connection does it have with justice? Not simply ethical justice—give to each what each deserves; primarily biblical justice, fidelity to relationships that stem from a covenant. What relationships? To God, to people, to the earth. Today a particularly crucial level of biblical justice is the second commandment of the law and the gospel, "You shall love your neighbor as yourself" (Mt 22:39). Love each human person, each man and woman and child, like another self, as if you were standing in his or her shoes. Especially "the poor, the crippled, the lame, and the blind" whom Jesus suggested we invite to our parties in place of "friends or brothers, relatives or rich neighbors" (Lk 14:12–13).

Why this command? Not because we are social workers consumed by compassion. Not because our neighbors, fortunate or unfortunate, are likable, lovable. Simply because each of these is shaped in God's image and likeness. Simply because each is a child of God as truly as you and I. Simply because each has been redeemed, caught up into God's love, by the blood of a God-man. Simply because each is meant for life with God days without end. In a word, it is our faith that does justice; it is because we accept Jesus for what he claims to be that we love one another as he has loved us, that in the hungry and thirsty, in the stranger and the naked, in the ill and the incarcerated we see Christ.

The Letter of James speaks volumes: "What good is it, my brothers and sisters, if you say you have faith but do not have works? Can faith save you? If a brother or sister is naked and lacks daily food, and one of you says to them, 'Go in peace; keep warm and eat your fill,' and yet you do not supply their bodily needs, what is the good of that? So faith, by itself, if it has no works, is dead" (Jas 2:14–17). And the First Letter of John is uncompromising: "It anyone has the world's goods and sees his brother in need, yet closes his heart against him, how does God's love abide in him?" (1 Jn 3:17).

This faith that compels justice explains Dorothy Day, who lived with society's outcasts amid rats and cockroaches, filth and vermin. Such is the faith that motivates Mother Teresa, who has housed 55,000 of Calcutta's dying, helps AIDS-afflicted to die with dignity, cradles orphans in Beirut and the homeless in D.C. Such was Archbishop Oscar Romero, slain by an assassin's bullet as he was offering the Sacrifice of Christ for the poor and downtrodden in El Salvador.

The faith Jesus was talking about was not a sterile, abstract faith, simply believing, accepting intellectually, everything God has revealed. Such a faith, James declares, the demons can claim: "Even the demons believe—and shudder" (Jas 2:19). No. The faith Jesus commended, the faith Jesus himself had, is a faith that is active, does something, a faith that does justice, a faith that can move mountains.[4]

III

A faith that can move mountains, that can uproot a mulberry tree and plant it in the sea—how does this touch us and our people? In at least two ways, at two points: our justice and our faith.

Our justice. The justice we are proclaiming from the pulpit, the only justice most of our Christian people recognize, is a very human justice. It may mean giving people what they can claim as a right: the right to life, to a decent job, to a family wage, to be treated with respect. Or it may mean what President Clinton meant when he said of the Oklahoma City bombers: We shall make sure they

receive justice, fit punishment for their crime. Fair enough for civilized living, not enough by half for Christian living.

You see, our people do not come to church for a lecture on
ethics, a class in philosophy or law. They may indeed have to be
reminded that sheer human wisdom dictates much of what we call
the common good. After all, it was not the Sermon on the Mount but
civil legislation that compelled us to acknowledge basic rights of
African Americans. And still we cheat our people if we limit the justice we preach to what the human mind can conceive through centuries of struggle, argument, and development; if we put the stress
on what people deserve or what we think they deserve; if we do not
proclaim the justice that is fidelity to our responsibilities to God, to
people, to the earth; if we do not insist, in season and out of season,
that the heart of our gospel is a single sentence of Jesus in the Gospel
of John: "This is my commandment, that you love one another as I
have loved you" (Jn 15:12). Not an invitation; a command.

Our faith. The faith we are proclaiming from the pulpit, the only
faith most of our Catholic people recognize, is the idea of faith with
which I grew up: There are certain propositions I must accept with my
mind. The creeds are summaries of such basic propositions: There is
only one God in three Persons; the Son of God became human for my
salvation; and so forth and so on. Faith indeed, important yes, but not
a faith that saves, not necessarily a faith that does justice.

The faith that saves is the faith that does justice, the faith that
not only accepts Jesus for all he claimed to be, but in that acceptance
puts unreserved trust and confidence in the power of Jesus. Not to
move mountains or uproot mulberry trees; the power to change
stubborn minds, ice-cold hearts, repressive cultures, to change a
world in peril of losing its soul. And that power of Jesus resides in
you and me, resides in our people, if...if we have even a smidgeon of
genuine faith.

Unbelievable? It would be, had not Jesus told us so. Might it
not be an excellent idea, then, as we struggle for justice under discouraging odds, to pray with the first apostles, "Jesus, increase our
faith"?

Cardinal Stritch Retreat House
Mundelein, Illinois
November 11, 1996

25

WIDOW'S MITE, SOCIETY'S SIN
Thirty-fourth Week, Year 1, Monday

- Daniel 1:1–6, 8–20
- Luke 21:1–4

Today's brief Gospel focuses on a widow, an Israelite widow. For simplicity's sake, let my reflections focus on two related facets that stem from this story. I mean the past and the present. I mean (1) what sort of life this widow lived in biblical days; (2) what sort of symbol this widow might be for you and me today.

I

First, the widow of our Gospel. We tend to focus on what the widow *gave*. But to grasp what she gave, we have to understand who the widow *was*.[1] Basically she was dependent. She had to dress in a special way. She could not inherit from her husband. If she had no children, she returned to her father's house. If she had no man at all to defend her rights, she was an obvious victim for a predatory creditor. Recall the widow who cried to Elisha, "A creditor has come to take my two children as slaves" (2 Kgs 4:1). She had no defender at law, was at the mercy of dishonest judges. Recall Isaiah's charge, "The widow's cause does not come before [your princes]" (Isa 1:23). Yes, God's law declared, "You shall not abuse any widow or orphan" (Exod 22:22); and Moses could proclaim, "Cursed be anyone who deprives...the widow of justice" (Deut 27:19). But in sheer fact so general a law had no practical effect, "was a lifeless ideal";[2] and the curse on injustice hardly deterred a scheming creditor. The pleadings of the prophets, of Isaiah and Jeremiah and Zechariah, reveal a

121

widow shamefully oppressed. So much so that Malachi has to make Yahweh Himself the protector of widows (Mal 3:5).

Remember Naomi in the Book of Ruth? She had lost not only her husband but both her grown sons. "Too old to have a husband" (Ruth 1:12), she found life so bitter, even food such a problem, that she said to her daughters-in-law, "The hand of the Lord has turned against me" (v. 13). When she returned with Ruth to Bethlehem, and the women of Bethlehem asked, "Is this Naomi?", she replied:

> Call me no longer Naomi [that is, Pleasant]
>   call me Mara [that is, Bitter],
>   for the Lord has dealt bitterly with me.
> I went away full,
>   but the Lord has brought me back empty;
> why call me Naomi
>   when the Lord has dealt harshly with me,
>   and the Almighty has brought calamity upon me?
>   (Ruth 1:20–21)

And here now is the widow of today's Gospel. Not indeed bitter like Naomi, but just as poor. For when she drops into the temple treasury "two small copper coins" (Lk 21:2), two of the smallest coins then in use in Palestine,[3] Jesus tells us that "out of her poverty she has dropped in all she had to live on" (v. 4). When this widow gave her two copper coins, she had nothing left off which to live. Absolutely nothing.

If that were all there is to the story, it would be more than enough. But there is more. Insightful Scripture scholars insist that Jesus is not heaping praise on the widow; he is lamenting "the tragedy of the day."[4] What tragedy? Recall the episode just before this: Jesus had condemned the Scribes "who devour the houses of widows" (Lk 20:47), what little estates widows had left. How? Perhaps they mismanaged the widows' property; perhaps they took the houses as pledges for debts that could not be paid; perhaps they sponged on widows' hospitality.[5] However they did their devouring, the tragedy of the day was this: "[This widow] has been taught and encouraged by religious leaders to donate as she does, and Jesus condemns the value system that motivates her action."[6] Displeased Jesus was over what the Scribes were doing to widows' estates; no more pleased is he when he sees a poverty-stricken woman persuaded by the hierarchy of her religion to contribute to the treasury her last penny.

Jesus is condemning a structure of sin, a social injustice.

II

My second point: What sort of symbol might the widow of today's Gospel be for you and me today? Here I commend to you for profound meditation an expression heard repeatedly across Latin America: "The poor evangelize us."[7] So many of the poor—young and aged, married and widowed, AIDS-afflicted and homeless, Africans and Afro-Europeans, Hispanics and Afro-Americans—have helped the churches discover what a 1979 conference of Latin American bishops called "the evangelizing potential of the poor."[8]

How do the poor actualize that potential, evangelize the churches, especially those of us who are not poor? They challenge us. How? By their overwhelming numbers, by their ever-worsening misery, by their Christlike endurance under domination and persecution, by their underlying gospel goodness, by their simplicity and solidarity, by their openness to God and what God mysteriously permits. In these and other ways the poor have in some measure turned the churches around, have compelled untold numbers of us to look more honestly within ourselves, have even stimulated profound conversion. Theologian Jon Sobrino has expressed it briefly and pungently: "When the Church has taken the poor seriously, it is then that it has become truly apostolic. The poor initiate the process of evangelization. When the Church goes out to them in mission, the paradoxical result is that they, the poor, evangelize the Church."[9]

Very simply, the poor are not just recipients of apostolic ministry; they are our teachers and educators...if we have eyes to see, ears to hear.

An example close to our daily experience takes us to the elderly who surround us—the elderly poor, the elderly lonely, the elderly ailing, the elderly in nursing homes. Two decades ago insightful Henri Nouwen penetrated to the heart of the matter: how the elderly can evangelize us, teach the teacher, preach to the preacher:

> Our first question is not how to go out and help the elderly, but how to allow the elderly to enter into the center of our own lives, how to create the space where they can be heard and listened to from within with careful attention. Quite often our concern to preach, teach, or cure prevents us from perceiving and receiving what those we care for have to offer....
>
> Thus care for the elderly means, first of all, to make ourselves available to the experience of becoming old. Only he who has recognized the relativity of his own life can bring a smile to the face

of a man who feels the closeness of death. In that sense, caring is first a way to our own aging self, where we can find the healing powers for all those who share in the human condition....[10]

Precisely here our Gospel widow returns to us. She evangelizes us. But, for us and our apostolate, she is not in the first instance a striking example of a poor believing woman who gives her last penny to God in the collection basket: "Go thou and do likewise." Her story is God's quiet but passionate rebuke to an unjust social system, a sinful structure that leaves her with only two copper coins and suggests that she surrender even these —"all she had to live on." God's quiet but passionate rebuke to our own contemporary sinful structures.

If "sinful structures" and "situations of sin" leave you cold or uneasy, take heart: John Paul II did not hesitate to speak this way. Listen to him: "...a world which is divided into blocs, sustained by rigid ideologies, and in which instead of interdependence and solidarity different forms of imperialism hold sway, can only be a world subject to structures of sin."[11] But John Paul has also insisted that a situation, a structure, an institution, society itself "is not in itself the subject of moral acts; therefore a situation cannot in itself be good or bad."[12] Such structures, such situations stem from "the accumulation and concentration of many *personal sins*"—men and women who cause, support, or exploit evil; don't eliminate or limit evil when they can; take refuge in the excuse that it's impossible to change the world.[13] Stem too from nations and blocs, from decisions "apparently inspired only by economics or politics, [but] are real forms of idolatry: of money, ideology, class, technology."[14] "Surely not I, Master?" (Mt 26:25).

So much from four verses in Luke? Our Gospel widow never knew she was taking us this far, never suspected that she and her innumerable sisters poor could evangelize us, could lead us to confront the personal sins within unjust social structures—our own sins included. But she does; indeed she does.

Mount Calvary Retreat House
Manchester, Jamaica, W.I.
November 27, 1995

FEASTS
AND
MEMORIALS

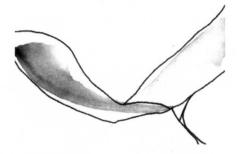

26
FOR JUSTICE' SAKE,
A SUFFERING SERVANT
Feast of the Baptism of the Lord

- Isaiah 42:1–4, 6–7
- Acts 10:34–38
- Matthew 3:13–17

The baptism of the Lord. A fascinating story; a fascinating liturgy. The all-important question is: What are we celebrating? Perhaps more accurately, what *should* we be celebrating? A word first about the biblical story, then a word about you and me.

I

First, the biblical account of Jesus' baptism.[1] There is something paradoxical about today's liturgy. You see, we call this feast "The Baptism of the Lord," but the focus of today's Gospel is not on Jesus' *baptism*. Oh yes, Jesus was baptized by John. Scripture scholars tell us "That Jesus was baptized by John is among the most certain historical facts in the Gospel tradition."[2] But notice what the four evangelists do with it. It begins with Mark's straightforward account: Jesus was baptized, the heavens opened, the Spirit descended, the Father spoke (Mk 1:9–11). But once Mark's story got around, the baptism became an embarrassment to the early Church. Why? Perhaps because Christians thought it utterly unsuitable, clearly contradictory, for the sinless Jesus to be baptized for the remission of his sins. Perhaps because it seemed to put Jesus in a subordinate position with respect to John.

So what do the other three evangelists do? Matthew tries to soften the seeming scandal: He introduces an explanatory dialogue between Jesus and John, and he mentions the actual baptism with a simple participle, "having been baptized" (Mt 3:16). Luke puts Jesus'

127

baptism in the middle of a sentence, in a subordinate clause: "Now when all the people were baptized, and when Jesus [also} had been baptized and was praying, the heavens opened" (Lk 3:21). And John? John is so embarrassed by the baptism that he omits it entirely; he has the Baptist hailing Jesus as the Lamb of God, the Baptist making it quite clear that after him, after John, comes a man who ranks ahead of him (Jn 1:29-34).

At any rate, today's Gospel has a different focus; all four evangelists have a different focus. It is only later in the Christian tradition that Jesus' baptism will become a model for Christian baptism, only later that Jesus' baptism will be seen as the first revelation of the Trinity, because Father, Son, and Spirit are seen as active together. What is the biblical focus? The person of Jesus: Who is he? Before Jesus begins his public ministry, it is necessary to make clear who he is and why he is significant.

How does Matthew accomplish this? The heavens are opened. What does this mean? Communication between heaven and earth is opened up, between God and humankind. This possibility is made concrete when the Holy Spirit descends upon Jesus and a heavenly voice speaks. All three images—heavens opening, Spirit descending, voice speaking—prepare for one revelation: Who is this Jesus? The answer: "This is my Son, the Beloved, with whom I am well pleased" (Mt 3:17). It is an allusion to our first reading, the passage from Isaiah:

> Here is my servant, whom I uphold,
>   my chosen, in whom my soul delights;
> I have put my spirit upon him;
>   he will bring forth justice to the nations.
>   (Isa 42:1)

"My Son...my servant." This unique Son of God is to be a unique servant, the Suffering Servant of God. In this unexpected sense he is to be the Messiah, the subject of the four Suffering Servant songs in Isaiah.[3] Though utterly innocent, he will suffer horribly for his people. He is the Servant who "will not grow faint or be crushed until he has established justice in the earth..." (Isa 42:4).

II

Splendid scriptural stuff, you will say, but how does it touch you and me?[4] One way struck me as soon as I linked the words from

heaven in Matthew to the words of Yahweh in Isaiah. In our very
baptism you and I are addressed in the words of our Lord:

> Here is my servant, whom I uphold,
>   my chosen, in whom my soul delights;
> I have put my spirit upon her (upon him);
>   She (he) will bring forth justice to the nations.

In the light of this first of the four Suffering Servant songs, three
words challenge us: justice, servant, suffering.

Justice. As for Jesus, so for you and me: Not ours to "grow faint
or be crushed until [we] have established justice in the earth." Not
simply the justice that is human—giving each man, woman, and child
what they can claim as a right: adequate food, decent housing, fitting
education, humane work, respect for their dignity as images of God.
Over and above all this, the justice that is divine: fidelity to relationships that stem from a covenant. A fidelity that is divine because God
is always faithful to God's promises. A fidelity that must be ours, that
introduces a fresh motivation, compels us to treat each man or
woman as a brother or sister, to treat the downtrodden and the marginalized as if we were standing in their shoes. A fidelity that inspires
us to love even our enemies as Jesus loves them, as Jesus has loved
us. A fidelity that makes our own the mission of Jesus:

> The Spirit of the Lord is upon me,
>   because [the Lord] has anointed me
>   to bring good news to the poor,
> has sent me to proclaim release for prisoners
>   and recovery of sight for the blind,
>   to send the downtrodden away relieved....
>   (Lk 4:18)

Servant. In doing justice, we take as spoken to us the pungent
words of Jesus to the Twelve: "You know that the rulers of the Gentiles lord it over them, and their great ones are tyrants over them. It
will not be so among you; but whoever wishes to be great among you
must be your servant, and whoever wishes to be first among you
must be your slave; just as the Son of Man came not to be served but
to serve, and to give his life a ransom for many" (Mt 20:25–28). Such
is our privilege as disciples of Jesus.

The problem is, it isn't easy to see ourselves as servants, to act
as servants, if we live in positions of power. If we can make decisions
that affect the lives of others. If we can say "Do this" and people do
it. If we haven't had to live powerless, begging for the bread we eat,

unable to discover decent work, crippled and without health insurance, agonizing over our ill-fed children.

How did Jesus do it? Remember the man who vowed to follow Jesus wherever he might go? Jesus' answer makes me shiver: "Foxes have holes, and birds of the air have nests, but the Son of Man has nowhere to lay his head" (Mt 8:20; Lk 9:58). As one Scripture scholar phrases it, Jesus "is en route; he lives the life of a homeless wanderer, having no shelter, no home, no family—none of the things that people usually consider requisite for ordinary life..... Even animals are better off."[5]

There are indeed servants of justice who live like that. Dorothy Day did. Mother Teresa comes close. Perhaps Bishop Ken Untener of Saginaw. But most of us do not seem called to so radical a life style. What all of us are called to, I believe, is to share *in some way* the suffering of the less privileged. Which brings me to the third demand.

Suffering. As I look back on 81 years, I can hardly claim to have suffered. Oh yes, I have agonized: over the deaths of my father and mother and only brother, over homilies and an irritable ileum, over affronts to my pride. But not the suffering that afflicts parents whose children are hungry, the suffering that wastes the cancer-ridden and the AIDS-afflicted, the suffering that agonizes the homeless and the hopeless, the suffering that torments the drug-addicted, the hundred-and-one afflictions of flesh and spirit that threaten to dehumanize God's images on earth.

And still, if I am to preach effectively on divine justice and human injustice, I have to experience to some extent, I have to at least feel deeply, the agony of the crucified. It can happen in varied ways: cradling an infant with multiple sclerosis, embracing an HIV-positive, serving the hungry at a soup kitchen, keeping a deathwatch with a family around a hospital bed—yes, even staring on TV into the hopeless eyes of war-ravaged, war-orphaned children.

Simply, I must experience what the Gospels keep repeating about Jesus: "He had compassion." Its literal meaning? To "suffer with." Not pity; for pity looks down on another from a perch above. No. Compassion means I feel what another feels; I put myself in a brother's or sister's shoes; I *am* my brother, I *am* my sister. It's not play-acting. What I felt when my only blood brother kept wasting away with cancer, that is what I feel when I see my brothers and sisters wasting away from "man's inhumanity to man."

Have I strayed from Jesus' baptism? Not really. My own baptism reveals my identity, tells the world who I am. I am, like Jesus, a servant sent to suffer for justice. And when I do, then the heavens open again, then the Holy Spirit descends dove-like, then the Father declares with pride, "You are my son/my daughter, whom I love. With you I am well pleased" (cf. Lk 3:22).

Notre Dame Retreat House
Canandaigua, New York
January 8, 1996

27

EAT MY FLESH...WASH THEIR FEET
Holy Thursday

- Exodus 12:1–8, 11–14
- 1 Corinthians 11:23–26
- John 13:1–15

Every year, on this sacred Thursday, worshiping Christians are puzzled. Puzzled by two quite different New Testament readings. Puzzled by Paul and John. Puzzled by Holy Eucharist and washing of feet. Puzzled by "This is my body that is broken for you" (1 Cor 11:24) and "Unless I wash you, you have no share with me" (Jn 13:8). Why, on this heart-swelling Thursday, not only bread and wine to nourish Jesus' friends, but water to cleanse their feet?

The solution, I suggest, the link between Eucharist and foot-washing, lies in the first verse you heard from John: "Having loved his own who were in this world, Jesus now showed his love to the very end" (Jn 13:1). He showed his love "to perfection."[1] *He showed his* love. A love that calls out for love in return. To make sense of this, three swift points: (1) Eucharist, (2) foot-washing, (3) you and I.

I

First, the love that is the Eucharist. On the eve of his crucifixion, a problem agonized Jesus. He had to go, and he wanted to stay. He had to leave us; "so it has been determined," he said, determined by my Father (Lk 22:22).[2] "If I do not go away, the [Holy Spirit] will not come to you" (Jn 16:7). And yet he wanted to stay with us; never had he loved his own as intensely as in that hour: "How intensely have I desired to eat this Passover supper with you before I suffer!" (Lk 22:15). Two loves in conflict: Which will yield?

132

That unique Thursday Jesus cut through the problem with a solution that still shocks our world. Neither love will have to yield. He will go, and he will stay; he will leave us, and he will remain with us. He will take from his disciples, from us, the sensible charm of his presence. No longer will his friends hear the music and thunder of his voice, sense the fascination of his smile or be touched by his tears. And still he will stay, will leave with us the reality, the truth, of that presence.

The solution? "This is my body.... This is my blood" (Mt 26:26, 28). Jesus took from us the God-man as Palestine saw him with the eyes of the body; he left with us the same God-man, whom you and I see with the eyes of our faith. Not only a real presence; not only is Jesus here. "Take [and] eat.... Drink of this, all of you" (Mt 26:26–27). It is the realization of his remarkable promise in Capernaum: "Whoever eats me will live because of me" (Jn 6:57). Communion: union with, oneness with our risen Lord. Not heaven, but awfully close.

Still, it is not enough to recall that Jesus loved us so intensely that, when he left us, he left us with his "real presence." The Eucharist is not a one-sided gift. It calls for a response. Love calls for love. Eucharist is exchange. Our reaction has to be an exchange of love. It is we who have to love. Rather than bore you with abstract theology, a single story.

1945, August 6, 8:10 in the morning, a malignant mushroom clouds Hiroshima's serene sky: the first atomic bomb. 75,000 dead or dying; 200,000 in need of medical care; 150,000 fleeing the holocaust in terror. A Basque Jesuit missionary to Japan, Pedro Arrupe, later the Society's superior general, walks for days through the ruins, with only aspirin and iodine, bicarb of soda and boric acid. With his brothers he piles up pyramids of once-human flesh, 50 or 60 at a time, pours fuel on them, sets them afire. After 15 days he comes upon an 18-year-old girl, her body one gangrenous mass, reduced to "a wound and an ulcer." Only one question from her dying lips: "Father, have you brought me Communion?" He had.[3] Must it take a catastrophe to rekindle our love for the Eucharistic Christ, to bring to Communion the 70% of American Catholics who rarely or never receive the Life that gives life?

II

Second, the love that is foot-washing.[4] I say "love" because this was a service that occasionally disciples would render to their teacher or rabbi as a sign of devotion, a service that might also be understood as a traditional act of love.[5] But for the teacher, the rabbi, to wash the feet of his disciples, of his pupils—not only unprofessional; undignified. Why, then, does Jesus wash the feet of the Twelve, the feet even of the Judas he knows is about to betray him? Jesus told us why: "Do you know what I have done for you? You address me as 'Teacher' and 'Lord'—and rightly so, for that is what I am. Now, if I washed your feet, even though I am Lord and Teacher, you too must wash one another's feet. For it was an example I gave you: You are to do exactly as I have done for you" (Jn 13:12–15).

Jesus' words take us back to an unforgettable Gospel scene. Do you remember how James and John asked of Jesus that they might sit at his right hand and his left hand when he comes into his glory? Do you remember how angry the other ten disciples were with James and John? Above all, do you remember how Jesus rebuked them? "Whoever wishes to become great among you must be your servant, and whoever wishes to be first among you must be slave of all. For the Son of Man came not to be served but to serve, and to give his life a ransom for many" (Mk 10:43–45).

"You are to do exactly as I have done for you." *Exactly*. Even to crucifixion. "Greater love than this no one has: to lay down one's life for those one loves" (Jn 15:13). What Jesus does so humbly at the Supper for the disciples he loves, this is symbolic of what he will do the next day on Calvary for all whom he loves. In incomparable humiliation he will die a bloody death for them.

III

Third, you and I. On two related levels: Eucharist and foot-washing. You see, there is a peril in frequent Communion—the peril that resides in anything we experience time and time again. Marriage, priesthood, a desk job, pizza pepperoni—early on, sheer delight; as time goes on, routine. The excitement of "the first time" disappears; we have to recapture its meaning. So too for Eucharist. We must recapture the feelings our grandparents had when Communion was not frequent but rare, the feelings you and I had at our very first Communion, the Communion that sealed your marriage. And so I commend to you a prayer before each Eucharist: "Dear Lord, grace me to receive you this day as if it were my first Communion, my last Communion, my only Communion." I delight to pray the poetry of theologian St. Thomas Aquinas, in Gerard Manley Hopkins' breathless translation of the *Adoro te:*

> Godhead here in hiding, whom I do adore
> Masked by these bare shadows, shape and nothing more,
> See, Lord, at thy service low lies here a heart
> Lost, all lost in wonder at the God thou art.[6]

But the Eucharist, Communion, our replay of the Last Supper is not a private party. As Jesus' own Eucharist, "This is my body given for you," led him to wash the feet of the Twelve he loved, so our Eucharist must take the Catholic from church to world, from altar to people, from Christ crucified on Calvary to Christ crucified not only in Bosnia and Belfast, in Rwanda and Uganda, but in the slums, the streets, the subways of New York and Washington, D.C.

You see, proclaiming our Eucharist as the Bread of Life will sound terribly hollow if we do not touch that life to the hungers of the human family. One example must suffice: our children. In the richest land on God's earth, one of every four children grows up hungry; close to a million youngsters sleep on our streets each night, "scared, cold, hungry, alone, and most of all, desperate to find someone who cares";[7] low-income children are suffering more abuse than others, physical, sexual, emotional.[8] In the capital city of our country, children are preparing not their futures but their funerals; for the deadly experience of several hundred playmates tells them they too will not be around very long.

My sisters and brothers in Christ: Our food divine is a dangerous food. It summons us to service. Not an invitation; a command. The command of Christ: "Love one another as I have loved you" (Jn 15:12). Love even if the cost is a daily dying.

Holy Family Church
New York, N.Y.
April 4, 1996

28

MY BODY...FOR YOU
Solemnity of the Body and Blood of Christ

- Genesis 14:18–20
- 1 Corinthians 11:23–26
- Luke 9:11b–17

Today I dare to confront you with a daring thesis: Today's liturgy is the touchstone, the test, the criterion by which you and I should measure our life, appraise it as success or failure. The crucial text is a remarkably brief sentence from the second reading, Paul's first letter to the Christians of Corinth: "This is my body [given] for you" (1 Cor 11:24; cf. Lk 22:19). That pithy sentence runs like a refrain through my three movements: (1) the body of Christ, (2) the body that is the Church, (3) the body that is you, your Loyola Foundation.[1]

I

First, the body of Christ. Not simply his flesh and blood, his bones and sinews, his veins and arteries. After all, the Son of God, in taking our flesh, did not become sheer matter, six feet of chemicals. He became a person, like us in all we are except for our sin. When Jesus walked the ways of Palestine, he was not a Middle East robot, triggered by button control from heaven. He learned by experience how to shape an idea and talk in Aramaic; learned by living to get angry at hypocrites and weep over his city Jerusalem and his friend Lazarus; knew what it feels like to be hungry and tired, to be called a madman by his relatives, to have no place whereon to rest his head. And when he died, he did not "pass away" serenely, with dear friends saying the rosary around his bed, a priest murmuring "May the angels receive you into paradise." He died in far greater agony than most of us, even feeling for a bitter hour that his own Father might not be there.

Very simply, when I say "the body of Christ," I mean a human being—intelligent, sensitive, emotional, loving. I mean someone so like us that for at least 30 years his own townspeople saw nothing special about him. Now that "body" came out of a mother's body, "grew in wisdom and years" (Lk 2:52), preached his Father's word and sweated a bloody death, for one reason. Never in over three decades was there a moment when he could not have declared, "This is my body [given] for you." That is what the Incarnation is all about: "for you," for me. But why? The answer comes from an astonished St. Paul: He "loved me and gave himself for me" (Gal 2:20). God's Son-in-flesh loved you— loved you enough to be born as you are, grow as you grow, die as none of you will ever die. Loved you so much that when he left you, he left his risen body with you under the appearance of bread, of wine. This is the body we celebrate this evening: the sacramental Christ, hidden indeed but remarkably real, because what is hidden is, as our age-old catechisms declare, "body and blood, soul and divinity." And, once again, "given for you." Christ did not leave himself in a consecrated host primarily to be worshiped. He is there, will be there till time is no more, for the reason he gave at the Last Supper: "Take, eat; this is my body" (Mt 26:26). Why? Because, in the inspired insight of Pius XII, if you have received worthily, you are what you have received. You are transformed into Christ.

It's a fact—this love we cannot fathom. We theologians have spilled centuries of ink and blood over it, have debated it unto frustration and heresy. And after mind is wearied and laser printer runs dry, we do best to lay aside our passions and our computers, kneel in adoration, and murmur to our hidden Lord with theologian Aquinas (in the rapturous translation of Gerard Manley Hopkins):

> Godhead here in hiding, whom I do adore
> Masked by these bare shadows, shape and nothing more,
> See, Lord, at thy service low lies here a heart
> Lost, all lost in wonder at the God thou art.[2]

His body...for you. From Bethlehem to Calvary, from a stable to a cross, his body...for you. Even now, in high heaven and in a helpless host, his body...for you.

II

Move now from the body of Christ to the body that is the Church.[3] In that same letter where Paul told the Corinthian Christians about the body of Christ given for them, he told them about another body that should shape their living. "By one Spirit we were all baptized into one body—Jews or Greeks, slaves or free..." (1 Cor 12:13). He compared it to the human body, to your body and mine. Look, he suggested, at your physical body. It's made up of myriad members. Happily, you're not all heart or hands, all stomach or spleen, all brain or buttocks. Why? Because it takes all sorts of parts working in harmony if the body is to be a body, if it is to be human, if you are to build ideas or cities, grow red with wrath or shame, frame words or run a marathon, waltz or break-dance, eye a sunset or hear a symphony, caress a child or taste a Big Mac, bake biscuits or make love. "The eye cannot say to the hand, 'I have no need of you,' nor again the head to the feet, 'I have no need of you'" (v. 21).

And so, Paul insisted, so it is with you: "You are the body of Christ and individually members of it" (v. 27). You play different parts indeed. Not everybody is pope or priest; not all are Thomas Mertons or Mother Teresas; not all are miracle-working Xaviers or exploring Marquettes; not everyone, thank God, is a Jesuit! But every single Christian is important if the Church is to be one. John Paul II cannot say to the Loyola Foundation, "I have no need of you." Not preacher to the pew, not white Christian to black, riches to rags, literate to illiterate, professor to pupil, lusty youth to doddering old. In Paul's words, "God has so adjusted the body...that the members may have the same care for one another. If one member suffers, all suffer together; if one member is honored, all rejoice together" (vv. 24–26).

"You are all one," Paul proclaimed, "all one in Christ Jesus" (Gal 3:28). But are we? In his time Paul had to flay fractious factions in Christian Corinth: "I belong to Paul," "I belong to Apollos," "I belong to Peter" (1 Cor 1:12). "Is Christ divided?" he asked. "Was Paul crucified for you? Were you baptized in the name of Paul?" (v. 13). In our time Catholics claw one another like cats in a sack: Prolife or prochoice? Mass with Bach or the St. Louis Jesuits? Women where I stand or males incorporated? Bedroom privacy or *Humanae vitae?* A pulpit is not the place to argue perplexing problems, passionately held convictions. In a church of humans, we shall always disagree. From Paul standing up to Peter in the first Christian century, through Thomas Aquinas condemned by the bishop of Paris in the 13th, to Marcel Lefebvre assailing the Second Vatican Council today, the body of Christ has never passed a perfect physical. I am neither damning discussion nor being permissive on heresy. Here I simply assert: If disagreement destroys our love, we are no longer the single body of Christ.

Oneness in mind and heart—an ideal, of course; but only if you and I slave towards that ideal will the Church ever come close to it, will Christ our Lord be able to proclaim proudly to the world outside our Christian gates, "This [this Catholic community] is my body [given] for you."

III

Finally, good friends, let me move from the body that is the whole Church to the body that is your Loyola Foundation. You see, you actually carry over into your concrete day-to-day existence the Christ of Bethlehem and Calvary, the Christ that is the Church, the Christ of the Eucharist. Together and individually, you can murmur honestly, "This is my body [given] for you." You are living the second great commandment of the law and the gospel, the commandment Jesus said "is like" the first, is like loving God, "You shall love your neighbor as yourself" (Mt 22:39), love every sister and brother like another I, another self. And your "neighbor" is not just the friend next door who shares your Bud Light. If the parable of the Good Samaritan is part of your gospel, "neighbor" is anyone and everyone who needs you (cf. Lk 10:25–37).

There is a problem here: a for-me culture. Sociologists claim we are witnessing a resurgence of late-19th-century rugged individualism: Look out for number one; get to the well first before it dries up; the race is to the swift, the shrewd, the savage, and the devil take the hindmost.[4] Nine years ago a prestigious university celebrating its 350th birthday reported the three top goals declared by the class of 1990: (1) money, (2) power, (3) reputation.[5] Not long after, a documentary in *Esquire* recalled "what everyone is saying these days": "money is the new sex."[6]

No, good friends. This Mass makes complete sense for you because the body of Christ you receive and the body of Christ of which you are a member thrust you from church to world murmuring, "This is my body [given] for you."

Given for whom? Not for an abstract mass called humanity. Rather for two very visible sets of people: those you meet each day, and those you don't. Those you meet day after day. I mean wife or husband, your children, the people with whom you work and play. Here it is that you must discover God, celebrate God, proclaim God. Here it is that the vocation built into you at your baptism comes to life: to bring Christ where you live and move and have your being, to help transform your acre of God's world into a city of justice, of peace, of love. Not primarily by preaching; basically by being. Being what? Simply the Christ into whom this Eucharist transmutes you. I mean a man or woman who attracts that world and challenges it. Attracts it because you are so splendidly human, challenges it because you are more than human, alive with a faith that triumphs over doubt, with a hope that overrides discouragement and despair, with a joy that leaps like John the Baptist from the barren womb of sorrow.

Your body given, second, for those millions most of you may rarely meet. I mean the dark side of our common humanity, at home and abroad: the homeless and the helpless, the lonely and the loveless, the drug-infested and the AIDS-infected, the thousand and one young runaways pimped and prostituted and angel-dusted—yes, those who sustain "the pain of being black."[7] They surround you, invade you, but you don't see them, save rarely. Wonder of wonders, unlike the priest in the Gospel parable you do not pass them by "on the other side" (Lk 10:31); for your eyes and your hearts and your purse strings have been opened to the crucified members of Christ's body.

"My body [given] for you." A powerful Presbyterian preacher once said: The religious man or woman is "a queer mixture" of three persons, "the poet, the lunatic, the lover."[8] Such is my provocative prayer for you as you gather this day from near and far. I pray that the poet may always find a place in you; for the poet is a person of profound faith, seeing beneath the appearances of things, seeing with new eyes—in your case, with the eyes of Christ. I pray that there may ever be a fair measure of lunacy in you: the wild idea, the foolishness of the cross, the mad exchange of all else for God; for herein lies your Christian hope. And I pray that, however radical the risk, even on your cross you will always be Christ the lover, arms flung wide, your body given to a whole little world for its redemption—its redemption and yours.

May the Eucharistic Christ continue to feed you...to lead you...to speed you.

Hay-Adams Hotel
Washington, D.C.
June 17, 1995

29
JUST A WORKER OR A JUST WORKER?
Celebration of St. Joseph the Worker

- Genesis 1:26–2:3
- Matthew 13:54–58

In Matthew's Gospel two words are particularly descriptive of Joseph. One tells us *what* he was; the other, *who* he was. What was he? A carpenter. Who was he? A just man. A word on each, then a word on you and me.

I

First, *what* Joseph was. It comes out unexpectedly. An adult Jesus has come back to Nazareth, where he had been brought up. He teaches in Nazareth's synagogue, apparently performs some astonishing works, perhaps a number of cures. But his fellow townspeople are puzzled, even a bit cynical: "Where did this man get this wisdom and these deeds of power?" (Mt 13:54). Why so puzzled, so cynical? Because they know his mother. And "Is not this the carpenter's son?" (v. 55).[1] Once again, familiarity breeds contempt.

The carpenter. He worked with his hands, worked with wood.[2] Long before the push-button age, centuries before technology, everything Joseph produced was crafted by his hands. It was genuinely his creation, his work of art. I find it significant that the Lord God put the protection of Jesus and Mary not in the hands of a man of power, of wealth, of reputation, not in the hands of a king or priest, of a scribe or Pharisee, of a landowner or a prosperous farmer, but in the hands of a laborer, a man who worked with his hands. It meant that Jesus himself would grow up a laborer, working with his hands.

How long Joseph lived, how many years he labored, Scripture does not say. He would not live to see his foster son leave home for his ministry, would not witness any of his miracles, would not weep for his crucifixion, would not rejoice to see him rise from the rock. This laborer simply did his work honestly day after day, read his Hebrew Scriptures, protected his Mary and his Jesus.

I doubt that Joseph had worked out a theology of work. Still, in point of fact, this image of God was imitating his Creator, sharing in God's own creative activity, unfolding the work God had initiated, helping to achieve in history God's own plan for man, for woman, for the earth.[3] Cocreator with God.

II

Second, *who* was Joseph? Joseph, Matthew tells us, was "a just man" (Mt 1:19). Immediately, in the context of Mary's pregnancy, this would mean that he respected the Mosaic law,[4] the law that commanded stoning unto death for an adulterous woman. Still, his obedience was tempered by compassion, which kept him from exacting the full penalty of the law.

But this was not the limit, the extent, of Joseph's justice. Recall what Scripture understands by justice. It is not simply what our President meant when he promised to bring the Oklahoma City bombers to justice.[5] And a just man or woman is not primarily one who gives to another what that other deserves. A just man, a just woman, is a faithful man, a faithful woman. Faithful to what? To relationships, to responsibilities, that stem from a covenant. A just man, a just woman, stands in right relationship to God, to humans, to the earth. To God, to the people of God, to the "things" of God. The crucial word is...fidelity.

Such was Joseph. Faithful to God. Recall his response when God told him not to be afraid to take Mary as his wife. Recall his response when God ordered him to take the child and his mother and flee to Egypt. Faithful to Mary and little Jesus. Recall his ceaseless protectiveness: protective of both on the laborious journey to Bethlehem, on the refugee road to Egypt; protective of Mary's God-given virginity; so caring of Jesus when they had lost him in Jerusalem and Mary chided him, "Your father and I have been searching for you in great anxiety" (Lk 2:48). And—perhaps new to our understanding—faithful, in right relationship, to the "things" of God, in his creative use of God's wood, God's trees. Not only Joseph the worker; Joseph the just worker. I wish some artist would sculpt a statue of Joseph with the focus on his hands, so strong and caring, so careful and creative, shaping God's "things" for God's people...for God.

Early Christians portrayed Joseph as elderly—to protect Mary's virginity. Forget it! Picture rather a robust young carpenter, faithful not because he was too old to be anything save good and chaste, but because God was faithful to Joseph, and Joseph to God. Not age but grace; not feebleness but the strength of virtue. Long before Sir Galahad, Joseph had "the strength of ten, because his heart was pure." Because he was singlehearted.

III

Third, what of you and me?[6] Over the years I have often been sideswiped by Jesus' comment, "When you've done all you've been told to do, say you are still unworthy servants: We've only done our duty (what we are obligated to do)" (Lk 17:10). Actually, it's a strong, perhaps paradoxical way of saying "Nothing you do is simply or primarily your own doing; all is gift, all is God."[7] Such is my emphasis this evening. No matter how "unworthy" or "unprofitable" your service, no matter that you've "only" done your duty, each of you is, by God's gracious giving, another Joseph. I mean...a just worker.

You see, each of you is privileged, by God's grace, to carry on, to implement, God's creative work, Christ's redemptive work. If the bombing of the federal building in Oklahoma City was a terrible act of biblical injustice—infidelity to relationships, to a God of love, to a people of life, to the things of earth that nourish our love and our life—your own work is a continual counteragent, a ceaseless expression of fidelity. Your preaching plays a major role in preacher/novelist Frederick Buechner's giant spider web that is humanity.[8] Day in and day out you preach that whatever we do, for good or ill, sets the whole spider web a-tremble. Touch one person with kindness or with hostility, that person will touch another, and this other still another, until, as Buechner puts it, "who knows where the trembling stops or in what far place and time my touch will be felt. No man [no woman] is an island."

And so you proclaim that, to be a Christian, it is not enough to love God with all my mind and heart, with my whole soul and strength. In fact, I do not really love God if I do not love every sister and brother, black or brown, red or yellow or white, like another I, as if I were standing in his or her shoes. You preach the uncompromising First Letter of John: "If anyone has the world's goods and sees his brother [or sister] in need, yet closes his heart against him [or her], how does God's love abide in him?" (1 Jn 3:17). You are not afraid to declare, with the U.S. Advisory Board on Child Abuse and Neglect, that violence in the home is as much a danger to young children as street gunfire is to teens. Not an exaggeration when 2,000 children die each year of abuse and neglect, 18,000 are permanently disabled, and 142,000 are seriously injured. Not when newborns are smothered to stop their crying, are dropped two stories to their death, are entombed in cement, are beaten and stuffed into a Christmas ornament box.[9]

But not people only, not only fellow humans. In harmony with God's own Word, you preach reverence for the "things" of God, for God's good earth, for the rain forest we ravage and the spotted owl we threaten, for the sparkling waters we pollute without thinking and the protected bears we poach without mercy. You preach reverence not only because these are God's handiwork. Not only because in ravaging them we are savaging ourselves. A strong but slender cord binds *all* God's creatures into a unique unity, incredibly interdependent—on Genesis' testimony, one remarkable society. More mysteriously, St. Paul insists that all creation is yearning, is groaning, to be set free from its enslavement to decay, to share the freedom of God's children (cf. Rom 8:19–23).

Have I gotten away from Joseph the worker? Quite the contrary. This past week I discovered the genuine Joseph. Not an aging Joseph sporting a lily; a virile, vibrant Joseph with the hands of a laborer. Not simply making a living with those hands; continuing the creation from which God "rested" on the seventh day (Gen 2:2–3); readying in his own way the coming of the kingdom by readying the coming of the King; faithful from beginning to end, responsive to his God, to family and townsfolk, to the things of earth he shaped for God and God's people.

Just worker Joseph, your example is precious to us. It triggers our own response to our call to care for each Jesus, each Mary, given us to cherish, to protect, to help grow. Especially today's "widows and orphans"—those alone and forgotten in the twilight of life, and those endangered at the dawn of life. Pray for us workers before the throne of grace: for courage in discouraging days, for confidence in hopeless situations, for joy in our heartbreaking service to God's children. This we ask through him whom you loved as your very own son, Jesus Christ, our Lord.... Amen.

Holy Family Retreat House
West Hartford, Connecticut
May 1, 1995

30

A SECOND BIRTH OF FREEDOM?
Memorial of St. Charles Lwanga and Companions, Martyrs

- 2 Peter 1:2–7
- Mark 12:1–12

The place: Uganda—a thickly populated country in east-central Africa, straddling the equator. The years: over a century ago, 1885 to '87. The situation: a vicious ruler, King Mwanga, commanding his young pages to have sex with him, condemning to death all who refuse, even such as counsel refusal. Three questions: (1) What happened in Uganda? (2) In what way is biblical justice involved?[1] (3) Can Uganda say anything to you and me?

I

First, what happened in Uganda? Twenty-two young men, all Africans, died terribly cruel deaths. Some were beheaded, like Joseph Mukasa, majordomo of the royal household, protomartyr of Bantu Africa. Others were burned to death, like Charles Lwanga, assistant to Mukasa in charge of the pages. On the night of Mukasa's martyrdom, Charles requested and received baptism. For months after, he protected the pages from Mwanga's demands, instructed the young men in the Catholic faith, in moments of crisis baptized the catechumens. Charles was singled out for an especially cruel death—by slow fire.[2]

Pages, a soldier, Catholic leaders—all African, all young, all ready to sacrifice life rather than their Christianity, prepared to say no to their king rather than to their Christ.

II

Second, what has the martyrdom of 22 young Ugandans to do with justice, specifically the justice we pondered this morning? Astonishingly much. If biblical justice is fidelity—fidelity to relationships, to responsibilities, that stem from a covenant; if biblical justice is a matter of right relationships to God, to people, to the earth—then justice is especially evident in the Ugandan martyrs. For they died precisely for God, for their sisters and brothers, for the land that is Africa.

You see, the dread-full task of these 22 was to be faithful. Dread-full, because fidelity would exact a terrible cost. To be faithful to God, they had to love God more than their own lives, over and above their trembling, their fear of sword and fire. They had to love God above their own hopes and plans, their desires and yearnings, for the next 30 or 40 years; love God more than the African love of life with wife, with children, with grandchildren.

To be faithful to Africa's people, they had to be loyal to their crazed king, but, as with St. Thomas More, God's servants first. They had to love the people of Uganda, Catholics and Protestants and animists, love them like other selves. Not only their blood sisters and brothers; not only their fellow Catholics; not only their fellow martyrs. They had to love non-Catholic Christians, found themselves protesting the martyrdom of Anglican Bishop James Hannington; had to love the native animists, yes even the maniac Mwanga, love him enough to say no to him.

And they had to love the land that sustained them, the way the Israelites loved their land, had to feel orphaned without Africa, apart from it; had to love Africa enough to leave it for ever, to die so that Africa might live more fully.

Yes, good brothers in Christ, martyrdom may well be biblical justice at its fullest: mimicking the justice of God, God's fidelity to God's promises, by fidelity to their own promises. Faithful to Africa's God, faithful to Africa's people, faithful to Africa's land. Faithful to the end, faithful unto blood.

III

This leads naturally into my third question: What might these 22 young Ugandan martyrs be saying to you and me?

To begin with, I said that these 22 young men died that Africa might live more fully. Africa has. These 22 martyrs should bring to realistic life for us the opening prayer of our Eucharistic liturgy: The blood of these martyrs has indeed been the seed of Christians. Take Uganda alone. In 1888, Catholics numbered 8,500; in 1905, 86,000; in 1923, 375,000; in 1993, over eight million, about 40% of the population.[3]

But there is something more significant than sheer numbers. In my effort to unearth the reality that is Ugandan Catholicism, I found uncommonly significant Pope Paul VI's visit to Uganda in 1969. He challenged Uganda's Catholics to cultivate an African soul of its own. He told them, "You may, and you must, have an African Christianity."[4] No longer may missionaries impose a European soul on Uganda, a Western-style liturgy on Africa. I found it splendidly symbolic when African drums first beat upon the walls of St. Peter's in Rome. I find it even more promising when African drums, African hymns, an African beat make the clouds tremble in Uganda—and this in the encouraging presence of the father of *all* Catholics.

That personal presence, John Paul II in February 1993, involved a homily, a written message, and a talk to the international diplomatic corps. Each highlighted issues far more complex than Uganda's 22 martyrs had to confront. The highly pastoral homily urged on Africans a "close, personal, monogamous union" that "is not of Western origin, but rather corresponds to God's plan for husband and wife."[5] To the ambassadors and personnel of the diplomatic missions and international organizations in Uganda, he expressed "profound anxiety" over warfare in Africa, six million refugees, 16 million displaced within their own countries, hunger, starvation, suffering, and death. And yet he could wax soberly optimistic: "Are we witnessing a recovery of that optimism for building sound societies which accompanied the transition from colonialism to independence? Is Africa experiencing a second birth of freedom? This is certainly my profound hope."[6]

John Paul's written message centered on AIDS. For Uganda, with more than 35,000 officially reported cases, may well be the epicenter of the African continent's AIDS crisis. The pope reached out to them:

> I know well that within one decade this dreaded disease has already affected so many of your people and left thousands of children without parental care. Many of you are already bedridden, many others diagnosed as seropositive, others living in constant fear of contracting the disease....

Adverting to the dangerous crisis of values that parallels the spread of AIDS, he added:

> You who suffer from AIDS have an important role to play in this vital struggle for the well-being of your country! Offer your sufferings in union with Christ for your brothers and sisters who are especially at risk! Your suffering can be a grace-filled opportunity to bring about the moral rebirth of Ugandan society.

Then he quoted the touching exhortation of Paul VI to hospital patients on his 1969 visit:

> Like our Lord on the cross, you cannot move about freely; but, like him you can hold your arms wide to the entire world and offer your sufferings for the salvation of men.... Let your hospital bed be an altar upon which you offer yourself completely to God to do with as he wishes; and your reward will be exceedingly great in heaven.[7]

Other issues raise the anxiety level of Africa's Catholics: desertion to fundamentalist groups sweeping much of the sub-Sahara; the low lot of women in church and society. And it is only recently that Catholic leaders have begun to speak out for social justice, against the disparity between rich and poor, between the powerful and the powerless.

Have we left Lwanga and his 21 companions? In a sense, yes. But more realistically, we have seen them in their suffering successors, in the AIDS-afflicted, in the widows and orphans, in the refugees and the displaced, in the poor and the powerless. Martyrdom comes in strange packages.

St. Charles, help us people of biblical justice, help us to expand our Christian vision, to see beyond Crookston and the District of Columbia, beyond the USA. Help us to realize that Uganda is not a foreign country; Uganda is part of our body, the Body of Christ. But in peering overseas, let us not forget what stares us in the face: the assault on aliens, the discrimination against immigrants, the prejudice against Native Americans, the color line that still divides blacks and whites in this "land of the free," makes two nations out of one. A cutting question: In this crisis of justice, this crisis of love, where am I? Where are my people?

Mt. St. Benedict Center
Crookston, Minnesota
June 3, 1996

31
HAPPIEST MAN OF ALL THE GONZAGAS
Memorial of St. Aloysius Gonzaga

- 2 Corinthians 9:6–11
- Matthew 6:1–6, 16–18

Almost four decades ago an insightful Jesuit observed that, as far as natural appeal goes, Aloysius Gonzaga died at an awkward age.

> At twenty-three he is an "in-between." He lacks the sparkle and charm of Stanislaus Kostka and Dominic Savio, and in comparison with these fresh and smiling stars he is, to many, a rather frosted moon. On the other hand there is wanting the mature touch of [Francis] Xavier or Pius [X] or Francis [de Sales] and other elder brothers in holiness. Yet to picture him as a black-robed, rather bleak-faced young religious, towering against a vacant sky, is to see less than half the man. It is to suggest an isolated, unfriendly figure, devoid of the human attractiveness which helps us to love the saints. In fairness to him, you must look to the circumstances; you must roll back the years; you must paint in the background, taking account of the riotous times in which he lived; and above all, you must remember that he was a Gonzaga, for that was in many respects the key to his life ....[1]

So then, let's look to the circumstances, roll back the years, paint in the background. Swiftly, of course: (1) the prince, (2) the Jesuit, (3) his significance for evangelizers.[2]

I

First, the prince. Aloysius was born to pride, to power, to possessions.[3] For almost four centuries (1328–1707) Gonzaga was the ruling family of Mantua. On the credit side, the Gonzagas produced able governors, built churches as well as palaces, commissioned magnificent art, made Mantua a center of culture. Less admirably, we discover rapacious rulers, unbridled power, internecine hatred. We discover artistic sense wedded to lust for blood, faith to immorality. We discover a Niccolò d'Este with 800 mistresses, beheading a son and a second wife on a single night. We discover tyrants born out of wedlock, adored by their subjects, murdered by their subjects. And so on, through seemingly endless corruption. "Though the Gonzaga family had no corner on high Renaissance ruthlessness and evil, by modern standards they make cardboard villains out of figures on...television,"[4] the corrupt cop, the coke king, the kid who kills for a Reebok.

Into such blood company was Aloysius born. From age five he was hustled from camp to court, from one court to another—that "education of a prince" which often meant spiritual devastation. Our contemporaries may ridicule his "modesty of the eyes," but it made good sense when it was quite common for women to abuse little boys at the great banquets and dances.[5] Apparently he was quite gifted intellectually: highly competent in the Latin classics, even more interested in mathematics and astronomy, knowledgeable about the Spanish Empire, enamored of that facet of philosophy which dealt with God—even argued in debate that the Trinity could be known from naked human reason. He had an innate talent for diplomacy; in his teens he traveled with his father on family business.

An imperial prince, Aloysius was his father's pride and joy—a father who saw in this son the fulfilment of all his secular hopes, the only son fit to succeed him, to govern his estates and cities, to lend a fresh glamour to the Gonzaga name.

II

With this as background, with the dreams his father fostered for so many years, imagine the rage—yes, rage—in the breast of Don Ferrante Gonzaga when Aloysius announced, "I want to become a Jesuit." A Jesuit? Vowed to poverty over against Gonzagan wealth? Vowed to chastity over against Gonzagan sexuality and fertility? Vowed to obedience over against Gonzagan unparalleled power?

Rage indeed. Gonzaga *père* threatened to flog his favorite son. He declared that, if Aloysius joined the Jesuits, the boy would no longer be his son. Then a fresh, more seductive strategy: Forget the Jesuits! Take more lucrative roads to holiness. Look at the good a Cardinal Charles Borromeo does. The Duke of Mantua promised him any ecclesiastical dignity in his power. All sorts of influential men were summoned to dissuade Aloysius: bishops and priests, uncles and cousins, members of religious orders. No effect whatever. So his father ordered Aloysius out of his house, out of his sight. And one day late in 1585, against all the odds, Aloysius delivered to the superior general of the Society of Jesus, Claudius Acquaviva, a letter from his father dated November the fifth. It read in part:

> ...In the past I considered it to be my duty to refuse to this my son Aloysius permission to enter your holy Society, for I feared that owing to his youth he might embark upon his enterprise without that firm resolution which were right. Now I think that I am sure that it is God who is calling him thither, and so I should feel it on my conscience were I to refuse him the permission that he has longed to receive, and has prayed for from me so urgently and so often. So, freely and willingly, with my mind at peace and full of God's consolation, I send him and commend him to Your Reverence, who will be to him a more helpful father than I can be. I have nothing here to add concerning the person of my son. I merely say that I am giving into Your Reverence's hands the most precious thing that I possess in all the world, and my chiefest hope, that I placed entirely in him, of maintaining and giving glory to my family....[6]

From Aloysius' Jesuit existence I choose only its close. 1591 was a disastrous year for Italy. "Scarcity had become famine, and famine bred the plague. From the blackened country districts, pitiable caravans of starving peasants poured into Rome, already congested with its own population, that festered in its tortuous streets."[7] Hospitals were jammed to overflowing; men and women were dying in the streets. Superiors gave Aloysius permission to minister to the sick and dying—a reluctant permission, for his health was precarious. Little reluctance in Aloysius. With intense joy he put the sick to bed, undressed them, washed and fed them—in fact, nursed with joy the most repulsive of the patients.

There is a tradition to the effect that Aloysius contracted a fatal infection, possibly from the poor fellow a famous statue represents as carried on his shoulders. An attractive tradition, but the evidence for this is slim at best. More likely, sheer exhaustion, intensified by his unremitting service of the plague-stricken, took a final toll on a flesh far from robust.[8] It was his dedication that killed him, his response to the call of Christ in the crucified. During the night of June 20–21, 1591, as the octave of Corpus Christi drew to its close, "the happiest man of all the Gonzagas"[9] returned to his God.

III

But what might such an Aloysius say to evangelizers? I take you back to 1975, to Pope Paul VI's remarkable apostolic exhortation *Evangelization in the Modern World.*[10] The pontiff insisted that, for all its complexity, two realities are utterly inseparable from evangelization: Jesus Christ and people.

First, Jesus Christ. As Paul put it, "Evangelization will always have as the foundation, center, and supreme focus of its dynamism the clear proclamation that in Jesus Christ...salvation is offered to every man [and woman] as a gracious gift inspired by God's mercy."[11]

But having anchored evangelization in Jesus Christ, the pope went on to declare:

> Evangelization cannot be complete unless account is taken of the reciprocal links between the gospel and the concrete personal and social life of [men and women].... In proclaiming liberation and ranging herself with all who toil and suffer for it, the Church cannot allow herself or her mission to be limited to the purely religious sphere while she ignores the temporal problems of [men and women].... The Church certainly considers it highly important to establish structures which are more human, more just, more respectful of the rights of the person, less oppressive and coercive.[12]

Here a young man in his 20s can inspire us. Not by his preaching. Rather by two realities in his life that must be ours if we are to preach with "fire in the belly": an intense commitment and a total involvement. The commitment? To Jesus Christ as "the foundation, center, and supreme focus" of our every waking moment. What emerges from Aloysius' life is what a distinguished French Jesuit spiritual writer, Joseph de Guibert, identified as the distinctive trait of Ignatian spirituality: enthusiastic love and rational judgment. Enthusiastic union with God and a relentless practical consideration of the best way to work God's will in the world—what we call discernment. For hours Aloysius would lie prostrate before a crucifix sobbing bitterly over the suffering of his Lord.[13] And for equal hours he could mull with dispassionate rationality over the most effective way in which he could serve his Lord and his sisters and brothers. As a prince or a pauper? In this religious institute or that monastic order?

From this wedding of reason and love was born his involvement. One reason why he joined the Jesuits was that the Society of Jesus explicitly embraced the work of conversion, the task of evangelization—in India, in Japan, in the New World.[14] From this wedding of reason and love was born the Aloysius who gave his life to the half-alive, to the dying. This is the Aloysius who today would be carrying the crucified of Calcutta to Mother Teresa's home, would be hugging the AIDS-afflicted and the drug-infected in Oklahoma City.

Not the destiny of Aloysius to change unjust structures, even Gonzagan structures. Not his to think and speak, his to think and do. A genuine son of Ignatius: a contemplative in action. Perhaps not quite "our kind of guy," our kind of saint. But Aloysius compels us to look deep inside ourselves: What actually triggers our commitment, our involvement? What are we doing here...and why?

Marriott Hotel
Oklahoma City, Okla.
June 21, 1995

32
BE CLOSEFISTED WITH ME, OPENHANDED TO THE POOR
Memorial of St. Robert Bellarmine

- 1 Corinthians 12:12–14, 27–31a
- Luke 7:11–17

Robert Bellarmine. Not an easy man to preach over; there's just too much. So then, let me first sketch what I shall *not* talk about. Then I shall spend a bit of time on the one facet of his life that might well be of more immediate concern to you and me.[1] I shall end on a brief personal note.

I

What shall I pass over? There's the professor of controversial theology at the Roman College, a discipline that at the time he took over "was a chaos and not a science."[2] There's the spiritual director of the Roman College, who had the future saint Aloysius Gonzaga in his loving care, prayed with him just before Luigi died.[3] There's the spiritual writer, with two themes towering above all others: the duties of the rich to the poor, and the obligation of bishops to reside in their dioceses, preach, and administer the sacraments to their flocks. There's the rector of the Roman College, who announced his policy as "Be among [your subjects] as one of them. Have care of them...and hinder not music"—by which he meant, "act the part of a good *maestro di cappella* who makes little fuss in his conducting, and directs the singers with a scarcely perceptible movement of his baton."[4] There's the archbishop of Capua, the pastor who thundered against the murders and suicides, the brawls and blasphemies that stemmed from the gambling to which his people were heavily addicted; the shepherd who knew each of his priests, their character, gifts, and virtues; the still-very-Jesuit prelate who renewed the lost fervor of religious communities, even wrote to a convent of nuns to express his "great disgust" that they received only girls of noble birth: "If the Blessed Virgin were on earth and wanted to become a nun, she would never be able to get into your convent, being a carpenter's wife."[5]

There's the cardinal, who wept in sadness while the red hat was conferred on him; for he had hoped that Pope Clement VII, "who regarded cardinals as little better than a necessary nuisance, would let him die in his Jesuit gown."[6] There's the theologian, who was involved in the bitter controversies on grace, free will, and predestination; who effected a doctrinal advance within the Church by stressing the purely spiritual power of the Church against those who claimed direct temporal power for the Holy See; who was unfortunately involved in the Galileo mess at 74, with a cast of mind that made it "pyschologically impossible for him to accept the revolutionary idea, which Copernicus, Kepler, and Galileo had intuitively grasped, that the solid earth under his feet was a planet in rapid motion around the sun."[7]

And there's the dying Bellarmine, suffering terribly but patiently from the zeal of his physicians. "The only humours which they did draw were the poor patient's tears."[8] With a cross on his breast, saying softly to himself "Jesus, Jesus, Jesus," he passed quietly, peacefully, to his Lord.

II

So much for what, like Roman prosecutor Cicero,[9] I shall *not* speak about. What, then, is the burden of my homily? Just this: Bellarmine had not been a cardinal long when the Roman slums christened him "il Padre de' Poveri," "Father of the Poor."[10] His house became the haunt of all the down-and-outers in Rome. Daily they crowded around the building, invaded the stairs, even his room. Upon returning home, he might find as many as 300 waiting for him. His reaction? He would rub his hands with delight, would say to his distraught almoner, "Peter, these are the people who will get us to heaven."

Everyone, simply everyone, was welcome—whatever the hour, however important the work he was about. Once each month, whatever surplus he discovered went to poor families or individuals, all listed in a book with details of situation and need. Each December 31 he repeated his standing orders to Peter, "Be as closefisted as possible with me, but as openhanded as you can to the poor." His principle? Every penny over necessary expenses belonged to the poor—not in charity but in strict justice.

Often Robert gave his cardinal's ring to a poor person, with a note stating it might be pawned; then, when money came in, he would redeem it. There were times when he gave even his mattress away. When his brother Thomas proposed that they erect a magnificent monument on their parents' grave, he replied, "Let it be a simple monument, for poor living people have greater need of my money than dead people have of rich tombs."

Even more impressive than *what* Bellarmine gave was *how* he gave. When anyone entered his room—anyone—he stood up and removed his cap. Nor did he "wait for misery to come and tell its tale. He sought it out."[11] Whenever he went driving, his head footman carried money to be distributed to hard cases along the way. Especially appealing to his heart were the respectable poor people in Italy whose pride was such that they preferred to starve rather than beg. Secret agents scented such cases out; their names and needs were recorded in "the book."

At home, he treated his household more as a father than a master. When they were sick, his own physician took care of them, and he paid all their expenses. Presents for his table went to their hall. He never ordered, always asked as if for a favor. He never suggested the slightest task after dark, in bad weather, during their meals or siesta. He despised the word "servant," spoke of them as "brothers and companions." He said Mass for them each day, preached to them on the greater feasts, never pried into their personal lives, but was very strict on behavior.

Like the Francis on whose feast day he was born, Bellarmine's compassion went out not only to people but to all living things. It always angered him, saddened him, to see a beast treated ill. At times he stayed at home rather than deprive his horses of their rest and refreshment.

III

Finally, a brief personal note: What might Bellarmine's life, particularly as "Father of the Poor," say to us? Not only as priests but as preachers of the just word. I focus on one aspect of the problem.

The Letter of James insists that Christians must be "doers of the word, and not merely hearers" (Jas 1:22). Transfer that to us, and James might well say, "Be doers of the word, and not merely preachers." Obviously, not all of us are called to "do the word" the same way. Robert Bellarmine did the just word by never refusing a single beggar's request, by sharing his surplus with the poor, by selling or pawning his precious possessions, by treating each of the disadvantaged with respect, as a person beloved of God. Closer to our time, Dorothy Day did the just word by living with the poor, sharing not only their homelessness but their lice and their vermin. Mother Teresa does the just word by bringing Calcutta's homeless dying into her own home. Jimmy Carter's Habitat for Humanity does the just word by building homes for the homeless. The Children's Defense Fund in Washington, D.C., does the just word by researching the state of the world's children, by flooding parishes with potential projects, by harassing Congress and the Administration to do justice to the most vulnerable of our society, Jesus' "little ones." Bread for the World does the just word by saving millions of children from starving. Missionary priests, married couples, young graduates of Catholic colleges do the just word by sharing the lot of the poor in Micronesia and Peru, in Nepal and Belize.

To do the just word, you and I need not abandon the turf we tread each day. Not mine to tell you exactly what to do; that revelation emerges from personal experience and from the dynamizing Spirit within us. But this much I can say: None of us can rest content with justice homilies. Necessary indeed, but not enough. We must gather our people, large numbers of them, to ask three questions: (1) What are the justice issues in our area—who are "the poor"? (2) What resources do we have to attack these issues, to "send the downtrodden away relieved" (Lk 4:18)? (3) What in the concrete shall we do?

Still not enough; we are still only talking. A neuralgic question this week: What do you want me to do, Lord? Can a Jesuit cardinal and theologian strike a spark? St. Robert Bellarmine, enlighten my mind, stiffen my will, share with me the courage that made you "Father of the Poor."

Holiday Inn
Wichita Falls, Texas
September 17, 1996

33
NOT FOR ME A HEART OF STONE
Memorial of St. Jerome

- Job 1:6–22
- Luke 9:46–50

The story persists that a Renaissance pope once came upon a painting of St. Jerome. It was one of those portraits that picture Jerome in the desert, gaunt and wild-eyed, on his knees before a human skull, beating his breast with a stone. And the pope, we are told, exclaimed, "Ah, Jerome! Had you not been discovered in that posture, you would not be on the Church's altars today!" The story raises intriguing problems.[1] The problem that engages me here should concern every priest, every preacher of the gospel, especially someone passionately provoked by the plight of the poor.[2] I mean passion, anger, outrage inside of us and in our proclamation. Two main steps to my dance: (1) Jerome, (2) you and I.

I

First, Jerome. To put it gently, he was a paradox. On the one hand, much in him was admirable. He was a humanist, so steeped in classical culture that he confessed he could no more forget it than the wine jar can lose the flavor of the wine, so enamored of Latin literature that he dreamt himself haled before Christ on the charge, "You are not a Christian, you are a Ciceronian."[3] He was a Scripture scholar, expert in Hebrew and Greek, a master of translation, with a love for God's Word that is summarized in his admirable advice: When your head droops at night, let a page of Scripture pillow it.[4] He was an ascetic who lived his last 34 years in Bethlehem, in the shadow of a manger, linking scholarship with monastic life: "Having

158

food and raiment I shall be satisfied, and the naked cross I shall naked follow."[5] He was an exciting controversialist, sometimes wrong but never dull, breaking lances with heretics and orthodox, on marriage and virginity, on solitude and celibacy, on grace and the Trinity, on the meaning of Scripture. Jerome was the most learned man of the fourth century, perhaps the most erudite figure in Christian antiquity.

On the other hand, Jerome puzzles us. The puzzle lies in his strong feelings, his sensitive, passionate nature. He analyzed it frankly: "I have no breast of iron, no heart of stone. I was not born of flint, was not suckled by Hyrcanian tigers."[6]

In the first place, Jerome was quick to be hurt. He turned petulant when Augustine questioned the value of his Old Testament translation from the Hebrew. He was distressed when monks of the desert called him heretic for his conception of the Trinity. He was wounded when his relations with a noble Roman ascetic, Paula, were misinterpreted. He grew violent when a priest, Vigilantius, censured him for his devotion to a controverted Christian writer named Origen. He brooded when his friends failed to write, complained when their letters were short.

Second, Jerome was slow to forgive. He left the desert bitter; his attitude, "it is better to dwell amid wild beasts than with such Christians."[7] He left Rome embittered; in his books Christian Rome was "Babylon."[8] The death of a former friend, Rufinus, prompted a raw valedictory: "Now that the scorpion lies buried in [Sicily]...and the hydra with its numerous heads has ceased its hissing against us...I will tackle the prophet Ezekiel."[9]

Third, Jerome's attacks on sin, on error, on hypocrisy, were dipped in mordant satire. He antagonized clerics by reminding them of a Greek proverb, "A fat paunch never breeds fine thoughts."[10] He assailed fasting women who "cover up their faces but manage to leave one eye open to watch the effect."[11] He warned consecrated virgins not to seek their Bridegroom "in the city squares."[12] He could question a man's motives as well as his orthodoxy, jest at his origins as well as his ignorance; he called Vigilantius an innkeeper who cut his wine with water in his tavern and in his theology.

Fourth, his very asceticism brought out Jerome's very human reactions. Two years he spent in the desert, blackened by a blazing sun. Lonely, he begged for letters. A gourmet with a weak stomach, he found desert food a penance. Even when his companions were scorpions and wild animals, his mind was invaded by "bands of dancing girls."[13]

Jerome's most sympathetic biographers find him an "irascible hermit." If only death arrested his ceaseless search for perfection, only death stilled the surging cry of his passions.

II

Second, you and I. At bottom, we do not differ much from Jerome. We have rational appetites we call emotions, the response of our spirit to our experience: delight in the *Swan Lake* ballet, sadness when my mother breathes her last, despondency when my hiatal hernia flares up, love when I contemplate Christ on his cross. But I am not pure spirit; I have strong feelings, passions, the reaction of my flesh to what I see, hear, touch, taste, smell.

By passion here I do not mean sexual arousal. I mean strong feelings such as Jesus displayed. I mean the *anger* that shook him when he whipped money-changers from the temple. I mean the *fear* that changed his sweat to blood when in the garden of his agony he begged his Father, "Don't let me die!" I mean the *indignation* that inflamed his flesh when he castigated Pharisees for putting the Sabbath before the sick and ailing. I mean the tears that wet his cheeks and wrung his heart as he gazed on a dead friend Lazarus and a dying city Jerusalem.

How does all this touch our justice preaching? Profoundly. If I am genuinely convinced that injustice is rampant in my country, in my parish, on my street, I should find it all but impossible to speak of it without passion. When I deplore a rich America that lets 25 percent of its children grow up in poverty, my face may well darken with anger. When I mention the teenagers in Washington, D.C., preparing not their futures but their funerals, because hundreds of their playmates have been blasted to bits by gunfire, my stomach might well revolt in fear for our young. When I cry out against the racism that burns black churches and desecrates Jewish synagogues, will it not be an anguished cry of indignation? When I sound the alarm over elderly men and women groping in garbage cans for the food I waste so thoughtlessly, tears may well course down my cheeks. When I read that each week 500 men, women, and children are being destroyed by land mines mostly manufactured in developed countries and sold in the developing world, how can I preach the just word calm, cool, and collected?

Our preaching must echo the declaration of a justice of the New York State Supreme Court, "A society that loses its sense of outrage is doomed to extinction."[14] Outrage not only deep within us; outrage on our faces, in our voices, in our gestures. An audible cry not only to our God but to our people, when we see children hurting, punished by Congress, discriminated against, deprived of an education for the sins of their parents. Yes, when we see developing humans cut off from life because they are an inconvenience, because in the womb they are not human, are things subject to our whims, an instant before birth have no rights.

But I shall not preach passionately unless I feel fiercely. I shall not preach passionately unless my life is a passionate protest against injustice. Jerome may have overdone the passion, bypassed the Thomistic definition of prudence, "putting reason into virtue." It is impossible to justify all his ravings and rantings. But that is not quite the point. The point is, Jerome felt fiercely. When he thought something unjust, someone hypocritical, when he was opposed or hurt, he rarely reacted with his head alone. The whole of Jerome reacted. To excess at times, yes indeed. But frankly, if I had to choose, I would rather be a Jerome than a cold, calculating thinker always in perfect control.

Why? Because it is the wedding of head and heart that shapes a preacher who can change heads and hearts. It is the wedding of reason and passion that shapes Christian congregations capable of denouncing and destroying the injustices that plague their acre of God's world. Cartesian clarity is good, but not good enough; necessary, but not sufficient. And so I pray: "Dear St. Jerome, indeed you puzzle me. But, more importantly, you inspire me. Help me not only to think clearly (your friend Augustine will do better there) but to feel fiercely. Ask our passionate Christ to put out his hand and touch my mouth, so that the word of God I preach may be tipped with fire. Not for me a breast of iron, not for me a heart of stone."

Mercy Center
St. Louis, Missouri
September 30, 1996

34
DIE NOW UNTO GOD OR LIVE A WHILE FOR OTHERS?
Memorial of St. Ignatius of Antioch

- Romans 1:16–25
- Luke 11:37–41

It was about the year 110. In Antioch of Syria, persecution racked the Christian Church. And the bishop of Antioch, Ignatius, was cast in chains. Flanked by ten Roman guards, he was hustled over land and sea to Rome, to die in the Colosseum. During that journey Ignatius managed to write seven letters—letters to six Christian communities and a single bishop—letters which have been termed the most beautiful pearls of ancient Christian literature.[1] What grips Ignatius is a passionate love for his crucified Lord, so overpowering that it breaks through grammar; language is inadequate, ideas tumble headlong one upon another.

But it is not Ignatius' rhetoric that attracts me this evening. It is rather his longing for martyrdom, his desire to die. I want to (1) contrast this with the attitude of another Ignatius, (2) reflect on what this contrast implies for genuine Christian discipleship, and (3) suggest briefly what all this might say for your life and mine.

I

Begin with Ignatius of Antioch. One letter, more than any other, has attracted the attention of the ages. Ignatius is writing to Christians who will soon see him, the Christians of Rome. He longs to see them, to embrace them, but he is afraid—afraid, he says, of their love; their love may destroy him. Their influence with civil authority may save him; and this he does not want. And so he writes one of the most moving passages the church of martyrs has bequeathed to us:

162

I am writing to all the churches and state emphatically to all that I die willingly for God, provided you do not interfere. I beg you, do not show me unseasonable kindness. Suffer me to be the food of wild beasts, which are the means of my making my way to God. God's wheat I am, and by the teeth of wild beasts I am to be ground that I may prove Christ's pure bread.... Then only shall I be a genuine disciple of Jesus Christ when the world will not see even my body. Petition Christ on my behalf that through these instruments I may prove God's sacrifice....

May nothing seen or unseen fascinate me, so that I may happily make my way to Jesus Christ! Fire, cross, struggles with wild beasts, wrenching of bones, mangling of limbs, crunching of the whole body, cruel tortures inflicted by the devil—let them come upon me, provided only I make my way to Jesus Christ.

...Him I seek who died for us; him I love who rose again because of us.... Permit me to be an imitator of my suffering God. If anyone holds him in his heart, let him understand what I am aspiring to, and then let him sympathize with me, knowing in what distress I am.[2]

Not long after, Ignatius died as he had desired, by the teeth of wild beasts in the Roman Colosseum.

Now turn the pages of history 14 centuries; turn to another Ignatius, Ignatius of Loyola. The Spanish Ignatius had a deep devotion to the Syrian. In honor of the martyr, he changed his name from Iñigo to Ignatius. The first of his maxims was a phrase from the first Ignatius, "My Love has been crucified."[3] He made the emblem of his Jesuits the first three letters (IHS) of the name of Jesus in Greek, because he had read in *The Golden Legend* that when the Romans tore out the heart of the martyred Ignatius, they found those letters graven on his heart in gold. And yet, as we listen to Loyola, we seem to hear a far different Ignatius. He is speaking to one of his first companions, James Laínez:

> *Ignatius:* Tell me, Master Laínez, what do you think you would do,were God our Lord to say: "If you want to die soon, I will release you from the prison of this body and give you eternal glory. If you prefer to stay alive, I give you no assurance as to what will become of you...." If our Lord told you this, and you thought that by remaining for some time in this life you could render some outstanding service to His Divine Majesty, which would you choose?
>
> *Laínez:* I must confess, Father, I would choose to go soon to enjoy God and to assure my salvation, and to avoid the perils in so important a matter.
>
> *Ignatius:* I certainly would not. If I thought that by remaining in

this life I could render some signal service to our Lord, I would
beg Him to leave me here until I had done it; and I would not
think twice of the peril to me or the assurance of my salvation.[4]

II

Two contrasting approaches to life in Christ, to the Christian
apostolate. Is one more Christian than the other? You know, several
critics have seen in Ignatius of Antioch a Christian fanatic. Back in
1951 a prolific author wrote of him: "This "strange saint, wandering
slowly toward Rome, left his mark on Christianity. All the wilder ele-
ments descend from him, from the terrible look in his eyes."[5] From
this point of view, the Syrian Ignatius is Christianity at its worst, sanctity at its most repugnant. This lust for martyrdom at all costs is a neurotic thing. This thirst for fire and cross and wild beasts is unnatural,
a weakling's flight from reality. Loyola's attitude makes Christian
sense. This is Christian humanism: to serve my sisters and brothers,
not to save me. This is Christian heroism: to risk not fire and sword
but hell itself. This is Christian realism: to lust for life, not for death.

The reaction is too facile. Whether I opt for a bloody dying
into Christ or a risk-laden living for others, the decision is not made
in abstraction, apart from concrete conditions. St. Paul recognized
how difficult the problem could be. Recall what he wrote to the
Christians of Philippi:

> To me, living is Christ and dying is gain. If I am to live in the
> flesh, that means fruitful labor for me, and I do not know which
> I prefer. I am hard pressed between the two. My desire is to
> depart and be with Christ, for that is far better; but to remain in
> the flesh is more necessary for you. Since I am convinced of this,
> I know that I will remain and continue with all of you for your
> progress and joy in faith....
>
> (Phil 1:21-26)

Ignatius of Antioch, Ignatius of Loyola, Paul of Tarsus—each
confronted a critical question: Given a choice between dying right
now unto God and personal salvation or living a while longer for
your sisters and brothers, which do you choose? Loyola apparently
had no problem: Go for the brethren! Paul confessed himself "hard
pressed," torn, in anguish. He knew what was "far better" for him in
isolation: "to depart and be with Christ." But he knew too what was
"more necessary" for his faithful, struggling people: "to remain in
the flesh." And so he opted to hang on.[6] The bishop of Antioch had

no doubts: "Pardon me—I know very well where my advantage lies. At last I am well on the way to being a disciple."[7] And so he opted for death.

"*My* advantage"? Here be careful. The attitude of our Syrian Ignatius was not dictated by self-love, divorced from his sisters and brothers. The Church knows no martyrs who have loved only God. "My love for you," Ignatius wrote to a Christian community, "overflows all bounds."[8] And to the Christians of Rome: "Remember in your prayers the Church in Syria, which now has God for her shepherd in my stead. Jesus Christ alone will be her bishop, together with your community of love."[9] Your community of love. Ignatius knew not only that God would watch over Syria with loving care (the original meaning of *episcopos*) but that the churches would rally round a church bereft of its bishop. Think of a man chained to a detachment of soldiers, yet thinking ceaselessly of Christians and their churches. He writes to thank them for their sympathy, to strengthen their faith, to warn against rampant heresies, to urge participation in the one Eucharist that is the flesh of Christ.

Each time I read Ignatius' letter to the Christians of Rome, I am utterly convinced that he was responding to a clear call from God. Listen to him:

> By this short letter I beseech you: Do believe me! Jesus Christ will make it clear to you that I speak the truth—he on whose lips there are no lies, through whom the Father has spoken truthfully.... What I write to you does not please the appetites of the flesh, but it pleases the mind of God. If I suffer, you have loved me; if I am rejected, you have hated me![10]

III

What might all this say to you and me?[11] Pressed by time, I simply suggest one topic for mulling some disenchanted evening. I suggest that our three protagonists exemplify three ways in which God speaks to us, three ways in which God calls for a response.

First, as with Ignatius of Antioch, God can be rather demanding. Not that God destroys our freedom. Not that we risk hell if we say no. Rather that there are situations when God's call is so clear that to say no to God is out of the question. Not only a terminal cancer; not only the moment before the life-supporting tubes are removed. Less life-threatening (in a physical sense) is God's demand that we live and preach biblical justice, fidelity to the demands of responsibilities that stem from our covenant with Christ. Love God above all else; love each sister and brother like another self; touch all of God's creation with reverence. No options here.

Second, as with Ignatius of Loyola, God can be quite relaxed. Not uncaring; simply open to options. Say, exactly how Christians will respond to the cries of the poor, the marginalized. Not all are called to the same response. Some will work alongside the poor; others will influence legislation or organize for greater effectiveness; still others may challenge our culture by powerful preaching, by courageous challenges to congregations unwittingly influenced by a resurgent rugged individualism.

Third, as with St. Paul, God can leave us uncertain, anxious. I don't mean simply your own delights and dislikes—the newly ordained priest who said to his first pastor, "I don't do hospitals." I mean the pressures that strait-jacket our priests today, unreasonable demands on time, energy, and abilities. For your people want you to be an efficient administrator *and* an inspiring preacher, one with God *and* one with them, genuinely prayerful *and* ceaselessly active, a model for the young *and* a companion to the elderly, continually studying *and* available to them 24 hours a day. You have to make choices, and whatever your choices, they will at times leave half your people unhappy.

No homily can supply you with push-button solutions. As a small beginning, I commend to you the advice an Ignatius of Antioch in chains gave to young Bishop Polycarp:

> Be concerned about unity, the greatest blessing. Bear with all, just as the Lord does with you. Have patience with all in charity.... To prayer give yourself unceasingly; beg for an increase in understanding; watch without letting your spirit flag. Speak to each [of your people] singly in imitation of God's way. Bear the infirmities of all, like a master athlete. The greater the toil, the greater the reward.[12]

Chula Vista Resort
Wisconsin Dells, Wisconsin
October 17, 1995

35

MOTHER OF IMMIGRANTS, PRAY FOR...US
Memorial of St. Frances Xavier Cabrini

- Wisdom 1:1–7
- Luke 17:1–6

A woman, an Italian woman, an immigrant woman—what possible connection can Frances Xavier Cabrini have with the justice of which Wisdom speaks, the justice you and I are committed to preach? Let's talk about (1) Mother Cabrini, (2) biblical justice, (3) you and me.[1]

I

First, Mother Cabrini.[2] Picture a young woman of mid–19th-century Lombardy. Frail of health early and always, young Maria Francesca still directs an orphanage for girls despite harassment and slander, calumny and threats. A religious congregation, the Daughters of the Sacred Heart, refuses to admit her. Not so much for her health; its superior general suggests she might be called to establish her own community to honor the Sacred Heart. She does: She founds a papal institute, Missionary Sisters of the Sacred Heart, writes its rules and constitutions. What are they about? Founding foundling homes, hospitals, and schools, visiting the housebound, the hospitalized, and the imprisoned. Not satisfied with local enterprises, she applies to the Holy See to begin missions in China. But Leo XIII has other plans for her. He is troubled by the poverty, material and spiritual, of large numbers of Italian immigrants in the United States. He asks her to go "not to the East but to the West." In 1889, age 38, she crosses the Atlantic. Her destination: Manhattan.

In New York Mother Cabrini and her sisters upgrade the life of Italian immigrants (there are over 100,000 of them): An orphanage arises, a school, even a hospital. For almost three decades this sickly little woman crisscrosses the country to assess the needs of Italian immigrants—in hospitals and prisons, in mines and plantations. Her foundations follow the streams of immigration: New York, New Jersey, Pennsylvania, Louisiana, Mississippi, Illinois, Colorado, Washington State, California. Naturalized in 1909, she multiplies missions in England, in France, Italy, and Spain, in Argentina and Nicaragua, in Panama and Brazil. This frail woman crosses the sea 23 times; in 35 years she establishes 67 houses. Though dubbed "Saint of the Immigrants," she is hardly a woman of tunnel vision; she finds time to found upper-class schools and institutions of higher learning that parallel her works for the poor. Her philosophy of education is a pedagogy of love, educating not only the mind but the heart—a synthesis of culture, faith, and life.

Not surprisingly, when Frances Xavier Cabrini dies in Chicago at 67, this "mother of immigrants" dies of malaria.

II

Second, what connection can Mother Cabrini have with the justice of which Wisdom 1 speaks, with biblical justice on the whole? As you have discovered,[3] the justice of which Scripture speaks is a complex reality. Still, we can say biblical justice rises above ethical and legal justice, is more than giving to others what they deserve. Biblical justice has for its focus fidelity. Fidelity to what? To relationships, responsibilities, that stem from a covenant. Relationships to God, to people, to the earth. Love God above all else; love the people of God, every human image of God, like another self; touch the things of God, God's earth, with reverence.

As far as God's human images are concerned, biblical justice demands a special concern for the poor. And the poor of Scripture are not simply the poverty-stricken, those without money enough to lead a decent human existence. Poor was the leper, ostracized from society. Poor was the widow, at the mercy of dishonest judges. Poor were the orphans with no parents to love them. Poor was the woman caught in the act of adultery.

But, strangely enough to our ears, the word "poor" did not apply to resident aliens, non-Israelites living in Israelite territory. Here the Lord's command was crystal-clear: "You shall not oppress a resident alien; you know the heart of an alien [you know how an alien feels], for you were aliens in the land of Egypt" (Exod 23:9; see

22:21). More than not oppressing, "You shall also love the stranger, for you were strangers in the land of Egypt" (Deut 10:19; see 24:17). What lay behind such ordinances? The land actually is God's; all humans, even Israelites, are aliens. "The land is mine; with me you are but aliens and tenants" (Deut 25:23).

Mother Cabrini's life was largely given to aliens, to immigrants, beginning with Italians. It was not primarily a natural reaction, the compassion of a tender heart that knew from experience what it meant to suffer. Hers was a *faith* that did justice. She lived what the First Letter of John expressed so powerfully: "If anyone has the world's goods and sees his brother [or sister] in need, yet closes his heart against him [or her], how does God's love abide in him?" (1 Jn 3:17). Again, "If you do not love your brother [or sister] whom you have seen, you cannot love God whom you have not seen. This commandment we have from [God], that he who loves God should love his brother [and sister] also" (4:20–21).

For 20 years, from 1889 to 1909, Mother Cabrini was an alien serving aliens; for eight more years, the American citizen still lavished her love on her struggling immigrants. I don't believe she ever discovered the meaning of biblical justice, rarely if ever did she preach justice; she simply lived it. She made it possible for untold thousands to live decently, to work honorably, to die in the peace of Christ.

III

And what of you and me? We are living at a moment in American history when immigrants, especially undocumented aliens, are at risk. Gone is our treasured memory of the words inscribed in 1903 on the Statue of Liberty in tribute to the "world-wide welcome" that "glows from [the] beacon-hand" of the "Mother of Exiles":

> ...Give me your tired, your poor,
> Your huddled masses yearning to breathe free,
> The wretched refuse of your teeming shore.
> Send these, the homeless, tempest-tossed to me,
> I lift my lamp beside the golden door![4]

I am not advocating an utterly unrestricted welcome to immigrants. I am agonizing over a whole new way of thinking, where the very word "immigrant" raises hackles on the American neck. Add now to the biblical poor the immigrant, the alien, the stranger.

A recent case in point is California's Proposition 187. The Proposition denies to any person suspected of being undocumented all but emergency health services; denies all public social services, including school breakfast and lunch programs for hungry children; denies all access to education from grades K to 12, through the California State University, University of California, and California Community College systems. Proposition 187 was blasted by California's bishops,[5] assailed in hundreds of Catholic pulpits. It threatens to put 300,000 to 400,000 children out of school; it imperils human rights, provides no long-term cure, fails to address root causes of the problem. And still Proposition 187 was approved by 59 percent of the voters. Of course the "common good demands an intelligent, humane, and just regulation of immigration," demands "control over illegal immigration."[6] But not this premature, panicky, pitiless reaction that stigmatizes all immigrants, is particularly punitive toward women and children. This from the children and grandchildren of immigrants. If possible above, Cabrini must be awash in tears.

The future of Proposition 187 lies largely in the hands of Californians—importantly, you and your people. But there is a related *national* issue that cries for Cabrinis across our country. In a November 3 open letter to President Clinton on the Op-Ed page of the *Washington Post*, Marian Wright Edelman, president of the Children's Defense Fund, begged him to "Say No to This Welfare 'Reform.'"[7] From extensive experience Ms. Edelman charges that both the Senate and House welfare bills are "morally and practically indefensible." Why? Because they will push millions of poor children and families deeper into poverty; will destroy the 60-year-old guaranteed safety net for children, women, and poor families; will leave millions of voteless, voiceless children to the vagaries of 50 state bureaucracies and politics; will end or weaken current ensured help for children day to day and during economic recessions and natural disasters; will exacerbate the current shameful and epidemic child poverty that no decent, rich nation should tolerate for even one child.

> It is moral hypocrisy for our nation to slash income, health and nutrition assistance for poor children while leaving untouched hundreds of billions in corporate welfare, giving new tax breaks of over $200 billion for non-needy citizens, and giving the Pentagon almost $7 billion it did not request.[8]

If we repeat this protest, are we priests entering politics? Indeed. Are we risking our own church's tax breaks? Possibly. Should we therefore shut up—grin and bear it? Absolutely not. Mother Cabrini would be marching up the Capitol steps, buttonholing our representatives, pleading like a Hebrew prophet for today's widow and orphan, the single mother and the fatherless child. Can we do less from the pulpit? Not solve complex issues; at least raise the issues, persuade our people to pray over them, to ponder them, to talk about them in small groups and large, to storm Washington with e-mail and telegram, with phone and fax.

I am told there are thousands of paid lobbyists in Washington. And still our children have no lobby. They have only the Cabrinis and the Dorothy Days, the Jack Egans and the Marian Wright Edelmans. And they can have us—and through us millions of layfolk who are fed with the body and blood of Christ, invigorated with the dynamism of the Holy Spirit, potentially with fire in the belly. That fire is ours to give, to share—but only if we are aflame ourselves.

So then, dear St. Frances Xavier Cabrini, "mother of immigrants," pray to the immigrant Christ for today's immigrants, especially the undocumented. But pray also for us. Pray that your likeness, enshrined in the immigration museum at the base of the Statue of Liberty, may be enshrined in the hearts of all Christians, in the hearts of all Californians, in my own heart.

Mater Dolorosa Retreat Center
Sierra Madre, California
November 13, 1995

WEDDING
HOMILIES

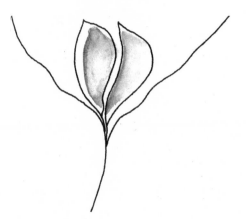

36
I CALL YOU MY FRIENDS
Wedding Homily 1

- Genesis 2:18–24
- Colossians 3:12–17
- Matthew 7:21, 24–29

Five years ago I received an unusual wedding invitation. The bride-
and groom-to-be, Georgetown graduates both, began the printed invitation with these words: "This day I will marry my best friend, the one
I laugh with, live for, love."[1] That sentence came vividly to mind when
MaryQ wrote me last month to declare, "The most important aspect
of our relationship is that Rogan and I are best friends." That being so,
I had best muse with you over friendship—a love that theologians insist
is the highest kind of love.[2] Not in abstraction, on Cloud Nine; rather,
the unique friendship that wedded love was divinely intended to be.
Usually I announce my three points in advance. This time I prefer to
keep you in suspense, save to promise that the three points embrace
three unforgettable facets of friendship.

I

First, there is a friendship of two, the friendship that Rogan
and MaryQ treasure between themselves alone, a facet of friendship
almost too intimate for even a Jesuit to intrude on. It shows in their
laughter, the humor which English novelist Thackeray described as
"a mixture of love and wit." They can laugh at themselves, because
they take themselves seriously but never too seriously. Each can look
in the mirror and smile; for each, like most of us, is a delightful bun-
dle of contradictions. I recall reminding Georgetown students:
"Aristotle said you are a rational animal; I say you are an angel with
an incredible capacity for beer." And each can often laugh at the

175

other, not in bitterness but the laughter than ends an argument, the laughter that spells sheer delight in the other.

I like the pride Rogan takes in MaryQ's gifts, she in his; how gentle they are with each other; the happiness each loves to see in blue eyes or green; their ceaseless effort to keep alive within them the child that often disappears as we grow more sophisticated, more skeptical, as childlike wonder gives way to adult boredom, as lovers cease to look with awe at the miracles that surround them, at the miracle that is the other, the beloved. At the same time, I like the ways in which they live out Kahlil Gibran's wise counsel, "let there be spaces in your togetherness."[3]

> Sing and dance together and be joyous, but let each of
> you be alone,
> Even as the strings of a lute are alone though they
> quiver with the same music.[4]

All of this is so important in our time, when violence owns our streets, when a chorus of hate floods hundreds of talk shows, when disagreement ends rarely in love, often in death. Friends like Rogan and MaryQ give reason to hope that a gentler age may lie ahead.

II

A second facet of friendship? I take you back to the Last Supper, the final discourse of Jesus the evening before he was pinned to a cross for love of us. What Jesus told his disciples then, he tells MaryQ and Rogan now: "I no longer call you servants [or: slaves], for the servant does not know what his master is about; but I have called you [my] friends" (Jn 15:15).

My point is this: Your friendship, Rogan and MaryQ, is not simply a *pas de deux*, a dance for two. A third person, a unique person, a wondrous wedding of divine and human, is part of your dance. You may call it coincidence, but how Kent and Philadelphia ever came together baffles human logic. I believe an imaginative Jesus was there almost five years ago, when MaryQ was compelled to watch Rogan's cricket match at Merion when she would rather have cheered the Eagles on. I believe the Jesus who was accused of eating and drinking with sinners joined your unexpected twosome at a bar named Marbles in Bryn Mawr. I believe the same Jesus has flown the Atlantic with you more than once to perfect your dance.

In a word, the friendship that links you two in lasting love is now deepened and heightened because it is gathered into the friendship of God's only Son. Never forget those six remarkable monosyllables, "I have called you [my] friends." Can you doubt that? When God's own Son took your flesh, was born as you were born, worked and wearied, sweated and slept as you do, was thought mad by his relatives and betrayed by one of his own, was lashed with whips and crowned with thorns, nailed to twin beams of bloody wood till he perished in agony? Why? Because he loved you two as if you were the only two humans in the world.

That friendship is thrillingly re-enacted here, now, during this sacred hour. For in a special way a friend is someone whose table you share, with whom you break bread and sip Chablis. And precisely this is what your Eucharist is all about—the words of Jesus that shortly will seal your friendship: "Take and eat; this is my body given for you. Take and drink; this is my blood of the new covenant. Do this in memory of me." For the first time as husband and wife, you will share together in the Supper of which Jesus promised, "I myself am the living bread that came down from heaven. Whoever eats of this bread will live for ever. And the bread that I shall give is my own flesh for the life of the world" (Jn 6:51). Was there ever such a supper, ever such a friend?

As if that were not enough, hear this! The same friend, the risen Jesus, has taken the simple, loving yes of two Christians and raised it to the dignity of a sacrament—like the Eucharist itself. What does this mean? It is not only you who promise to be true to each other, utterly faithful, in good times and bad, in sickness and in health, in poverty and wealth. The moment your vows express your total gift of self to each other, Jesus himself promises to be true to you, unfailingly faithful. Never forget what St. Paul wrote to his beloved Timothy: "If we are faithless, [Christ Jesus] remains faithful; for he cannot deny himself" (2 Tim 2:13). Wherever you are, you will never escape him. Wherever you are, there he will be. Unseen guest? No. Better still, faithful friend.

III

Friends with each other, friends with Jesus. Remarkable, but your wedded friendship is not yet complete. For the recessional that closes this Eucharist, your joyous jaunt down the aisle to the music of Mendelssohn's *Wedding March,* is not primarily a swift path to the

Merion Golf Club before we selfish folk reach the bar. The recessional is strikingly symbolic. It is a movement from church to world, from altar to people, from Christ under the appearance of bread and wine to Christ hidden in the men and women you will touch each day. A movement to...friends.

Many who are already your friends you will wave at on your way out, hug at the reception, greet over a delectable dinner. These are not here as spectators, privileged ticket holders at a spectacle. They are here because each has played a part, feature or supporting, in the love, the friendship, that reaches a significant high point today. They are here because each presence is a precious promise that, whatever the future holds, their friendship is unbreakable, even an Atlantic shall never sever them from you.

But I make bold to suggest that an unpredictable number of men, women, and children out there are friends-in-the-making, still await your friendship, may even need it to live a human existence. I mean especially those less fortunate than you. I mean those of whom your special friend Jesus was speaking when he promised to say to you at the Last Judgment:

> Come, you that are blessed by my Father, inherit the kingdom prepared for you from the foundation of the world. For I was hungry and you gave me food, I was thirsty and you gave me something to drink, I was a stranger and you welcomed me, I was naked and you gave me clothing, I was sick and you took care of me, I was in prison and you visited me.

Then you will answer him:

> Lord, when was it that we saw you hungry and gave you food, or thirsty and gave you something to drink? And when was it that we saw you a stranger and welcomed you, or naked and gave you clothing? And when was it that we saw you sick or in prison and visited you?

Then Jesus will answer you:

> Truly I tell you, just as you did it to one of the least of these who are my brothers and sisters, you did it to me.
>
> (Mt 25:34–40)

Jesus' brothers and sisters; our sisters and brothers. I mention this crucial Christian text because your recessional will be a burden and a privilege. Blessed by God, you go forth together to a paradoxical world where God's good earth is rich in promise and a billion humans fall asleep hungry; where men of the same race and blood love one another and kill one another. You go forth hand in hand to the two countries you cherish most, an America and an England where children are an endangered species, the only two industrialized countries where in the past 20 years the lot of children worsened.[5] You go forth as one to cities captive to coke and crack, where minorities are still second-class citizens, where black and white live a tenuous truce.

I mention this not to cast a pall over your joy. Quite the contrary. Here is the broader arena of your love, where your friendship with each other in Christ confronts the most arduous of Christianity's challenges, the new commandment Jesus stressed the night before he died for us: "Love one another as I have loved you" (Jn 15:12). The kind of love Christ Jesus lived for you and me from Bethlehem to Calvary, the kind of love St. Paul summarized when he said, "The Son of God loved me and gave himself for me" (Gal 2:20), such is the love Christ demands of you. Not an invitation; a command.

Indeed a difficult kind of friendship: the gift of yourself to the less fortunate, the marginalized: the child abandoned and the elderly left alone, the wife abused and the teenage mother unwed, the AIDS-infected and the drug-addicted, the immigrant newly despised and the convict on death row, the homeless and the helpless, the unnumbered thousands who hunger for food or affection, for a warm smile or a kind word.

No homilist can tell you precisely where to lavish your love, just where to unfurl your friendship. I simply submit that your love for each other and for your friend Jesus is deep enough, rich enough, to embrace always some stranger who experiences more of Jesus' crucifixion than of his resurrection. And I can promise you this: Rarely will you experience such joy as when together you bring hope to the eyes of the hopeless, a smile to the lips of the tear-worn, love to the life of the loveless. Rarely will your own friendship be so enriched as the day you can murmur to a troubled stranger, "I no longer call you a stranger; I call you my friend."

Here, Rogan and MaryQ, here is Christian marriage at a new high: when together you love a sister or brother like another self, another I. Another Jesus. Another...friend.

St. Matthias Church
Bala Cynwyd, Pa.
May 19, 1995

37

IN GOD'S IMAGE, AFTER GOD'S LIKENESS
Wedding Homily 2

- Genesis 1:26–28, 31
- Colossians 3:12–17
- John 15:9–17

Good friends all: Three profound passages have just been proclaimed to you: from the Hebrew Testament, from a letter of St. Paul, from the Gospel of John. Here a danger lurks. You can listen patiently, even piously, to such readings. After all, isn't this a religious ceremony? In such a setting, isn't it appropriate to read from Scripture, from God's own Book? A "nice" touch before the exchange of vows, somewhat like the Star-Spangled Banner before an Orioles baseball game. But thank God we are finally coming to "where the action is at."

I'm afraid not. You see, these passages were selected not by me but by Dan and Kathleen—carefully chosen from a host of possibilities—1805 pages in my Bible. Together Kathleen and Dan chose these texts for one overpowering reason: because these three passages, passages inspired by God, express for these two precious people three relationships, three sets of responsibilities, that sum up their wedded oneness. What relationships, what responsibilities? To God, to each other, to the world around them. Let me spell these out, hoping I can be faithful not only to the Word of God but also to the expectations of Kathleen and Dan.

I

First, the Genesis story: how Hebrew wisdom expressed our relationship to God. "God said, 'Let us make humankind in our

180

image, after our likeness.... So God created humankind in [God's] image...; male and female [God] created them" (Gen 1:26-27).

Have you ever heard anything so amazing, so difficult to believe, so preposterous at first hearing? Each human being born into this world is...like...God. Here is our basic dignity, each one of us. Male or female, rich or poor, healthy or encephalitic, black or white, red or brown or yellow—each of us comes forth from a mother a mirror of God, an image of divinity. What does it mean? Concretely, how do we mirror, reflect, resemble God? Genesis itself does not tell us, does not reveal its secret.[1] And so, for 2500 years Scripture scholars, talented theologians, all manner of mystics have spilled oceans of ink struggling to plumb this mystery.

From all these efforts I suggest simply one. It goes back to the New Testament, to the First Letter of John—John's three monosyllables that seek to express the mystery that is God: "God is love" (1 Jn 4:8). Not "God loves"; "God *is* love." And so, when our imaginative God decided to shape images of God, what kind of creature came forth? Someone with an incredible quality: the capacity to love, to give of myself to another, to live for another, even to die for another.

More imaginatively still, out of God's dream for us came not just one human image: "Male and female God created them" (Gen 1:27). Two images of God, similar indeed, but not the same. And so, after several million years of living and loving, after unnumbered unrecorded ancestors and events, two images of God called Kathleen and Daniel have come together to continue God's dream for our human story. Very much like the billions who have preceded them; unlike because each is unique, unrepeatable, one only Dan and one only Kathleen. Each an image of God, each gifted to love, but each mirroring God, expressing love, in a distinctive way—Dan his way, Kathleen her way. Neither of them reshaping the other into his or her image; each helping to fashion the other more fully into God's image. Dan his own person, Kathleen her own; but paradoxically, each needing the other for a still richer sharing in the inexhaustible Beauty that is God. Not slavish dependence, only total sharing.

Your first love, Kathleen and Dan? The God who was the first to love you; the God who, before time began, shaped you from love, for love; the God who from eternity held both of you passionately in the palm of God's hand; the God who at this moment lives not in outer space but deep within you; the God who, if only you want it, will ceaselessly reshape your wondrously human love into an image of love divine. Please God, with each passing day you will love more and more as God loves.

II

Second, the passage from Paul: how Dan and Kathleen are to mirror God's love in their love for each other.[2] Paul is ever so blunt. Three remarkable expressions: Be forgiving, be compassionate, be thankful.

Forgive. Why such stress on forgiving? Because to forgive is terribly difficult, and to forgive is wondrously divine. Difficult because I hurt, because at times my heart has been broken, because it is impossible to forget. How does the husband of Susan Smith forgive his wife when she has drowned their two children in a locked car? How do Bosnians forgive Serbs who murder their children, rape their women? How does Coretta King forgive her husband's assassin? How can Jews forgive Nazis for six million executions? How does Randy Weaver forgive the federal agent who shot his wife as she held their baby in her arms? How does a wife or husband forgive betrayal, infidelity, "I will love and honor you the rest of my life"? More to the daily marital grind, how do you forgive the "little" things—the curt word, the silent stare, the loveless kiss? How do you forgive being taken for granted, like a picture on the wall? How do you forgive playing second fiddle to the idiot box?

Not because you are remarkably human; usually because you are wondrously divine. Because by grace, by God's gracious giving, you are images of the Jesus who pleaded for his executioners from a bloodstained cross, "Father, forgive them, for they do not know what they are doing" (Lk 23:34). Oh I know, there are situations where a heart is too bitter to forgive, where forgiveness still calls for punishment. All too often there is no easy solution, where distance is demanded, where separation or divorce is inevitable. But before our eyes there must always be the ideal Paul sets before us: "Just as the Lord has forgiven you, so you also must forgive" (Col 3:13).

Be compassionate. Literally, to be compassionate means I feel what another is feeling, I even suffer when the other is suffering. It's a profound facet of genuine love. We sense it in a mother living her infant's multiple sclerosis, in Martin Luther King sharing unto blood the frustrations of black sisters and brothers, in Mary of Nazareth beneath the cross of her Son. And yes, compassion is what basically binds two lovers together in marriage. Not pity; that's looking at the other from above. No, Kathleen hurting when Dan hurts, Dan reacting to the pain in Kathleen's eyes. It shows in a look that needs no words, in a touch that brushes a tear away, in a kiss that heals.

Be thankful. Each day, clouds or blue sky, thank God for the gift of the other. Thank God for the miracle of your meeting, that first conjunction of hazel eyes and light green. Thank God for the chemistry that drew you together. Thank God you enjoy so much in common, can disagree without civil war. Thank God you use words to explain rather than excoriate, to heal rather than flay. Thank God you are surrounded with love, from parents who have lived for you, from siblings who for some reason think you're cute, from friends who crowd this house of God to show their affection, their respect. Thank God you enjoy the good things of this earth, and yet you esteem being over having, sharing over clutching. Thank God you worship the same God each in your own way, and still together. Thank God you can share the same Eucharist, receive on your palms and in your inmost flesh the same Christ who died for you, the Christ who presides over this liturgy, presides over your vows, presides over your life.

III

Third, the command of Jesus in John's Gospel, "Love one another as I have loved you" (Jn 15:12). Not an invitation; a command. A frightening command. For it turns Dan and Kathleen together to a whole little world where love is tangled with hate, hope with fear, compassion with competition; where the race (sociologists claim) is often to the swift, the strong, the savage; where human persons, images of God, die for one another and kill one another. And Jesus commands, "Love each one of these bewildering creatures as I have loved you." As Jesus has loved us. And how did he love us? Why, God's only Son was born as we are born, grew up as we grow, hungered as we hunger, died as we die—only more cruelly than most. Why? Paul tells it in accents of wonder: "He loved me and gave himself for me" (Gal 2:20). He lived and died for every human from the first Adam to the last Antichrist. Not only for the "nice" people, the people who loved him, his disciples, his mother, but for the Judas who betrayed him for silver and the Pilate who washed his hands of him, for the soldiers who flogged him and the soldier who pierced his side with a spear.

There is a sobering vocation here, where Kathleen and Dan are called to carry their love for God and for each other beyond Lake Forest Drive, to help transform the earth on which they dance so lightly into God's own acre of peace and love. For, as I insist at every wedding, the recessional is not a rapid run to the reception, a shrewd move to the Meridian bar before the selfish get there. The recessional is a movement, Dan's and Kathleen's, from church to world, from altar to people, from Christ crucified on Calvary to Christ crucified on the highways and byways of our world. And none of us need fly to Bosnia. The crucified surround us, invade our turf.

One crucified class pleads especially to the married: our children. Every day in America 3 children die from child abuse, 15 from guns, 37 from poverty, 95 before their first birthday. Every day in America 1340 teenagers give birth, 2217 drop out of school. Every day in America 8189 children are reported abused or neglected, 2350 are in adult jails, 100,000 are homeless, 135,000 bring guns to school, 1,200,000 latchkey children come home to a house where there is a gun.[3] If Kathleen and Dan, if each married couple, can look into the eyes of a single one of these children, change those eyes from dullness to hope, your own love will glow anew.

Dan and Kathleen, two months ago, Val Kilmer, the star of *Batman Forever,* reported his own experience of marriage:

> The reality of love is that it's hard to do. It's a darn shame that as a species we've convinced ourselves love should be fun, that it's got some kind of pastel color to it, that it tastes good and should make our lives easier. Love is hard!
>
> But I believe that the more we love, the more alive we are. And, other than your relationship to God, who your partner is in life is the most important thing.... Each experience we have is an opportunity to express the truth of our life, an opportunity to confront our fears, to take a chance with love and go out and live! I think that notion is what life's about...[4]

Good friends all: No one of you is simply a spectator here. You are here because each of you has played a role, feature or supporting, in the love that reaches new heights today. But the good news: Your role is not over. If Kathleen and Dan are to live as images of God, live for each other, live for the world around them, they will need your ceaseless support: your hands and your heart, an awareness of your love and a sense of your presence whatever the distance in miles. In a special way, let me suggest to the married among you that, when Dan and Kathleen vow themselves to each other, you join your own hands and murmur in your hearts, with fresh conviction, the promise that thrilled you a year ago or 50: "I take you to have and to hold, for better for worse, for richer for poorer, in sickness and in health, till death do us part. I will love you and honor you all the days of my life."

No wedding gift could make Kathleen and Dan happier; for you are linking to them your own wedded love. You are promising them...yourselves.

St. Aloysius Church
Washington, D.C.
September 2, 1995

38

LOVE FROM ABOVE, LOVE LIVED BELOW, LOVE SHARED
Wedding Homily 3

- Tobit 8:5–7
- Colossians 3:12–17
- Matthew 22:35–40

You have just listened to three passages from God's own Book. Not chosen at random, not just there by chance. From roughly 1800 Bible pages, Beth and Carlos have opted for these passages. Why? Because they sense a special message for themselves, because each passage says something significant to this man and this woman promising love until death. Since today's intense joy and the swift passage of those texts from tongue to ear may have lessened their impact on you, let me try to recapture their significance. Three texts, three insights: (1) Love is from above. (2) This love from above has to be lived here below. (3) This love has to be shared.

I

First, an age-old Hebrew insight: Love is from above. The text of Tobit was fashioned probably two centuries before Christ. It has been called "A fascinating amalgam of *Arabian Nights* romance, kindly Jewish piety, and sound moral teaching."[1] And still the Catholic Church regards it as inspired, part of Scripture. Much of the story centers on Tobit's son, Tobias. Tobias goes off to a distant land and, on the advice of an angel, marries a Jewish woman named Sarah. It is Tobias' prayer on their wedding night that Carlos and Beth have plucked for their life and our meditation:

> "Blessed are you, O God of our fathers....
> You made Adam and gave him Eve his wife
> as a helper and support.

From them the race of humankind has sprung.
You said, 'It is not good that the man should be alone;
    let us make a helper for him like himself.'
...Grant that [we] may grow old together."
And [Sarah] said with him, "Amen [So be it]."

(Tobit 8:5–8)

Tobias' prayer takes us back to Genesis, to the beginning of creation. And Genesis tells us that love did not come about because in prehistoric times two evolving apes were chemically attracted to each other. Love, lifelong love, was born because a loving God, in an imaginative outburst of self-giving, shaped not one type of human but two. Two who would be similar but never the same. Two who in their love would be like the God of love, he in his unique way, she in hers. Two humans whose love would bear fruit in a third person—whose love would be the source of human society, the expression on earth of the love in heaven that is the secret life of God.

Yes, Beth and Carlos, before you were born your love was crafted in heaven. Your love was born in the loving mind of God. A mind-boggling fact: Before anything but God existed, God knew you—knew you in your separate reality, knew you in the loving oneness you share today. And when God made you, God loved you. Could not fail to love you, for what God had shaped was a man and a woman in God's own image. Uncommonly like God this very day, for today, in your total gift of self each to the other, you image God's own love: the love of Father, Son, and Holy Spirit, the love that is perfect because there is indeed "I and thou," distinct persons, but never "mine and thine," what St. Augustine called "those ice-cold words."

Indeed, Carlos and Beth, indeed love is from above. Your love. Your love for each other. From the God of love.

II

Second, this love from above has to be lived here below. Here St. Paul enters in. So much that he says is inspiring, uplifting. Put on love, because love ties everything together. Let Christ's peace rule in your hearts. Teach one another. Even sing together! But two commands are particularly pertinent.

First, forgive each other. Not an easy command, if only because it collides with a contemporary conviction coined by Hollywood: "Love means never having to say you're sorry." Nonsense! Hogwash! Ever since the first man bit into forbidden fruit, "I'm sorry" has to fall as frequently from our lips as "I've sinned." Within the human story, "I'm sorry" sums up a sad litany of sins against God and against the human images of God. But the saving centerpiece is the prayer from the parched lips of the crucified Christ, his prayer for those who had crucified him: "Father, forgive them; for they do not [really] know what they are doing" (Lk 23:34).

Is there an unforgivable sin within marriage—a sin a spouse might not forgive even if God does? A homily is not the place to argue that agonizing question. I do say that marriage is a bond, a covenant, a pact, not between a god and a goddess, but between a man and a woman, between two imperfect images of God, frail and forgetful for all their good will, self-willed for all their self-giving, amazingly unleashing their frustrations on those they love. Little wonder St. Paul counsels you, "Put on, as God's chosen ones, compassion, kindness, patience, putting up with one another." And then that compelling comparison, "As the Lord has forgiven you, so you also must forgive" (Col 3:12–13). A glorious Greek word that implies a free and gracious giving. In a Christian context, forgiveness is not a weakness; it is a sharing in Christ's own reason for borrowing our flesh, his own reason for Bethlehem and Calvary.

Second, that pithy precept of Paul, "Be thankful" (v. 15). It says so much. The word has a rich history—found frequently on ancient inscriptions where cities and their people etch "thank you" to their benefactors. It is the Christian word for Eucharist, our supreme act of thanksgiving to God.

So too, Beth and Carlos, for you: Be thankful. You would not stand here in love, were it not for others. I mean especially those who bore you and fed you, changed your diapers and endured your adolescence, gave of their substance for your education and set you free to live and to love. I mean all those who surround you this day, invited by you to celebrate your love because in varied ways unknown to me but vivid to you they have helped to shape you, in large measure or small have brought this day to dawn. I mean so many, bound to you by blood or otherwise linked to you in love, who share this day in a singular way because they share what we call "the communion of saints," the faithful men and women who have died but are alive as they have never lived before, and in the Lord's presence are holding heavenly gossip, insatiably curious about whom each of you is marrying. Never cease to be thankful, for experience has already taught you that your acre of God's earth will never cease to be crowded with women and men without whom your life together would be less human, less Godlike.

III

Move now to a final point: This love of yours must be shared. There are two attractive "heresies" that plague Christianity today. They have to do with the passage Beth and Carlos have selected for their wedding Gospel. It is the striking sentence Jesus has plucked from the Hebrew Testament, from the Book of Leviticus: "You shall love your neighbor as yourself" (Mt 22:39; Lev 19:18). Among all too many Christians, two mighty mistakes.

First mistake: Who is my neighbor? Not simply the lady next door; not only the people I like, who like me. The neighbor, in Jesus' eyes, is every human fashioned in the image of God. The same Jesus who said "Love your neighbor" said "Love your enemies and pray for those who persecute you, so that you may be [children] of your Father who is in heaven" (Mt 5:44-45). It's a tough command; not an invitation, a command. My sister, my brother, is in a special way every man or woman in need—each of God's unfortunates pleading for bread, for justice, for love.

Second mistake: Taking "love your neighbor as yourself" as a psychological balancing act: As much or as little as you love yourself, so much or so little shall you love your neighbor. No. What Jesus commands is that we love every single one of God's human creatures like another self, like another "I," as if we were standing in his or her shoes. It is Jesus' startling precept at the Last Supper, "This is my commandment, that you love one another as I have loved you" (Jn 15:12).

Why is all this so important? Because the recessional, Beth and Carlos waltzing down the aisle together to the strains of Handel's *Water Music,* is not a swift movement to the reception. The recessional is symbolic: It is a movement from church to world, from altar to people, from Christ crucified on Calvary to Christ crucified on the crossroads of our country.

Not to burden you with all the crucified who call for bread or justice or love, I commend to you the children who will intersect your life. I mean children born with AIDS; children with one parent or none; children with bellies swollen from hunger; children coming to school with deadly weapons; children giving birth to children; children sleeping on our streets; children maiming their minds and debasing their bodies with crack and coke. I commend to you the children in my Washington back yard, preparing not their futures but their funerals; for with over 200 of their playmates gunned down in D.C. streets they do not expect to grow up. Small wonder that in 1991 the National Commission on Children declared that addressing the needs of America's children is no longer a matter of choice. "It is a national imperative as compelling as an armed attack or a natural disaster."[2] Pope John Paul II put it bluntly: "...in the Christian view, our treatment of children becomes a measure of our fidelity to the Lord himself."[3]

Beth and Carlos, I have no wish to restrain your ode to joy. I simply submit that your wedding in Christ lays a burden on you that is also a privilege. For if the land we love is to survive as a "land of the free," if the children who are our future are to grow up human, it is in large measure couples such as you that can effect it. You are young and still restless; you are highly intelligent and impressively vigorous; you are gifted with imagination and compassion; you are committed to sharing what you have and who you are; you have God's grace coursing through you like another blood stream. One day, God willing, you will be blessed with children of your own. I know no better preparation for the fruitful days ahead than your care for those crucified images of the Christ Child who seem to be "children of a lesser god."

A final suggestion. In an adventure as demanding as marriage, Carlos and Beth dare not go it alone. God's support they will surely have; what they need as well is your own. I mean in particular the example of husbands and wives who for one year or 50 (1) have recognized that their love comes from above, from the God of love; (2) have forgiven what they cannot forget and been ever thankful for the love that surrounds them; (3) have shared their love not only with those who can return it, but also with the most vulnerable and helpless of their sisters and brothers, today's Christ child with "no room in the [world's] inn" (Lk 2:7). And so, when Beth and Carlos join their hands once for all, I ask the wedded among you to link your own hands and murmur again the promise that thrilled you a year ago or 50, "I take you to have and to hold, for better or worse, for richer or poorer, in sickness and in health, as long as we both shall live."

No more precious wedding gift can you give to Carlos and Beth; for in this gift you are giving them...yourselves.

Mount St. Mary Chapel
Newburgh, N.Y.
October 21, 1995

39
LOVE IS FROM GOD
Wedding Homily 4

- Genesis 2:18–23
- 1 John 4:7–13
- Mark 10:2–9

Good friends: Over a half century of weddings, I am still struck, daily delighted, by the passages brides and grooms pluck from Scripture. Today my delight stems from the First Letter of John, four momentous monosyllables. They were indeed read to you. But those short syllables sped so swiftly from our reader's lips that we risked missing their meaning. Especially when our minds and hearts were fixed not on four lifeless syllables but on two living persons we love. And yet, those four words are for ever part of these two persons. The four monosyllables? "Love is from God" (1 Jn 4:7). Let me probe those four words in three stages. First, why does Scripture say "Love is from God"? Second, what demands do those four words lay on Debbie and Mark? Third, what might they suggest for you who have gathered here out of love?

I

First, why does Scripture say "Love is from God"? Before all else because, as John says a bit later, "God is love." Not simply "God loves" but "God *is* love." Love tells us not only what God does but what God is. And it is precisely because God is love that God has wrought such wondrous works of love from the Garden of Eden down to our own day. Out of love, God shaped humankind in God's own image, shaped each man and woman in the likeness of God, in the likeness of God's own love. Out of love, God fashioned a small nomad tribe into God's own people, graced them with the capacity

191

to love: to love God, to love people, to love the earth that nourished them. Out of love, God blessed the Hebrew people with their own land, their own kings, their own priests and prophets. When the people complained, "The Lord has forsaken me, my Lord has forgotten me," God responded:

> Can a woman forget her nursing child,
> 　　or show no compassion for the child of her womb?
> Even these may forget,
> 　　yet I will not forget you.
> See, I have inscribed you on the palms of my hands.
> 　　　　　　　　　　　　　　　　　(Isa 49:14–16a)

From this Hebrew people, out of love, God's only Son took our flesh. Out of love, Jesus Christ was born as we are born, grew as we grow, lived as we live, died as we die. Why? The Letter of John answers with two thrilling sentences: "God's love was revealed among us in this way: God sent His only Son into the world so that we might live through him. In this is love, not that we loved God but that [God] loved us and sent His Son to be the atoning sacrifice for our sins" (1 Jn 4:9–10). From Christ's crucified love our own love stems.

And today, Debbie and Mark, today you enter this house of God because you are wondrously aware that *your* love is from God. Not only the love that graces each of you as an individual; from God is your love for each other. I refuse to believe that this love is mere coincidence, that by sheer chance you shared an ice-cream party during Mark's freshman orientation at Georgetown. Not that God forced love upon you; God never does. Only that behind your love is divine love, a providential care that mysteriously brought you together, allowed blue eyes and brown to meet, rejoiced in the attraction, the recognition, the love that followed, the love that has survived separation and togetherness, the love that has touched Vermont and California, Asia and Africa and Alaska. Divine love that, when you join hands and hearts some moments from now, will make you ministers of a fresh sacrament. For when you say "I take you to have and to hold," each of you will become a channel of God's grace to the other, a guarantee of God's endless love over your life together.

II

Indeed, Mark and Debbie, your love is from God. But the Letter of John does not rest satisfied with "Love is from God." John goes on to say, "Since God loved us so much, we also ought to love one another.... If we love one another, God lives in us, and His love is made perfect in us" (1 Jn 4:11–12).

The point is, the love of man and woman for each other dare not stop there. Some years ago a penetrating woman psychologist put it splendidly:

> A love that is not for more than itself will die—the wisdom of Christian tradition and the best we know from psychology both assure us of this truth. It is often very appropriate at the early stages of a relationship that the energy of romance and infatuation exclude the larger world from our vision. But over the long haul an intimate relationship...which doesn't reach outward will stagnate.[1]

A remarkable facet of the love we celebrate this evening is that "the larger world" is intimate to that love; the love of Debbie and Mark does "reach outward." In a country where the most vulnerable of humans are our little ones, the unborn and the newborn, Debbie not only ushers them lovingly into the world but keeps in loving touch with their parents—an outgrowth of her care for children in small but tight communities of Alaska and Africa. In a land where, sociologists tell us, we are witnessing a resurgence of late-19th-century rugged individualism, where the race is often to the big and powerful, Mark has moved his rich legal talents to the Hill on behalf of small business.

For Mark and Debbie, this is not simply a very human compassion. Their commitment to the "little ones" of their world stems from their realization that there are *two* great commandments of the law and the gospel. It is not enough to love God above all else. A second commandment, Jesus insisted, "is like" the first: "You shall love your neighbor [each human shaped in God's image] as yourself" (Mt 22:37–39). Not a psychological balancing act: As much or as little as I love myself, so much or so little love shall I lavish on my sisters and brothers. No. We are commanded to love each human like another "I," a second self, as if we were standing in his or her shoes. It is simply the strong assertion of Jesus, "This is my commandment, that you love one another as I have loved you" (Jn 15:12).

To love as Jesus loved—such is the love our loving Lord asks of Mark and Debbie; such is the love their lives already promise. I suspect that this love was fostered in their Georgetown years. There, each year, I watched ten-or-so graduates leave for a year with the poor in Nicaragua or Peru. None of them returned to the States the same; all had lived the hurts of the poor, experienced a conversion that changed them to the depths of their being. I remember talking to a Georgetown girl who was spending hours in downtown D.C. with drug addicts, battered women, prostitutes. College life had taken on a different look; even the university Pub looked different—not bad, just a little sad. I remember Georgetown choir members who sang liturgy at the D.C. jail. They touched what it feels like to live without windows, wear the same old jumpsuits, have nothing to do that delights you, languish for months before coming to trial, give birth to your baby behind bars and have the infant torn from you. Words of the Mass that had slipped so facilely from their lips took on meaning: "May the Lord accept this sacrifice at our hands...*for the good of all God's Church.*" All God's people...the prisoners they had come to know.

Such is the love Jesus lived; such is the love Mark and Debbie promise. A special care for the helpless, the powerless, those who seem to be "children of a lesser god."[2]

III

Finally, let me touch "Love is from above" to you who have gathered here with such enthusiasm, such joy. You see, no one of you is simply a spectator at a spectacular, like a Redskins fan at JFK. You are here because each of you has played a role, feature or supporting, in the love that reaches a certain apex today. Put another way, you are here because you love. Because in varied ways, from diaper stage through school days to hospitals and the Hill, your love has touched the two lives that become one this evening.

This love too, your love, is from God. The miracle of that love, your love for Mark and Debbie, is that it dare not end with today's sacred rite. The adventure on which they embark this evening involves a twofold risk: (1) how to keep alive the flame of love for each other in a society increasingly unable to say and live the words "for ever," and (2) how to keep their love reaching outward to the less fortunate of Christ's images in a culture entranced by money, by power, by fame. The day of the Lone Ranger is dead. What Debbie and Mark need is communities of support. Hospital personnel indeed; companions on the Hill of course. But more importantly, a community of love such as surrounds them in this house of God. Let your presence here be a profound promise that in the days and years ahead your hands, your hearts, and your homes will always be open to them.

In a special way Debbie and Mark will need the support of the wedded among you. I mean those who, for one year or 50, have experienced the highs and the lows, the ecstasies and the agonies, the delights and the doldrums of life together. I mean those of you who find your joy in reaching out together to the child abused or the elderly alone, to the cancer-ridden or the AIDS-afflicted, to the countless men, women, and children who hunger for bread or justice or love. And so, when Mark and Debbie turn to each other and declare their total self-giving, I would ask the married among you to join your own hands and murmur once again the words that thrilled you this year or half a century ago: "I take you for better for worse, for richer for poorer, in sickness and in health, in good times and bad, till death do us part. I will love you and honor you all the days of my life."

A superb wedding gift, I assure you. Not as obvious perhaps as Waterford Glass or Limerick Lace, but in a way more profound; for in such renewed self-giving you are promising Debbie and Mark...your deepest selves.

St. Aloysius Gonzaga Church
Washington, D.C.
November 4, 1995

40
JOYFUL, JOYFUL WE ADORE THEE
Wedding Homily 5

- Isaiah 40:28–31
- Colossians 3:12–17
- Matthew 5:13–16

This evening one emotion makes all of us one. I mean...joy. Joy in the joy of a man and a woman inexpressibly precious to us. And yet, this very joy contains a hidden danger. We are so caught up in the joy of the occasion, in our happiness for this dear couple, that we may not have heard what Maureen and Mark are trying to tell us. Tell us how, where, when? Very simply, through the three passages just proclaimed to you. Readings not required by Rome, not wormed in by wily Jesuits. Rather, passages carefully culled by Mark and Maureen from the hundreds of pages in God's own Book. Chosen because these inspired passages summarize three facets of their life together, three aspects of their covenant in Christ that are uncommonly meaningful to them, each an "amazing grace."

Let me try to recapture why this is so. The three names to remember, the three characters who speak, believe it or not, are not Michael Jordan, Cal Ripken, and Shannon Miller.[1] The names are...Isaiah, Paul, and Jesus. A word on each.

I

First, Isaiah. This section of Isaiah is called the Book of Consolation. For the Jews, the year 587 B.C. was catastrophic. Jerusalem and its temple had been destroyed by the Babylonians; the important people were deported to Babylon. No city, no temple, no priests, no power. Against all the odds, what Isaiah preached was a message of hope. This is not the end; Jerusalem will rise again, purified—if the people put their faith, their hope, in God.[2] It is in this context that these breathtaking words were proclaimed to Israel in God's name, were heard in recent months by Maureen and Mark, were just now proclaimed to you and me:

> [The Lord] gives power to the faint,
>   and strengthens the powerless.
> Even youths will faint and be weary,
>   and the young will fall exhausted;
> but those who wait for the Lord shall renew their strength.
>   they shall mount up with wings like eagles,
> they shall run and not be weary,
>   they shall walk and not faint.
>
> (Isa 40:29–31)

Maureen and Mark have experienced some of the crucifixions inescapable in human living. Five deaths that scarred Maureen in a single year left their pain on Mark as he tried to share an unfamiliar sorrow. As Maureen says, "we've already been through some of the pain and disillusionment that many couples don't experience until they've been married several years." Knowing each other's wonders and limitations, aware that the future likely holds "some nasty twists and turns," aware that "the blessings sure to be in store for [them] may be mixed with sacrifice and tears," they will still say a faith-filled yes to God and to each other. Their source of courage? The promise of Isaiah: "Those who wait upon the Lord," whose hope rests in the power and compassion of God, "shall run and not be weary, shall walk and not faint." For to "wait upon the Lord" is to be aware of two things: how powerless I am of myself, and how powerful God is to redeem, to save.[3]

It is not a high I.Q. that keeps love alive in marriage, not vibrant personalities, not hazel eyes and green. It is profound trust in a God who shaped man and woman for each other, trust in a God who has a vested interest in each love story, trust in a God who made the love of man and maid a striking symbol, the most powerful reflection of the love that links Christ and the Church that is his body, his bride.

It is not by sheer chance that Maureen and Mark became engaged in a lovely little courtyard behind the Jesuit church on Farm Street in London; not by a toss of the coin that they wed for life in Georgetown's Dahlgren Chapel. Whether in London or D.C., wherever they may be, for them the most important reality is the real presence of the Christ who literally loved them to death, the Lord in whose strength "they shall mount up with wings like eagles, run and not be weary, walk and not faint."

II

Second, St. Paul. Why have Mark and Maureen chosen a section from a letter of the apostle Paul to the Christians of an insignificant town in Asia Minor? Primarily for a single sentence. Listen to Paul: "Bear with one another and, if anyone has a complaint against another, forgive each other; just as the Lord has forgiven you, so you also must forgive" (Col 3:13). Now listen to Maureen and Mark: "We chose Colossians because 'forgive the other' reminds us of the choices we will be asked to make day after day, to love the other when we'd rather scream at the other, to put the other one first when we'd rather put ourselves first."

Forgive. Do you remember a movie called *Love Story?* One swift sentence from the script I have never forgotten: "Love means never having to say you're sorry." Fifty-five years a priest, I have rarely experienced a definition so untrue to genuine love. Love may well have been crafted in heaven, but it has to be lived on earth. It is lived by us humans, terribly frail even with God's grace, at times thoughtless, often insensitive, plagued in our culture by a rugged individualism where the most important letter in the alphabet is I. Even the first paradise, the Garden of Eden, was not safe from it, from blaming the other. Asked by God how he came to eat of fruit forbidden, Adam responds, "*She* did it!" Asked by God what she had done, Eve blames the serpent. It is the human story repeated down the ages.

The solution? "As the Lord has forgiven you, so you also must forgive." Not only in your heart—with your lips as well. Somewhat as the Son of God in our flesh spoke it from bloody lips over those who had nailed him to a cross: "Father, forgive them; for they do not know what they are doing" (Lk 23:34). When the days are darkest, when stubbornness locks the lips of one and hurt dries up the heart of the other, look long at your crucifix, preferably together, then look at each other as you look at each other today, and let love's most difficult words break out: "I'm sorry." "And I—I forgive you."

Is it always possible? Frankly, I don't know. The statistics on sundered marriages are sobering. There are indeed sins that destroy love. There are hurts that wound mortally the strongest of human bonds. If you want to watch them in living color, stare at the early-afternoon "soaps"—TV's daily round of how to hurt the one you love. Count on one hand this exchange: "I'm sorry for what I've said and done; for I love you." "I know, and I forgive you; for I love you." The words don't come easily to "the bold and the beautiful"; this is not the way "the world turns."[4] It suggests graphically that "to forgive is [indeed] divine," that in major marital crises the power to forgive is not of our human making, that a tortured "I'm sorry" and a crucifying "I forgive" are amazing graces, gifts of God to bent knees and fractured hearts.

III

Third, Matthew. "Let your light shine before women and men, so that they may see your good works and give glory to your Father in heaven" (Mt 5:16). There's a "sleeper" here, more than meets the eye.

You see, this liturgy of love will close with a recessional: Maureen and Mark, the wedding party, skipping down the center aisle to the strains of "Joyful, Joyful We Adore Thee." For years I have insisted that the recessional, joyful as it justly is, is not primarily a swift exit to the reception before the congregation gets to the cocktails. The recessional is strikingly symbolic. For it is a movement from church to world, from altar to people, from Christ crucified outside Jerusalem to Christ crucified at the crossroads of every large city, crucified in D.C. and London.

The point of this? Maureen and Mark will not live their wedded love on some fantasy island, in splendid isolation. Perhaps not in the eye of a hurricane, but surely where love and hate intermingle, where men and women die for one another and kill one another, where the haves and the have-nots tell a "tale of two cities," where the younger you are the poorer you are, where all too many experience more of Christ's crucifixion than of his resurrection. Into this context Maureen and Mark can integrate what a woman psychologist has expressed so perceptively:

> A love that is not for more than itself will die—the wisdom of Christian tradition and the best we know from psychology both assure us of this truth. It is often very appropriate at the early stages of a relationship that the energy of romance and infatuation exclude the larger world from our vision. But over the long haul an intimate relationship...which doesn't reach outward will stagnate.[5]

Mark and Maureen: You know far more intimately than I how richly God has blessed you. Mothers and fathers without whose gift of self this day would never have dawned; siblings who in ways delightful and discomforting have challenged you to grow up; happy Hoyas and generally genial Jesuits. With these, gifts of intelligence and love. Gifts given you not to be greedily grasped; gifts given you to give away. To each other indeed, but more lavishly still. Turned so touchingly to God and to each other, you now turn together to a whole little world. You let your good works shine, a light to the world. Not for the world's applause; for the world's salvation: to help make some of God's children more human and more divine. Wherever you travel, there will be crucified images of Christ: a child with Down's syndrome, a runaway kid pimped and angel-dusted, an adolescent drug-addicted, a teenager pregnant and unprepared to parent, a grown man homeless and helpless, an aged lady alone and loveless. So many who are dreadfully weary, often so weary of living that they ask someone to help them die.

This is not to put a damper on your joy. Quite the contrary. The joy you now experience *in and from each other* stems in largest measure from your self-giving, from your gift of self each to the other. That experience should pervade *your total existence.* It is the Christian paradox expressed so pithily in the Prayer of St. Francis of Assisi: "It is in giving that we receive, it is in loving that we are loved." When the love you share with each other broadens out to touch a youngster with MS, when you can hug an infant born HIV-positive, when you carry your warmth to the homeless or the elderly unloved, when you bring hope into the eyes of the hopeless, then the joy that floods your whole being will be the joy Jesus promised "no human being will take from you" (Jn 16:22).

With your gifts of nature and grace, you can transform the turf on which you dance so lightly and many trudge so heavily. The new adverb in your life is "together." Together you can, together you should, together you will make a difference. The way you care, you will light with hope eyes that are dull with despair. A child will chuckle who has forgotten how to laugh. A graying lady will not wonder why it is taking so long to die.

Come now, Maureen and Mark, and let the Christ who once died for you, the Christ who now lives for you, join you together in a oneness unique on earth. Come now and let your lips and your hearts say to each other, to our dear Lord, and to a whole little world the transforming words of the Eucharist, "This is my body, [this is my whole self], and it is given for you" (Lk 22:19).

Dahlgren Chapel
Georgetown University
Washington, D.C.
July 27, 1996

MEDLEY

41

A NEW TIME, A NEW HEART
45th Assembly, Greater Dallas Community of Churches

- Ezekiel 11:17–21
- Ephesians 4:1–7, 11–13
- Luke 22:19

"A new heart for a new time." This rallying cry from your Annual Assembly[1] is not simply a neat phrase stolen in part from the Hebrew prophet Ezekiel. The biblical context is strikingly pertinent. In the year 598 before Christ, a Babylonian army had sacked Jerusalem, had carried off thousands of its leading citizens into exile; 8000 captives, presumably including Ezekiel, were brought to Babylon. Years later political leaders who remained in Jerusalem were claiming that it was the exiles of 598 who were guilty of idolatry and therefore no longer had any claim on the land given by Yahweh to His people. On the contrary, cried Ezekiel, God is with the exiles. In God's good time God will restore them to the land as an obedient and purified people utterly loyal to their God. Those who remained in Jerusalem will be destroyed for their idolatries. The "new heart" is a *single* heart: Israel will become singlehearted in its loyalty to Yahweh, no longer a people with a heart seeking both Yahweh and the idols.[2]

With this biblical context in mind—one true God and many false idols—I suggest two stages for our meditation this evening: first a new time, then a new heart.

I

A new time. Fifty-four years a priest, I come to the eve of Christianity's third millennium torn in spirit. Why? Because the American landscape for our ministry is so diversified, so complex, so contradictory that it defies definition, forbids easy analysis. For our purposes, two sets of realities. One set disturbs me, because it sets up barriers to the gospel, false idols; the other encourages me, because it evidences the powerful presence of the Spirit.

What realities disturb me? I limit myself to five. First, *communication without community.* Increasingly, the world is ours by remote control. Eyes glued to CNN, we cross oceans to grasp with miraculous speed events historic or forgettable: the heart attack of Russia's Yeltsin, the assassination of Israel's Rabin, a rape by American soldiers on Okinawa, 8000 Muslims massacred by Serbs in Bosnia, fluctuation of the yen in Japan, narrow defeat for an independent Quebec, arrest of a government official in Italy for association with the Mafia. Not to forget Internet: person to person, here and everywhere, adult conversation and child pornography, all at the touch of a finger. And against all the odds, community collapses: neighborhoods of barred windows, color lines uncrossed, poor arrayed against rich, teenagers in gangs, coke and crack to escape reality, the elderly left to waste away lonely, a nationwide clamor for capital punishment, liturgies of strangers—the list is all but endless.

Second, *rugged individualism versus the common good.* Not a jeremiad against the type of individual resourcefulness that made America great and enviable. Rather, the late-19th-century rugged individualism sociologist Robert Bellah saw resurgent in our time, where success comes to the swift, the shrewd, and the savage, and the devil take the hindmost; where in the end each of us is alone, responsible to no one save myself. The individualism that gave us the Savings & Loan disaster, the Wall Street scandals. No longer the well-being of the people, the public welfare of the political community. The individualism Bellah saw taking over the followers of Christ, when he told us Catholic theologians that Catholics, proudly describing themselves as the Body of Christ, potentially the counterforce to rugged individualism, are little different from their unbelieving neighbors.

Third, *a culture of consumerism,* of having over being. As Pope John Paul II saw it, this "consists in an *excessive* availability of every kind of material goods for the benefit of certain social groups," and it "makes people slaves of 'possession' and of immediate gratification, with no other horizon than the multiplication or continual replacement of the things already owned with others still better."[3] If a papal encyclical fails to stir you, listen to Lee Atwater, the architect of presidential politics who almost singlehandedly turned the Bush campaign around in '88. Dying of a brain tumor at 40, this gifted man made this poignant confession:

> The '80s were about acquiring—acquiring wealth, power, prestige. I know. I acquired more wealth, power and prestige than most. But you can acquire all you want and still feel empty.... It took a deadly illness to put me eye to eye with that truth, but it is a truth that the country, caught up in its ruthless ambitions and moral decay, can learn on my dime.[4]

Fourth, *parents not parenting.* Statistics I have not; but prolonged experience across the States persuades me that all too many parents, good Christians too, abdicate parentage when their sons and daughters acquire their first adolescent pimples. Give them whatever keeps them from rebelling; be pals rather than parents; let them choose their own schools; don't force your morality on a new age; keep the liquor overflowing at adult parties while denouncing youthful marijuana, coke, and crack. Mull over the latest Gregg Araki film, *The Doom Generation.* "Not every kid may be as mad and morose as Araki's lost boys—sophomores who can't bear to live till junior year. But a lot are...." "And the magic number for everything (the price of a burger meal, the address of a motel, even Amy's cumulative SAT score) is 666, the mark of Satan in Revelation."[5]

Fifth, *neglect of the most vulnerable in our society–our children.* One child in every four is growing up in poverty; all told, nearly 16 million. Not the genteel poverty of Jesus, Mary, and Joseph; our poverty means children with stunted minds and bodies, most without medical care and insurance, children who will rarely really grow up. Each year 1.6 million innocents are forcibly prevented from ever growing up. And so vicious is the violence against the young that in my own back yard, the District of Columbia, children are planning their own funerals: how they want to be dressed, how to look, where to be waked. (My colleague Father Raymond Kemp was asked by a teenager on the Donahue Show if he would officiate at her funeral.) And so little concern for children surges among our lawmakers that the president of the Children's Defense Fund, Marian Wright Edelman, has written an open letter to President Clinton charging that both the Senate and the House welfare bills "are fatally flawed, callous, anti-child assaults. Both bills eviscerate the moral compact between the nation and its children and its poor."[6]

II

What realities encourage me? Again I limit myself to five. First, a growing *hunger among Americans for the spiritual.* Much of the hunger is vague, indeterminate. Hard to judge how deep it is, how superficial. All too often a "search for the sacred" fails to find it, or even to look for it, in our extraordinarily rich Christian traditions; many look to the East, to Buddhism and Islam; some are fed by psychics. These efforts I do not disdain; I simply weep over our own failures to satisfy a basic human hunger that has its roots in the Holy Spirit, a thirst that the Son of God took our flesh to satiate.

Second, a persistent *idealism among our young.* I have experienced it in 12 years at Georgetown University: graduates spending a year with the poor in Peru, in Nicaragua; students spending nights with the homeless, hours in conversation with prostitutes; the choir celebrating liturgy in the D.C. jail, experiencing briefly but poignantly what it means to live without hope. Few of them return home, return to the campus, the same.

Third, *the African American example.* Most are used to a struggle for survival. They experience what it means to do without: without food, without education, without work, without luxuries. So many resemble the Hebrew Testament *anawim,* downtrodden indeed, but so conscious of their spiritual need that they look to the Lord for strength and help. In so many there is an openness to rescue, to the power of God. Intimate to them is a sense of healing. Not so much from doctors and ministers; rather the expectation that God will bring healing. God cares, God heals (even if God doesn't always cure); somehow God will make it come right.

Fourth, a *deep-seated generosity* in the American spirit. If someone is hurting, we rarely pass by on the other side. A busload of children crushed by a train outside Chicago; relentless rains flooding Midwest farms; another quake in California; devastation from a hurricane in Florida; a child who needs a special wheel chair; turkeys for the poor on Thanksgiving—the examples are legion. We are, on the whole, a compassionate people, even if we tend to close in on ourselves when the going gets rough, when immigrants or affirmative action threaten our way of life. This very Presbyterian parish is a breath-taking mirror of American generosity. I shall never forget the words of a Missouri rabbi after he had helped serve lunch to 400 hungry men and women at the Stewpot here:

> As I looked into the faces of those to whom I served water, and as they looked into mine, a voice within me spoke saying,

"Behold, God is in this place. God's face shines in the faces of those who gratefully give and gratefully receive. You made a difference today. You showed these people respect. You gave them hope. Give thanks to God and praise God's name."

Fifth, a widespread sense among Christians that the *Holy Spirit is proclaiming a new Pentecost* in our land. The evidence multiplies from all sorts of sources: not only Protestant Pentecostals and Catholic cursillos, not only those who speak in tongues, but more generally a surprising number of less obvious Christians, young and old, rich and poor, white and black, whose lives have been transformed unexpectedly by the inbreaking of the Spirit.

III

This leads neatly into my second principal point: a new heart. It goes back to the Lord's promise in Ezekiel:

> When [the exiles] come back [to the land of Israel], they will remove from it all its detestable things and all its abominations. I will give them a new heart, and put a new spirit within them; I will remove the heart of stone from their flesh and give them a heart of flesh, so that they may follow my statutes and keep my ordinances and obey them.
>
> (Ezek 11:18–20)

For us Christians living in "a new time," what is the "new heart"? I suggest that for us the heart we yearn for is not utterly new. My authority for this is the word of God proclaimed in Paul's letter to the Christians of Ephesus: "Speaking the truth in love, we must grow up in every way into him who is the head, into Christ" (Eph 4:15). We must *grow*. Ceaselessly grow. It is a process of growing, of intensifying and expanding what we already have. Call it a *new* beginning if you will, since everything God works in and through us has a certain freshness about it. But Paul's stress is on growing. And such is my own stress in your regard and mine. Concretely, how? Here five ways.

First, and before all else, we must grow into *Christ*. It is the basic Christian task: union with our risen Lord. This is a struggle, a striving, that is never ended. It is a oneness with which we can never be content at any given moment. It is Paul's heartfelt cry, "This one thing I do: Forgetting what lies behind and straining forward to what lies ahead, I press on toward the goal..." (Phil 3:13–14).

Second, we must grow into the *Body of Christ*. After 450 years of icy silence and theological assassination, we Christians have grown strikingly in our awareness of the whole Christ. Your Assembly is a vivid illustration; it is ecumenism in microcosm. And still we have a long road to travel before we live the prayer of Jesus, "As you, Father, are in me and I am in you, may they also [who believe] be one in us, so that the world may believe that you have sent me and have loved them even as you have loved me" (Jn 17:21). A long, rocky road before we are one as the Father and Christ are one. An ideal surely unattainable in our earthbound existence, but unless we struggle towards it despite all obstacles, we are to that extent unfaithful to our Lord.

Third, we must grow in *love for the poor,* the less fortunate, the marginalized. Not only action for the poor; within that action, love. Your programs for children and youth, for poor families, for the hungry and the imprisoned—these are not simply the efforts of social workers; with your commitment you are playing Christ, living the second great commandment of the law and the gospel, "Love your neighbor as yourself" (Mt 22:39). That injunction is not a psychological balancing act: As much or as little as I love myself, so much or so little love must I lavish on my neighbor. Scripture scholars tell us it means I must love each human, each brother and sister, like another I, another self, as if I were standing in his or her shoes. Free meals are indispensable. But, I ask myself, what ever happened to hospitality as Jesus described it: "When you give a banquet, invite the poor, the crippled, the lame, and the blind" (Lk 14:13)?

Fourth, we must grow in *respect for gays and lesbians.* In one of our Catholic parishes, a priest asked a mother why her son, an AIDS-afflicted gay young man, did not come to church. Her response? He would never think of doing that. He knows that, if he sashayed down the aisle of this church, if he walked there the way he walks here, people would break out in laughter. And that would break his heart.

Demanded of heterosexuals, if we are to grow in Christ and within the Body of Christ, is forthright denunciation of "violent malice in speech or in action directed against homosexuals"[7] and an insistence that gays and lesbians share in the "intrinsic dignity of each person," a dignity that calls for respect not only "in word [and] in action" but "in law" as well.[8] Seared on my heterosexual heart is a rebuke tendered by the editor of the *New Republic,* a Catholic with an evident respect for Catholic tradition. He finds no *positive* approach in the Catholic Church to gays and lesbians. Some have been wounded by brusque treatment. In his own home parish, there is "almost no ministry to gay people, almost no mention of the subject.

It is shrouded in complete and utter silence."[9] Here is a whole population "desperately seeking spiritual help and values. And the church
refuses to come to our aid, refuses to listen to this call." Just a question would encourage: "How can we help you?"[10]

Fifth, we must grow in our *understanding of justice.* You see,
when the prophet Micah declared to Israel, "What does the Lord
require of you but to do justice?" (Mic 6:8), he was not imposing on
God's people simply or primarily an ethical construct: Give to each
man, woman, and child what each deserves, what each has a strict
right to demand, because he or she is a human person, has rights
that can be proven from philosophy or have been written into law.
Basic to biblical justice is fidelity. Fidelity to what? To relationships,
to responsibilities, that stem from a covenant with God. To be just is
to be in right relation: to God, to people, to the earth. Love God
above all else; love each sister and brother like another self; touch
the earth, all of God's creation, with reverence. In the Christian perspective, to be just is to love as Jesus loved—even unto crucifixion.

A tough love indeed, this new heart. In fact, it is an impossible
love—save for one reality. Our "new spirit" (Ezek 11:19) stems from
the Holy Spirit. Never forget what Jesus cried out on the last day of
the Feast of Tabernacles: "If you are thirsty, come to me. If you
believe in me, drink. As the Scripture says, 'From his belly [from
within Jesus[11]] shall flow rivers of living water.'" John adds: "Here he
was referring to the Spirit which those who came to believe in him
were to receive" (Jn 7:37-39).

That is why I insist that what is new in this Assembly, your "new
heart," is not the Holy Spirit. What is new is letting the Spirit within
you loose. You know, you can have the Spirit within you and not be
dynamized by the Spirit. Look at the staggering number of Christians who would never dream of sinning, of breaking a single one of
God's commandments, like the elder brother of the prodigal son,
but do no more than follow the rules. I mean the contradiction we
call "Sunday Christians." What a dreadful waste! Waste of divine
Power—capital P. Within the millions of us who comprise the Body
of Christ is the potential to change our acre of God's world. It is not
high IQs that can destroy today's idols: communication without
community, rugged individualism, a culture of consumerism, violence arrayed against violence, disdain for life, neglect of our children, nihilism among the marginalized, divisions that rend us
within. It is the dynamism of the Spirit, not somewhere in outer
space but deep within us, that makes each heart a single heart, refusing to serve both our God and today's idols. Remember how 12

"uneducated and ordinary men" (Acts 4:13) were transformed once the Spirit filled them. Fellow Jews thought them drunk, and in a sense they were—intoxicated by living waters.

So then, my sisters and brothers in Christ, shake the Spirit loose! You already do. My point is, there is no end, no limit, to what the Spirit can accomplish through you. Shake the Spirit more and more, shake like men and women intoxicated. Shake so that this Body of Christ which is your Community of Churches may "build itself up in love," may "grow in every way into him who is the head, into Christ," may "attain to maturity," to full-grown adulthood, an adulthood measured by "the full stature of Christ" (Eph 4:16, 13). Such is your calling. Nothing less can transform our culture; nothing less does justice to the Spirit within you.

First Presbyterian Church
Dallas, Texas
November 16, 1995

42
OUR LADY, SYMBOL OF MY JESUIT EXISTENCE
Sixty-five Years in the Society of Jesus

- Acts 1:12–14
- Luke 1:26–38

To celebrate my 65 years as a Jesuit in appropriate liturgical style, I have chosen a Votive Mass of our Lady.[1] Not only because I entered the Society on the feast of Our Lady of Lourdes; even more because the life of Jesus' mother symbolizes for me three significant aspects of my own Jesuit existence. A word on each.

I

First, youthful Mary did not receive from God's messenger a script, a scenario, for her life as a mother. Gabriel did not tell her: "Now, Mary, before you say yes or no, you should know what a yes entails. Your husband will think you have been unfaithful, will plan to separate from you. Your baby will be born far from your home, in a feeding trough for animals. To escape the rage of a king, you will have to flee with your infant to far-off Egypt. For three decades you will live in this backwater town, and no one will know who your son really is. You will watch your neighbors try to cast him from a cliff, your relatives claim he is mad, the authorities accuse him of blasphemy. He will not outlive you, not die of natural causes. He will breathe his last a criminal on a bloody cross, between two bandits. But not to worry, Mary: Three days later you will see him again."

None of this. The only promise? "The Holy Spirit will come upon you, and the power of the Most High will overshadow you" (Lk 1:35). Knowing only that God had spoken, that God would be with her, Mary spoke her once-for-all yes: "Here am I, servant of the Lord. Let it be with me as you say" (v. 38).

So too for me, just out of Xavier High. No script from Father Provincial, no scenario. The pleasures of patristics and preaching, the fascination of the classroom and the lecture hall, the challenge of the written word and the just word, the sadness of family deaths and the closing of Woodstock—of these and so much more, no slightest inkling. Only a conviction that God was somehow calling. No struggle; not even a Mary-like "How can this be?" No intimation that the Church would change so radically with Vatican II, hundreds of friends find priesthood bereft of meaning and joy, Jesuit vocations in my province drop from sixty a year to six. Only an increasing sense that whatever might happen, the Holy Spirit will still be overshadowing me and my world, the risen Christ shaping his kingdom in his own time, his own mystery-laden way. An increasing conviction that what Jesus did with twelve, the Holy Spirit might well do with six!

II

A second significant way Mary symbolizes my Jesuit existence, specifically in recent years: her Magnificat. For the Magnificat is, as one biblical expert puts it, the "prayer of a woman between the times, prayer of a woman who is a symbol and model of faith. It is a prayer with a sociopolitical theme, filled with memory and with hope."[2] Take simply several verses:

> [God's] mercy is for those who fear him
>   from generation to generation.
> He has shown strength with His arm,
>   has scattered the proud in the thoughts of their hearts.
> He has brought down the powerful from their thrones,
>   and lifted up the lowly;
> has filled the hungry with good things,
>   and sent the rich away empty.

(Lk 1:50–53)

This is the Mary whose sights are set beyond little Nazareth, who proclaims biblical justice, not the justice of men and women but the justice of God: fidelity to relationships that stem from a covenant. Mary takes us back to God's mercy in the election of a band of enslaved tribes, their exodus from Egypt, the covenantal dispositions, the prophetic witness. Mary takes us forward to the hope that stems from Jesus, who fulfils all justice, whose kingdom is a kingdom of justice, making all things right; forward to the Jesus of the judgment (Mt 25:31–40); forward to the ideal community envisioned in Acts (4:32–35).

Such is our Lady's influence on my latter days, Preaching the Just Word. Sights set beyond little old Woodstock, beyond even the Beltway. Sights set on a country that is discouragingly deaf to the cries of its enslaved poor, its abused women and homeless men, its million youngsters sleeping on its streets each night, its elderly rummaging for food in garbage cans, its prisoners on death row. Sights set each year on 40,000 infants who will not see their first birthday, 1.6 million little ones who will never see the dawn of a day. Sights set on those who should be preaching passionately to their people with the prophet Micah: "What does the Lord require of you but to do justice, and to love kindness, and to walk humbly before your God?" (Mic 6:8). Preachers who should be echoing the mission of Jesus: "The Spirit of the Lord is upon me, because [the Lord] has anointed me to bring good news to the poor, has sent me to proclaim release to the captives and recovery of sight to the blind, to let the oppressed go free" (Lk 4:18).

III

A third significant way Mary symbolizes my Jesuit existence: a single sentence in the Acts of the Apostles. "[The apostles] were constantly devoting themselves to prayer, together with certain women, including Mary the mother of Jesus, as well as his brothers" (Acts 1:14). One word sums it up: community. Concretely, Mary sharing food and conversation, prayer and memories, with Jesus' closest friends, with men and women who had shared his hopes and his fears, his travel and his travail, his agonies and his ecstasies, his life and his love.

From 1931 to 1996, from St. Andrew overlooking the Hudson to Gonzaga skirting the Potomac, my Jesuit life has been shaped in uncommon fashion by Jesuits. I would not have it otherwise. I am not blinding myself to reality. I have experienced large communities (as many as 300 inhabitants) and small (as few as five). I have been affected by the famous (Murray and Weigel, Healy and Dulles) and the hidden (coadjutor brothers from wise infirmarian Cummings in Poughkeepsie, through German-born tell-it-like-it-is Spiess at Woodstock, to our own day-after-day devoted Dixon). I have known the cordial good-mornings and the expressive silences, the empathies and the envies, the laughter and the tears. They have molded me and scolded me, inspired me and irritated me, healed me and (rarely) wounded me. To all, yes to all, I say a heartfelt "thank you"; for all without exception have been a grace to me, an unmerited gift from above.

In consequence, I can say of the Society of Jesus: In the midst of a world gone mad with passion and power, I find here a tradition of intelligence, of reason. Though occasionally dampened by the demands of obedience, I find here a freedom beyond compare. Despite the pettiness that can stalk unisex existence, I find here a community of openness, of love, a community that supports me without strangling me, a community on which I depend without being enslaved to it. And so I shall never cease, please God, to be grateful to my brothers in Christ, never cease saying to the Society of Jesus what the exiles in Babylon said to their own mother:

> If I forget you, O Jerusalem,
>   let my right hand wither!
> Let my tongue cleave to the roof of my mouth,
>   if I do not remember you,
> if I do not set Jerusalem
>   above my highest joy!

Our Lady's Chapel
Gonzaga High School
February 12, 1996

43

TO SUCH AS THESE HEAVEN BELONGS
Baptism of an Infant

• Matthew 19:13–15

Katherine Stephanie Christin Maria: I wish you were just a few years older. I don't mean you are not unbelievably lovable right now; I simply wish you were old enough to understand two breath-taking things that are going to happen to you a quarter hour from now. Two miracles of God's grace. A word on each, then a final word about us who surround you with our love.[1]

I

The first miracle is symbolized in the Gospel story that was just read over you (Mt 19:13–15). Listen to it again.

> Little children were being brought to [Jesus] that he might lay his hands on them and pray. The disciples spoke sternly to those who brought them; but Jesus said, "Let the little children come to me, and do not stop them; for it is to such as these that the kingdom of heaven belongs." And he laid his hands on [the children] and went on his way.

This afternoon your mother and father have brought you to Jesus. This time there are no disciples protesting, no one commanding them not to disturb the Master: He's tired; little children trigger his hiatal hernia; he doesn't have time for squalling babies. No. This afternoon Jesus will lay his hands on you, pray over you, and as blessed water flows over your forehead, something only our imaginative God could have conceived will happen to you.

215

You see, God always loved you—loved you from the moment your mommy and daddy gave you life. But God was reserving something, keeping something from you the way we keep gifts for special days—birthdays, Christmas, graduation. St. Paul—you don't know him, but one day I hope you will—St. Paul put it powerfully: "If anyone is in Christ, he/she is a new creation" (2 Cor 5:17). A new creation. The first creation took place when your parents gave you life, made it possible for you to be, to be alive in this world of ours. The new creation, baptism, makes it possible for you to be alive "in Christ."

Kate, hold on to those two marvelous monosyllables, "in Christ." They express your new life. They meant so much to St. Paul that in his letters he uses that expression 165 times. Why? Because to be in Christ means you and Jesus are unbelievably one.

That oneness is not easy to put in simple language. Let me try a comparison. Remember how for nine months you shared your mother's life when you were growing within her? During those precious months we could truly say that her life was your life. You actually lived off your mother, could not have lived without her. Well, somewhat like that experience, you will share Jesus' life after your baptism. From your baptism on, you will be able to say just as truly that Jesus' life is your life. Your Christian life—believing, hoping, loving—you will be living off Jesus. You can exclaim with St. Paul, "It is no longer I who live, but it is Christ who lives in me. And the life I now live in the flesh I live by faith in the Son of God, who loved me and gave himself for me" (Gal 2:20).

Very simply, for you to be "in Christ" means that you live in Christ and Christ lives in you.[2]

II

But that is not all, That miracle of God's grace, you in Christ and Christ in you, goes hand-in-hand with another miracle of grace. Once the blessed waters flow over you, you will be one not only with the Christ who walked the roads of Palestine, who rose from the dead and is gloriously alive right now. You will be one with what St. Paul calls "the body of Christ" (1 Cor 12:27). I mean the community we call the Church, all of us who believe and hope and love.

Today we welcome you into this community of ours, this Catholic Christian community. We do so without asking your permission. Not only because you are so small and we can take advantage of you. More importantly because we are convinced, from our experience, that this is where you belong, that here, with our loving help, is where you will experience God's love more fully than anywhere else. For this community will be the air you breathe, the atmosphere within which you believe, act, and worship.

Kate, I wish with all my heart that you could unwrap the gifts God will lavish on you in these sacred waters. Hidden within you, unknown even to you for a while, will be the power to believe what passes proof: to believe in a God who shaped you out of nothing but love, believe in God's Son who loved you enough to die for you. Hidden within you will be a Power to say yes to what is good and no to what is evil, a Power that is a Person, the Holy Spirit. And before very long you will share with us, week after week, daily if you wish, our supreme experience of worship, the Eucharist where our hidden Lord will rest in your hand, on your tongue, in your body.

III

A brief third point, Kate. It has to do with something I said almost five years ago, when we welcomed your big brother, Frans-Joseph, into our Christian community. You see, the baptism we are forcing on you today lays a heavy burden on us who know and love you. As you grow into childhood and adolescence, you will have to grow into faith and hope and love—into Christ. How you grow into Christ will be mightily affected by what you see, what you experience, in us—in your father and mother, in your godfather and godmother, in relatives and friends, in all of us who take such joy in your baptism into Christ.

And so we who surround you have to ask ourselves: What will you see in those of us who claim to love you more than a little? I believe I can speak for all of us here when I promise you our own baptismal gift. We shall try our level best, with God's grace, to reveal to you a community that tries to live the two great commandments of the Mosaic law and the gospel. We shall make it our primary effort to love God above all else. It means we shall reject the idols that have captured our culture. I mean, for example, what Pope John Paul II called "the civilization of consumption or consumerism," which "makes people slaves of 'possession' and of immediate gratification,"[3] that puts the emphasis on having rather than on being—especially being "in Christ." We shall make an equal effort to live the commandment Jesus said "is like" loving God. I mean loving every man, woman, and child like another self, another I, as if I were standing in their shoes—especially the unfortunates who share more of Jesus' crucifixion than of his resurrection.

In a word, we shall try, as you grow, to show you by our lives that to live is to love: to love as Jesus loved. In that spirit we move now to a remarkable act of community love. With Jesus we take you in our arms to waters that give life, God's life. Waters that will make you even more lovable than you are now; for when you rise from these waters, you will rise... "in Christ." Then it is that we shall say even more truly with Jesus, "To such as [you] the kingdom of heaven belongs" (Mt 19:14).

Holy Trinity Church
Washington, D.C.
February 17, 1996

44
MY WORLD, YOUR PROFESSION, CHRIST'S GOSPEL
A Medical School Graduation

- Deuteronomy 6:4–7
- Colossians 1:3–4, 9–14
- Matthew 5:13–16

Two years ago, a perceptive Presbyterian preacher remarked:

> Part of what the preacher is about is knowing what the issues
> are, the questions being asked, which define a culture in a given
> time and place. The preacher must read and listen and see and
> participate in the world in which the congregation lives. We
> need to know what is being written by novelists, poets, journal-
> ists, essayists. Kathleen Norris in her wonderful bestseller
> *Dakota* says that Lemmon, South Dakota, is so small that the
> poets and preachers have to hang out together.[1]

I dare to address you this morning, not because I share your
professional proficiency, your medical art and science. Only because
I "read and listen and see and participate in the world" in which you
doctors will live, will work. That, I suspect, is why I have been privileged to address your Surgery Grand Rounds; why yours is my third
round of GUMed graduates; why I have contributed to your volume
on the Jesuit tradition in medicine. I have even been restored to gas-
troenterological and cardiological health on your floors. This next
quarter hour you may regret your Medical Center's skills that have
brought me here!

So then, three questions: (1) What is this world in which you
will live, will work, as women and men of medicine? (2) Is there
any connection between that world, your profession, and the
gospel I preach? (3) What realistic challenge dare I hurl out to yo'
today?

I

First, what is this world like, this world you are about to invade—31 States and the District of Columbia?[2] Not only the world of unnumbered illnesses; importantly, too, the world of ideas and feelings, loves and hates, hopes and fears that impact your profession. In a sense, that world can be summed up as...people. And this people is a paradoxical people.

Why a paradox? Because we out there are wonderfully and fearfully diverse. Thousands of talents that ceaselessly re-create our pulsing planet, energize your own profession. Hundreds of languages that impede genuine communication, even rival your medical rhetoric for obscurity. Some of us venerate you; others are afraid of you; still others suspect you.

A paradox because we out there are a rainbow of colors: black and white, red and brown and yellow. And we bring to you not only an ulcer or a cancer, but our colorful history: beaten down or beloved, choked or cherished, neglected or encouraged, from poverty or plenty. We come to you with all manner of diseases, some of which still resist your research. We are little children not knowing why our tumorous head hurts; elderly folk aware that this day may be our last; middle-agers who have never been sick a day, ran a 10K just minutes before we collapsed. We are the affluent who can afford you, the millionaire hoopster with a damaged knee, the entertainer needing a face lift. But we are also the homeless and hopeless, the jobless and penniless, who cannot expect dialysis or a new kidney. And somewhere in-between, the average American, nothing special about us, uncomplaining, undemanding, grateful for any attention, a kind word, a smile. All of us, however, have a single feature in common. In your hands each of us becomes one terribly dull word: a patient, a nonperson.

You see, on your wards, in your ORs and ERs, we experience our littleness. Each one of us is in reality a person, an individual; and each of us wants to be treated as a person, an individual, not as a wrist tag, a room number, a medical chart. But that backless gown, not shaped by Priscilla of Boston, removes our individuality, makes us feel helpless, not quite but somewhat like the nakedness of the Jews in Auschwitz.

We are terrified by the changing world of health care, where 37 million of us have no insurance, where healthy legislators are plotting health cuts that won't lose our votes, where a balanced budget takes priority over our incurable cancer, where the time you can give us may be dictated by an impersonal HMO. We are agonizingly anxious over our potential powerlessness; some of us with Alzheimer's are afraid that our relatives may now appeal to compassionate courts for physician-assisted suicide—for our own good, of course.

II

Terribly selective, I know, only hints of the raw reality. But enough to ask a second question: Is there any relation between that world, your profession, and the gospel I preach? Those three realities—world, profession, gospel—come together in the Jesus who proclaimed his mission in the synagogue of his hometown: "The Spirit of the Lord is upon me, for [the Lord] has anointed me. He has sent me to preach good news to the poor, to proclaim release for prisoners and sight for the blind, to send the downtrodden away relieved" (Lk 4:18). To send the downtrodden away relieved. With that mission the awesome syllables addressed by a God-man to his followers, to you: "You are the salt of the earth, but if salt has lost its taste, how can its saltiness be restored? You are the light of the world. Let your light shine before others, so that they may see your good works and give glory to your Father in heaven" (Mt 5:13–14, 16).

Send the downtrodden away relieved...salt the earth...let your light shine. My point? For the Christian, medicine is not only a science, not only an art; medicine is a vocation. A call. In the Christian vision, a call from God. You've heard it all before, from elementary school on. But this you may not have heard: Yours is not a vocation just like any other—banker or baker, astronaut or astrophysicist, garbage collector or Wall Street speculator. You have an uncommon call; God calls you in God's own surprising way. You never touch simply a diseased body. Not a man *with* melanoma, not a woman *with* scarred uterus. *He* is sick, not his chest; and *she* is sick, not her womb. You never touch simply a spirit gone astray, a neurosis, a paranoia. *She* is neurotic, not her mind; *he* is paranoid, not his spirit. Always and everywhere, what you touch in a unique way, uniquely intimate, is a person.

Not some abstraction called "person." This person, each patient, is unique; each is unrepeatable; no one else quite like him, no one exactly like her. For each is an image of God, and each reflects God in his or her own inimitable way. Each has a story, each *is* a story. And the story comes to a critical point in your presence, your insight, your diagnosis, your hands, your scalpel. Critical because, from a

Christian perspective, each is a person-in-process-of-redemption. Each at that moment—aware of it or not—is working out his or her destiny as a person. If disease diminishes me, it diminishes my Christianness. If sickness strengthens me, I take a giant step toward my salvation.

Here not only the hospital chaplain comes in, with cross and Communion. Here medicine as a vocation reveals itself with uncommon clarity. One of your profession, a surgeon with a touch of the poet, has paralleled it to priesthood.

> I must confess that the priestliness of my profession has ever been impressed on me. In the beginning there are vows, taken with all solemnity. Then there is the endless harsh novitiate of training, much fatigue, much sacrifice. As last one emerges as celebrant, standing close to the truth lying curtained in the Ark of the body. Not surplice and cassock but mask and gown are your regalia. You hold no chalice, but a knife. There is no wine, no wafer. There are only the facts of blood and flesh.[3]

Poetry? Perhaps. But poetry that comes alive in a distinction (Jesuits always make distinctions). Not only the distinction between curing and failing to cure. Even more importantly, the distinction between curing and healing. It suggests my third point: my realistic challenge to you.

III

From my experience, an increasing issue for medicine women and medicine men is disenchantment. The glow is gone. It's a job. For ever so many reasons. Routine: doing the same things day after day, year after year. Atmosphere: blood and bones, mucous and metastasis. Stress: how harness patients, continuing education, insurance companies, fear of lawsuits, the time HMOs allow for patients? How recapture the excitement of your youth? How keep your salt from losing its taste?

One solution has for persuasive testimony your own profession. Listen to Jewish holistic physician Bernie Siegel, at times criticized, yet speaking from a lifetime of experience, convinced that the most powerful known stimulant of the immune system is unconditional love.[4] Siegel struck it swiftly and starkly: "Remember I said love heals. I do not claim love cures everything but it can heal and in the process of healing cures occur also."[5]

Love heals. Heals the patient, and in the process can heal you.

Oh, not some vague, gossamer, soap-opera love. Here love means you care—always care, at times agonize. Care knows no cases; only persons. Each has a name. Each has a story not irrelevant to the disease. Each needs not only a prescription or a placebo, not only an anesthetic or a scalpel. Each needs a doctor who cares, especially when the prognosis is dismal. The miracle of touch, the pain in your eyes, the smile on your lips, the encouragement in your voice—these are ways God speaks to the sick. Only rarely does God appear in person at a hospital bed. God is there through you, in you. Not mouthing pious platitudes; simply being very human. Like Jesus holding the fevered hand of Peter's mother-in-law; like Jesus taking little children into his arms when the disciples tried to whisk them away.

In the process love can heal *you* as well. Have you seen *Les Misérables?* Remember the last scene, the song of Jean Valjean? "To love another person is to see the face of God." That piece of music is not fantasy. It is good theology with a realistic bite. To love is to care; to care is to play Jesus Christ to men and women who have been shaped in the image of God, have been fashioned after the likeness of Christ. In your profession, to care for women and men who share more of his crucifixion than of his resurrection. All genuine human loving is an experience of caring. It's true not only of husband and wife; it's true of all authetically human relationships. But it is especially important for a relationship that professionally seems one-sided: You give and I receive. Sorry, good friends. That is not the way it should work, not the way medicine should work. Love was never meant to be a one-way street. Love heals the healer, love heals the lover.

Last week a pertinent, or impertinent, thought struck me: For a doctor, caring doesn't take any more time than not caring. It's simply being a person. Not a person in an ancient definition: a rational animal, someone who stands tall, independent, existing in himself and for himself—a solitary god in a white coat. No, a person alive is a man or woman who is "for others." Especially for those who depend on you if they are to come alive again.

A swift summary. In you three awesome realities come together: my world, your profession, Christ's gospel. My world? People, infinitely diverse, but all one in coming to you terribly afraid, no longer persons, only patients. Your profession? No patients, only persons; no cases, only caring; sometimes curing, always healing. Christ's gospel? Care without ceasing, and your salt will never lose its saltiness. Heal even when not curing, and your light will constantly shine before us your paradoxical world, and your healing will give glory to your Father in heaven. For this were you fashioned: to give healing to people, to give glory to God. Both with the same hand, both with the same heart.

Holy Trinity Church
Washington, D.C.
May 25, 1996

45

WITH WHAT SHALL I COME
BEFORE THE LORD?
University Mass of the Holy Spirit

- Isaiah 42:1–3
- 1 Corinthians 12:3–13
- Luke 4:16–21

I come to you a stranger, a sheer name, at best another wise man from the east. Somewhat like the politician who began his address with today's prize for the unbelievable: "I come from Washington; and I'm here to help you." But the name is not important, the message is. And the message is important because it translates God's own Word to you, the message you heard from Isaiah and Jesus. Important too because it is your generation of Christians who must breathe new life into that message, into an American Church that enters its third millennium in peril, searching for its identity, a church whose young look upon it largely with suspicion or indifference.

A homily is not a blueprint for a millennium. I offer you a single word from God's Word, a two-syllable word that can focus your human and Christian striving, all you are and do, at Creighton and beyond, as few other words can. The word? You heard it this morning when Scripture declared that God's servant "will bring forth to the nations...justice" (Isa 42:3). The problem: What does it mean? Three stages to my song and dance: (1) how *we* understand justice; (2) how *God* understands justice; (3) how God's understanding, in this liturgy and in every liturgy, can transform your lives and my life. Not a lecture; Cartesian clarity indeed, but with the stress on excitement, on feeling, on the human heart.

I

First, what do most Americans understand when they hear the word "justice"? In an ethics course, you are just when you give to another, to each man or woman, what he or she *deserves*. Deserves because it has been written into law or can be proven from philosophy. You have a right, say, not to be mugged, a right to a job and a family wage, a right to decent housing. At times the word "deserves" takes on ominous overtones. Remember how President Clinton vowed that the Oklahoma City bombers would be brought to justice? They would indeed get what they deserve.

Such an understanding of justice is unavoidable, important for human living, for civilized behavior. And it touches today's burning issues. What do the poor without a job deserve? Do African Americans, do women, deserve affirmative action? Do illegal immigrants deserve public education for their offspring? Does a murderer of children, a rapist, a terrorist deserve the gas chamber, a lethal injection, a rope around his neck?

Ethical justice, Aristotle and Plato, John Rawls and Michael Walzer, I leave to your classrooms, to your native intelligence, to your gift for distinctions. Not because it is unimportant; simply because there is a justice even more important, a justice without which you cannot claim to be Christian. Which brings me to biblical justice, the justice proclaimed in Scripture, God's imaginative grasp on a richer reality.

II

Cast your mind back 2800 years. Imagine a Hebrew prophet named Micah, unafraid of powerful princes, pretentious priests, unjust judges, manipulative merchants. His charge to Israel is blunt: "With what shall I come before the Lord? With burnt offerings, calves a year old, thousands of rams, rivers of oil, my firstborn for the sin of my soul? The Lord has told you what is good. What does the Lord require of you but to do justice, love kindness, and walk humbly with your God?" (Mic 6:6–8).

Do justice. Not simply or primarily, give others what they deserve. Remember, Israel was not a nation of rugged individualists. To "live" meant to be closely linked to others. How? "King with people, judge with complainants, family with tribe and kinfolk, the community with the resident alien and [with the] suffering in their midst, and all with the covenant God." This was the world in which life was played out.[1] In that context, biblical justice was a single, potent, all-embracing word: fidelity. Fidelity to what? To reponsibilities, to relationships, that stem from a covenant with God. What responsibilities, what relationships? I am just with the justice of God if I am in right relation in every facet of my existence. Simply, in right relation to God, to people, to the earth.

To God: Love God above all else, with all your mind and heart, all your strength, above every creature, every person or thing God ever created, however lovely, attractive, tempting. Love every human person who crosses your path, touches your life, reaches your eyes in newsprint and on TV. Love them not because they are likable, lovable, but because they are children of God, images of the Christ who died a crucifying death for them. Touch the earth with reverence; for each "thing" (that ice-cold word) God ever fashioned— each bluebird gracing the air with its song, each redwood lifting its arms to the sky, each mountain majestic in its lordly solitude—speaks of its Creator; each is a trace of God, would not even exist did it not reflect its divine Artisan.

This is the tradition that sparked the ministry of Jesus. He summed it up in the synagogue of his native Nazareth: "The Spirit of the Lord is upon me; for [the Lord] has anointed me, has sent me to preach good news to the poor, to proclaim release for those in chains and sight for the blind, to send the downtrodden away relieved" (Lk 4:18). This is the tradition that sparked the early Christian communities. Matthew summed it up in Jesus' startling declaration: If *anyone* is hungry or thirsty, naked or a stranger, sick or in prison, it is always Christ who clamors for bread or water, Christ who cries to be clothed or welcomed, Christ whom you visit on a bed of pain or behind bars (Mt 25:31–46). Here is a vision of community where, as Paul puts it, no one, absolutely no one, can say to any other, "I have no need of you" (1 Cor 12:12 ff.).

III

Lovely, you say; the preacher is a poet. But how does this touch you, your campus existence, this liturgy and every liturgy till your very last? Few of you will remember Dorothy Day, Communist turned Christian. She walked picket lines, struggled against segregation in Georgia, was jailed for supporting Mexican itinerant workers, even squared off against a New York cardinal in defense of cemetery strikers. She argued passionately that "the poor do *not* have the Gospel preached to them." To preach it to them, she lived with them, "with the criminal, the unbalanced, the drunken, the degraded...with rats, with vermin, bedbugs, roaches, lice...."[2] Why? Because Dorothy Day

> could not go to Communion and be insensitive to the reality that someone was hungry; she could not enjoy the warmth of Eucharistic consolation and know that she had a blanket while her brothers and sisters did not; she could not "go to the altar of God" and be aware that someone was sleeping over a grate on the sidewalk....

This liturgy, each liturgy, suggests or declares biblical justice, right relationship to God, to the human community, to material creation.[3] To God above all. For in a few moments the Eucharistic prayer will begin—begin with a soul-searing confession, not to be uttered mindlessly by priest, not to be passed over passively by people. Translated from the Latin with insight, it should begin: "It really is proper, it is a matter of justice, that we should always and everywhere give you thanks." For all of us who are privileged to serve the less fortunate, there can be no messiah complex; the cause is God's; God's too are the power and the glory. "Not to us," sings the Psalmist, "not to us, O Lord, but to your name give glory" (Ps 115:1).

Right relationship to the human community. For the liturgy is a ceaseless "we." And we stand to our brothers and sisters "not as the rich to the poor, the strong to the needy, the clever to the simple; we stand rather as the poor to the poor, the weak to the weak, the loved to the loved."[4] In point of fact, most Eucharistic assemblies, perhaps this your gathering, reflect not the justice, the right relationships, of God's kingdom but the divisions of social groupings. This constitutes a tension rather than an achievement; we are not yet one the way Jesus envisioned it, not yet one as he and the Father are one. Still, the tension must be preserved, even in the liturgy, if we are not thoughtlessly to accept our unjust world.

Right relationship to material creation. For when Jesus took the bread, blessed it, broke it, and shared it, he showed us in striking symbol how we are to use this earth, all material things. They are not to be clutched in hot hands; they are to be given, to be shared. Not only my love but my learning, not only my possessions but my compassion. "This is my body, [and it is] given for you" (Lk 22:19). When Jesus took the cup of his blood and passed it among his disciples, he revealed the joy that comes from not claiming anything as simply our very own— even life itself. And he forbade us to turn the creation committed to our care into weapons of power, instruments of destruction.

Good friends in Christ: I am stirred profoundly, mightily

moved, by Creighton's concern for the less fortunate. I find you in Appalachia and on Indian reservations; I find you with the poor in the inner city, with Hispanics in Texas and Colorado, serving a semester in the Third World; I find your health professionals in the Dominican Republic. You may call it charity, because it seems to be service above the call of Christian duty; you might reach heaven without it. Scripture calls it justice, because you are faithful to responsibilities that stem from your covenant with Christ, faithful to relationships that mark every human as your sister or brother; you are loving as Jesus loved—and that is not an option for Christians. Only a faith that does biblical justice is a living faith. With such faith you can declare, as God's own Son-in-flesh declared, "The Spirit of the Lord is upon me." For only through the Power that is the Holy Spirit can you love as Jesus loved. Hence the supreme importance of this liturgy: your University Mass of the Holy Spirit.

I have but one regret. Never quite satisfied with all the justice you actually do, I regret that not all of you are involved. I regret it not only literally for Christ's sake, but for your own sake as well. For you will rarely know a deeper joy than when through your love you see hope light the dulled eyes of a child AIDS-infected from the womb; stunted minds opening to an idea, a vision, a future; elderly hands coming to life at your touch; even the earth and its riches renewed. And scout's honor, I promise you this: Young or aging, busy or retired, as long as you are doing biblical justice, as long as you love God above all else, love each crucified image of Christ like another self, and touch God's "things" with reverential care, as a vestige of divinity, you will never be bored! Never.

Creighton University
Omaha, Nebraska
September 11, 1996

46

WITH WINGS LIKE EAGLES
175th Anniversary of Gonzaga College High School

- Isaiah 40:28–31
- Philippians 2:1–11
- Matthew 20:20–28

How does a homilist recapture 175 years? It's like Maria in *The Sound of Music*, "How do you hold a moonbeam in your hand?" Fortunately, a homily is not a history, though a homily should praise God for what history has wrought. Nor is it a teary attempt at nostalgia, a yearning for the days of old. I mean those earliest years in midtown; later, the years within sight of what Pat Buchanan called "the ladies from 48";[1] the riots next door in '68; the down days in the early 70s (Will Gonzaga die?) and the Eagle's resurrection; the days of Barter and Bellwoar, Carmody and Clements, Delaney and Dooley, Hanley and Herlihy, Joyner and Kozik and Lelii, McGonigal and McHale and McKenna, Sampson and Sweeney, Troy and Petrik, Wheeler and Woodward and Ward.

For a preacher the overriding question is: What has the past wrought? Whereto have the decades brought us? What sort of man, what kind of human, what manner of believer is now at the heart of Gonzaga? Where are we? And what does it have to do with the Christian gospel, with Jesus Christ?

No homily can provide a complete response. My own gaze on Gonzaga can be summarized in one phrase with three subheads. The phrase: an adventure in discovery. The subheads: discovering God, discovering things, discovering people. Always there in Jesuit education, but freshly encountered in each age, more deeply discovered, by each new Novotny or Ciancaglini, each new Warman or Freburger, each new Howell or Collins.

230

I

An adventure in discovery. I begin with God, because here is where each of our young eagles has to fly frighteningly high. Somehow, from the Gonzaga experience, each youngster shapes a picture of his God. I am reminded of a young African American child in Mississippi who drew a picture of herself, then said: "That's me, and the Lord made me. When I grow up my momma says I may not like how He made me, but I must always remember that He did it, and it's His idea. So when I draw the Lord He'll be a real big man. He has to be to explain the way things are."[2]

Each Gonzagan, know it or not, draws a picture of God here. Various paints, different colors go into it. He learns to paint with biblical colors, colors that reproduce God's own scenario for us from Genesis' primitive garden to John's heavenly city, from the first man through the God-man to the last of humans. He learns from master painters called theologians: some of them masters of abstraction, others masters of impressions, some drawing mystically in clouds of unknowing, others painting in the grime and grit of human sin and folly. He learns to draw his God within a church that claims to have its original of God from God, a unique God who walked our earth in our flesh. He listens to painters who are cynical, who refuse to paint a God who they claim isn't "for real," doesn't exist, clearly doesn't weep when we bleed.

And as each has done since 1821, today's Gonzagan leaves here with a picture. Childish perhaps, a God in designer jeans, Oriole or Redskins cap on backwards; perhaps surprisingly mature, a Son of God who for love of sinful humans "emptied Himself, being born in the likeness of men and women, humbled Himself, obedient even unto death on a cross" (Phil 2:7–8). An angry picture possibly, because the God he paints weds divine love to inhuman poverty and sexual abuse, links love for life to wars that blast life to bits. A confusing picture maybe, because his God conceals what is divine in the all too human face of a church that does not always image the Christ who created it. A disappointing picture at times, because he doesn't like the way his God made *him*.

In any event, in each case the beginnings of discovery. In books he studies and the Eucharist he feeds on, in the fine arts and films from *The Ten Commandments* to George Burns's *Oh God!*, from Bergman to Fellini. Not the end of discovery, only a beginning, a sketch for the future. But terribly important, crucial, for the years that beckon ahead. Hence our hopeful, fearful prayers for him.

II

An adventure in discovery. But discovery at Gonzaga is not limited to "three Persons in one God." Essential even to eagles that fly high is discovering the things of God, God's nonhuman creation—the earth and sky, the land and waters, the birds and fish and animals of which an imaginative God said after six days, "It is very good" (Gen 1:31). A cynical observer once defined education as "the inculcation of the incomprehensible into the ignorant by the incompetent." I am not suggesting that Gonzaga has never been guilty of this particular felony. I do submit that Gonzaga puts its eagles in touch with the world that sustains them—a search for understanding. On a level very human, and on a level distinctively divine.

On a human level, in the sciences, Gonzagans learn to touch the earth with reverence, to "handle with care." One example: The life they touch in biology is itself life-giving. Without plants and animals we could not survive. That is why they tremble when they read the 1992 declaration issued by the Union of Concerned Scientists over 1575 signatures that said in part: "Human beings and the natural world are on a collision course. Many of our current practices put at serious risk the future that we wish for human society and the plant and animal kingdoms, and may so alter the living world that it will be unable to sustain life in the manner that we know."[3]

The more they experience the things of God, the more profoundly Gonzagans can relate to John Paul II's warning against exhaustion of the soil, uncontrolled deforestation, unbridled consumerism, instant gratification; can realize with him that "their responsibility within creation and their duty toward nature and the Creator are an essential part of their faith"; can accept his challenge to contemplate nature's beauty, recognize its restorative power for the human heart; can learn to imitate St. Francis of Assisi, who loved all of God's creatures—not only the poor but animals and plants, natural forces, even Brother Sun and Sister Moon.[4]

On a level divine, Gonzagans learn, as Ignatius Loyola learned, to find God in everything that exists. Why? Because simply everything, majestic mountain and giant redwood, blue marlin and scarlet tanager, each carries a trace of its imaginative Maker—if we have eyes to see. Like a painting of Rembrandt, a scherzo of Chopin, an architectural gem of Saarinen, every single artistry from God's hand sings of its Creator—if we have ears to hear. Because our God is active—Ignatius said Christ "behaves like a laborer"[5]—in all that is: gives not only intelligence and love to each of you, but gives being to billions of stars, life to over four thousand varieties of roses, smell and smiles to the dolphins of Disneyland.

Little wonder that Gonzagans learn to care for God's world with respect, as a gift received from God.

III

An adventure in discovery. Not only God; not only the things of God; discovering the people of God, God in others. It is the song of Jean Valjean at the close of *Les Misérables:* "To love another person is to see the face of God." Especially on the faces of the less fortunate. Seeing in the McKenna Center not so much the refuse of humanity as what Horace McKenna saw: ravaged images of the crucified Christ. Spying the face of Christ on the face of a *Dead Man Walking,*[6] a murderer eying electrocution.

Gonzaga is not a head trip. The mind is indeed important. As is faith. But even more important is "the faith that does justice." Not just ethical justice, giving people what they deserve, because it can be proven from philosophy or has been written into law. More broadly, biblical justice, fidelity to relationships, responsibilities, that stem from our covenant with God in Christ. Realizing that Jesus' command "Love your neighbor as yourself" (Mt 22:39) is not a psychological balancing act: As much or as little as you love yourself, so much or so little love shall you lavish on others. It means loving each brother, each sister, like another self, as if you are standing in their shoes, particularly the paper-thin shoes of the underprivileged. Hence Gonzaga men on service, like the Christ who came among us "not to be served but to serve" (Mt 20:28). Servants especially of the disadvantaged: orphans in Guadalajara, the poor in Puerto Rico, students of Holy Redeemer, the hungry on North Capitol, the elderly at J. B. Johnson. This is not a fad at Gonzaga, not sheer requirement— you don't graduate unless...; this is education for realistic living. Here head and heart come together, knowledge and love, belief and action, understanding and passion, Christ crucified not only on Calvary but at the crossroads of D.C. This is carrying on the tradition of St. Aloysius Gonzaga, dead at 23 as he spent the last ounce of his fragile strength on the plague-stricken in Rome.

A final word, good friends. A delightful film surely familiar to you has made me think of Gonzaga, indeed of all Jesuit secondary schools. The title: *Mr. Holland's Opus.* The principal character: Richard Dreyfuss, frustrated composer, exciting teacher. Let me leave with you three sentences from that celluloid, sentences no teacher, no parent, no student can afford to forget.

First, to Gonzaga teachers I commend imitation of Mr. Holland's excited advice to a frightfully bad young flutist: "There's a lot more to music than notes on a page. It's fun, it's feeling, it's heart!" When she realizes that to play the flute is to enjoy the playing, then it is she begins to make music. Not that high school is rollicking laughter, belly spasms. Simply that when teachers make God's things, God's people, God's very self come wondrously alive, then it is that young eyes, young ears, young hearts, even young mouths open in wonder. Second, to Gonzaga parents I commend what the teacher of Mr. Holland's deaf son says to Holland himself: "The most important teacher your child will ever have is you." For parents are the first to create or destroy; parents are the first to inspire or deaden. Third, to Gonzaga students I commend what Holland says to Rowena Morgan, gifted student singer: "If you have the passion, if you have the hunger, you can do anything."

Teachers who excite their students, parents who inspire their sons, students who hunger to know and to love: Here is Gonzaga at its noblest, here eagles fly highest. Gonzaga's opus, Gonzaga's music, is its students, its alumni: You are Gonzaga's symphony, the music of our lives. Unfinished indeed; will never be finished until Christ comes again. But the music is not "notes on a page," your sheer biography. Gonzaga's music is the human and Christian joy you take in coming alive, in thinking and feeling and loving, in sharing that joy with your acre of God's tearful, fearful world.

It's the astonishing admission of the British Olympic runner in *Chariots of Fire:* "When I run, I feel God's pleasure." Like the fastest man in the world, Michael Johnson in Atlanta last month: first to the tape, first with eyes to heaven, first with knees to the ground. It's the Gonzaga ideal: Whether you are thinking or talking, studying or teaching, praying or playing, loving a dear one or feeding the hungry, dunking the round ball or tickling the keys, you feel God's pleasure.

Such, I believe, is Gonzaga's greatest gift. So then, this blessed day if any day, feel God's pleasure! All of you. Your God loves you, your God lives in you, your God died that you might come alive. Student or alumnus, parent or teacher, please...come...alive!

St. Aloysius Gonzaga Church
Washington, D.C.
September 29, 1996

47
ALIVE, NOW AND FOR EVER
Homily for a Mass of the Resurrection

- 1 Corinthians 15:12–20
- John 11:17–27

Today, dear friends, we give back to God a precious gift God has given to us. Because the gift is so precious, our hearts are torn. And still we gather in God's presence to celebrate that gift. Something of a paradox, I know—sadness and celebration. So then, let one person who was privileged to share that gift try to make sense out of the paradox, put sadness *and* celebration into each of our hearts. Not a head trip; a cry from the heart. For the inspired passage we heard from the Gospel of John speaks to us on two levels. It reproduces the emotion in our hearts and it forces on our minds an all-important message of Jesus.

I

First, the emotion in our hearts. We do right to mourn, to weep. Rather than get lost in abstractions, let me relate one story I have never before revealed.

The date: August 17, 1967. The place: the theological seminary at Woodstock in Maryland. The event: a summer program called "Search and Service," retitled by some of my theological students "Search and Destroy." One participant attracted me immediately: a student at Wellesley in her late teens—bright-eyed, energetic, highly intelligent. We were rapt in conversation when word came to me that my closest friend, Father John Courtney Murray, had died of a heart attack in a taxicab on Long Island. Utterly unexpected, too sudden to take in. Tears rolled down my cheeks; I thought my heart would break. Without a word, that teenager put her arms around me, held me, till the storm subsided.

Such was Eileen Flanigan Serene. Someone incomparably dear to us has been taken from each of us. Her smile, her quick wit, the depth of her ideas, the love in her eyes, the compassion in her heart—all this and more we shall experience no more. Each of you has your own memories of her, most more intimate than mine. For one dear family, it is your own flesh and blood you mourn today.

And so, with Martha in John's Gospel we cannot help asking, Why? We cannot help repeating, "Lord, if you had [really] been here, our daughter, our sister, would not have died." Where were you when we needed you? Where were you when without warning life was stolen from her? When she was touching the flower of her life—children growing, law career promising, husband and parents and siblings surrounding her with love.

There is no answer that will satisfy the philosopher. In the face of innocent suffering, human wisdom is bankrupt. Peace will come not from logic but from trust—trust that stems from love, love of a God who, John's Gospel tells us, "so loved [us] that He gave His only Son" to an excruciating cross (Jn 3:16). Peace will come only when, as with Job in the Hebrew Testament, God shows His face to us—not for us to experience explanation, only to experience love. If only we can love God as we love Eileen, then it is that we will "see" in the darkness that God has richer plans for those He loves, richer plans for Eileen, than we have for ourselves and her.

Where were you, Lord, these painful months? Where were you that fatal Sunday evening? Closer to Eileen than ever before. Because every gethsemane is your garden, and every calvary is your cross. Thank you for being with Eileen as she shared your agony; thank you for being near her as she died your death.

II

Second, the Gospel passage, the mystery-laden message of Jesus. As you listened to the Gospel, did you notice that Jesus was not satisfied with Martha's act of faith? Oh yes, she believed, believed in life—but in *another* life: "I know that [my brother] will rise again in the resurrection at the last day" (Jn 11:24). No, says Jesus, that's not the point. "Whoever lives and believes in me shall *never* die" (v. 26). Shall never die.

This is not pious exaggeration. This is not spiritual pap, soft food for feeble Christians, a sop for those who mourn. For me, the most rapturous, the most consoling words in the Gospel are the short words our Lord spoke to his apostles the night before he died: "I have life, and [so] you will have life" (Jn 14:19). Here is the pith, the marrow, of John's Gospel, summed up in today's reading: "Jesus said to [Martha], 'I am...the life'" (Jn 11:25). Jesus not only *has* life, he *is* life—because the Holy Spirit, that Spirit who gives life, is his Spirit, and this Spirit, this life, this Spirit of life, he gives to us. In John's vision, in the Christian vision, we die only if and when the Spirit of life leaves us. At the moment Jesus died, his body was indeed lifeless; and yet he was gloriously alive, because the Spirit of life, God the Holy Spirit, was still and for ever his Spirit, his life.

And so for Eileen. Indeed, there is much to mourn, as there was much to mourn on Calvary. We shall have to wait for "the resurrection at the last day" (Jn 11:24) before we see the smile light up Eileen's eyes again, before we feel the gentle pressure of her touch. And that is sad, no matter how profound our faith. But the thrilling truth remains: Eileen is alive! Alive with the life of Christ, because even in death the Holy Spirit never left her. More alive than she ever was before, because every tear is past, every malignant growth, every infirmity of our fragile humanity. In the presence of God, there is only God, there is only love. And you know who was utterly convinced of this? Yes...Eileen.

And we who remain, what of us? We have our memories, of course, and they are precious. Like Mary in Bethlehem—and after Calvary—we can "[keep] all these things, pondering them in [our] heart" (Lk 2:19). But there is more, much more. Eileen is not merely a memory; she is part of us, part and parcel of each one of us. She is inescapably built into our lives. How? I cannot speak for you, only for myself. Who and what I am, Eileen has helped immeasurably to shape. Her courage and her laughter, her Christlike compassion and her limitless love, these have seeped into my blood. Because of Eileen, I am not only more Christian; I am more human. Can any of you say less?

Mary Ann and Pierce, Joe and Peter and Stephen, Pierce and Kathy and Anne and John, and all of you who held and hold Eileen so dear, one final word that perhaps sums up all I have said: For the way she lived, Eileen is alive with God. By the way we live, let us keep Eileen alive in ourselves.

> Our Lady's Chapel
> Gonzaga High School
> October 10, 1996

NOTES

Homily 1

1. On the imminence of the Parousia, Paul's thinking underwent some development; see Joseph A. Fitzmyer, S.J., *Paul and His Theology: A Brief Sketch* (2nd ed.; Englewood Cliffs, N.J.: Prentice-Hall, 1989) 46–49.
2. Hilary of Poitiers, *Commentary on Matthew* 2.5 (Patrologia latina 9, 927).
3. Cyril of Alexandria, *Commentary on John* 1.9 (ed. Pusey 1, 141).
4. So E. Mersch, *The Whole Christ: The Historical Development of the Doctrine of the Mystical Body in Scripture and Tradition* (London, 1949) 273.
5. For a summary of explanations, see my chapter "The Body of Christ: Patristic Insights," in *The Church as the Body of Christ*, ed. Robert S. Pelton (Notre Dame, Ind.: University of Notre Dame, 1963) 69–101, at 73–74.
6. I am aware that Paul is speaking in the context of reconciliation between Jew and Gentile; I am extending his meaning, but not, I believe, without justification.
7. This homily was delivered at a Vesper service at the Washington Theological Union.
8. Augustine, *Sermon 272* (Patrologia latina 38, 1247–48).
9. Title of a powerful film dealing with capital punishment.

Homily 2

1. This homily was preached during the retreat/workshop Preaching the Just Word for priests of the Archdiocese of Baltimore, March 5–10, 1995.

2. Hugh Sidey, "Where's His Wheelchair?" *Time* 145, no. 9 (March 6, 1995) 105.

3. Ibid. The information and quotations that follow are taken from the same page.

4. Roland J. Faley, T.O.R., "Leviticus," in *The New Jerome Biblical Commentary,* ed. Raymond E. Brown, S.S., Joseph A. Fitzmyer, S.J., and Roland E. Murphy, O.Carm. (Englewood Cliffs, N.J.: Prentice-Hall, 1990) 4:38, p. 73.

5. Pertinent here is the observation of Benedict T. Viviano, O.P., "The Gospel according to Matthew," *NJBC* (n. 4 above) 42:133, p. 666: "The commandment [as cited by Jesus, Mt 22:39] includes a right form of self-love."

6. The only other OT reference to love of self occurs in Proverbs 19:8a, "To get wisdom is to love oneself," which John McKenzie paraphrases as "he who acquires wisdom takes good care of himself" (*Dictionary of the Bible* [New York: Macmillan, 1965] 520).

7. McKenzie, ibid.

8. See, e.g., Daniel J. Harrington, S.J., *The Gospel of Matthew* (Sacra pagina 1; Collegeville, Minn.: Liturgical, 1991) 358–60.

9. John P. Meier, *Matthew* (New Testament Message 3; Collegeville, Minn.: Liturgical, 1990) 302. See also ibid. 304: "The stunning universalism of this revelation must not be blunted by restricting 'the least of my brethren' to Christians, to poor or insignificant Christians, or to Christian missionaries. The phrases used in such passages as 10:42 ('little ones'...'because he is a disciple') and 18:6 ('these little ones who believe in me') are different, and the context in such places is clearly ecclesiastical; they lack the sweeping universalism of this scene."

10. John R. Donahue, S.J., "The 'Parable' of the Sheep and the Goats: A Challenge to Christian Ethics," *Theological Studies* 47 (1986) 3–31, at 30.

11. For details of the reactions and an intelligent appraisal of the various criticisms, see John Langan, S.J., "The Pastoral on the Economy: From Drafts to Policy," *Theological Studies* 48 (1987) 135–56.

Homily 3

1. The traditional site; but note the observation of Benedict T. Viviano, O.P.: "*a high mountain:* A mountain symbolic of revelation, a kind of Galilean Sinai, perhaps then Carmel rather than the traditional Tabor or the visually appropriate Hermon, though no localization is necessary" ("The Gospel according to Matthew," *The New Jerome Biblical Commentary,* ed. Raymond E. Brown, S.S., Joseph A. Fitzmyer, S.J., and Roland E. Murphy, O.Carm. [Englewood Cliffs, N.J.: Prentice-Hall, 1990] 42:107, p. 660).

2. Daniel J. Harrington, S.J., *The Gospel of Matthew* (Sacra pagina 1; Collegeville, Minn.: Liturgical, 1991) 255.
3. For illuminating details see Raymond E. Brown, S.S., "Three Gospel Stories That Should Change Your Life," *St. Anthony Messenger* 103, no. 10 (March 1996) 29–34.
4. Ibid. 32.
5. Ibid. 33; italics in text.

Homily 4

1. See my collection *Speak the Word with Boldness: Homilies for Risen Christians* (New York/Mahwah: Paulist, 1994) 25–28.
2. Ibid. 27.
3. This homily was delivered to priests of the Archdiocese of St. Louis, Missouri, during a retreat/workshop in my project Preaching the Just Word.
4. From *The State of America's Children Yearbook* (Washington, D.C.: Children's Defense Fund, 1995) [108].
5. Quoted ibid. 3.
6. Marian Wright Edelman, ibid. 4–5; emphasis mine.

Homily 5

1. Vatican II, Constitution on the Sacred Liturgy, no. 7.
2. See Joseph A. Fitzmyer, S.J., *The Gospel according to Luke (X–XXIV)* (Garden City, N.Y.: Doubleday, 1985) 1559, 1568.
3. Thomas Aquinas, *Sum. theol.* 3, q. 35, a. 2, ad 1m. I have been helped in this area over the past three decades by a highly useful chapter, "The Resurrection: History and Confession," in Avery Dulles' *Apologetics and the Biblical Christ* (Woodstock Papers 6; Westminster, Md.: Newman, 1963) 45–60.
4. See *Time* 147, no. 15 (April 8, 1996).
5. Lest I seem to be depreciating the custom of egg rolling, I am aware that this age-old, originally Egyptian folk custom (part of a spring ceremony) is based upon use of the egg as a symbol of life; but I suspect that the symbolism is rarely recognized or mentioned in our culture.
6. I am aware that this exclamation is recorded as uttered by "the Eleven and their companions" to whom Cleopas and friend returned in Jerusalem (vv. 33–34); but it is likewise clear that the two from Emmaus uttered substantially the same declaration (v. 35).

Homily 6

1. Tim Unsworth, "This Is a Messy Church of Varieties and Quirks," *National Catholic Reporter* 32, no. 26 (April 26, 1996) 13.
2. For arguments against and for Petrine authorship, see William J. Dalton, S.J., "The First Epistle of Peter," *The New Jerome Biblical Commentary,* ed. Raymond E. Brown, S.S., Joseph A. Fitzmyer, S.J., and Roland E. Murphy, O.Carm. (Englewood Cliffs, N.J.: Prentice-Hall, 1990) 57:2, p. 903.
3. Note that Dalton, ibid., prefers to take this phrase as two nouns, "a royal house, a body of priests," rather than as a noun with an adjective.
4. Or "let yourselves be built."
5. Leo I, *Sermon 1 on Christmas.*

Homily 7

1. For this interpretation see Raymond E. Brown, S.S., *The Gospel according to John (xiii–xxi)* (Garden City, N.Y.: Doubleday, 1970) 727.
2. Here it is important to note that this homily was delivered during the Preaching the Just Word retreat/workshop for priests of the Archdiocese of Montreal at Manoir d'Youville in Quebec.
3. Jerome, *In die dominica Paschae* 52–54 (Corpus christianorum, series latina 78.550). For illuminating biblical and theological information on the Ascension, important for preachers, I am deeply indebted to Joseph A. Fitzmyer, S.J., "The Ascension of Christ and Pentecost," *Theological Studies* 45 (1984) 409–40.
4. Fitzmyer, ibid. 425.
5. On the punctuation of vv. 37–38, see Brown, *John* (n. 1 above) 320–21. Most of the Eastern Church Fathers and a number of modern commentators translate as follows: "If anyone thirst, let him come to me and drink. He who believes in me (as the Scripture says), 'From within him shall flow rivers of living water.'" Such a translation makes the believer, not Jesus, the source of the water.
6. Brown, *John* (n. 1 above) 732–33, has rich suggestions on the meaning of the Greek word *thlipsis* (suffering, affliction, persecution) in v. 33.
7. See ibid. 733.
8. Ibid. 653.
9. Reference to *Mass Appeal.*

Homily 8

1. I am aware that the three astrologers from the east followed a star; but the call in that instance was not explicitly to "follow" Jesus; after all, they

did return home after their Christmas visit. I am also aware that our Lady is often perceived as the first Christian disciple, but her call did not come precisely from Jesus.

2. Léon-Joseph Suenens, *Coresponsibility in the Church* (New York: Herder and Herder, 1968) 31.

3. Second Vatican Council, Decree on the Apostolate of the Laity, no. 5.

Homily 9

1. This homily was delivered during a retreat/workshop, Preaching the Just Word, for priests and deacons of the Diocese of Santa Rosa, California.

2. Here I have profited from the exegesis of Heb 9:11–28 by Myles M. Bourke, "The Epistle to the Hebrews," in *The New Jerome Biblical Commentary*, ed. Raymond E. Brown, S.S., Joseph A. Fitzmyer, S.J., and Roland E. Murphy, O.Carm. (Englewood Cliffs, N.J.: Prentice-Hall, 1990) 60:51–56, pp. 936–38.

3. For the Semitic use of "many" meaning "all," see J. Jeremias, *"Polloi,"* in *Theological Dictionary of the New Testament*, ed. G. Kittel and G. Friedrich (Grand Rapids, Mich., 1964–76) 6.536–45.

4. An interesting sidelight here: When the Roman Canon speaks of the *oblatio rationabilis*, usually translated "reasonable sacrifice," it is quite likely that *rationabilis* is an effort to translate *logikos*. *Logikos* can indeed mean "reasonable," but in the Eucharistic context I find that "of the Logos" makes much better sense. See William J. Lallou, *The* Quam oblationem *of the Roman Canon* (Washington, D.C.: Catholic University of America, 1943).

5. For a succinct presentation of the pertinent data, see the booklet by Richard G. Brown, *"The Griefs and Anxieties of This Age..."*: Facts and Figures* (3rd ed.; Washington, D.C.: Woodstock Theological Center, 1994).

Homily 10

1. For factual data I am much indebted to Alexander A. Di Lella, O.F.M., "Sirach," *The New Jerome Biblical Commentary*, ed. Raymond E. Brown, S.S., Joseph A. Fitzmyer, S.J., and Roland E. Murphy, O.Carm. (Englewood Cliffs, N.J.: Prentice-Hall, 1990) 32:1–83, pp. 496–509.

2. Ben Sira is clearly not concerned with the theological question whether one can keep the commandments without divine grace. An important question indeed, but not Ben Sira's concern. His main point is, no one is ever compelled to sin against his will.

3. Jerome Murphy-O'Connor, O.P., "The First Letter to the Corinthians," *The New Jerome Biblical Commentary* (n. 1 above) 49:19, p. 602.

4. "Though the rule sounds barbarous today, its original intention was

humanitarian, to limit revenge (only *one* eye for one eye, not two or three) to an exact reciprocity. When first introduced, it constituted genuine moral progress. By the time of Jesus the rabbis already felt it too harsh and began the process of commuting the penalty to fines, but the principle of corresponding restitution remained dominant in legal thinking" (Benedict T. Viviano, O.P., "The Gospel according to Matthew," *The New Jerome Biblical Commentary* [n. 1 above] 42:34, p. 643).

5. I have borrowed this story from an article by Dennis Burke, "Why Priests Can't Preach: It's All in the Preparation," *Commonweal* 122, no. 7 (April 7, 1995) 15–17, at 17.

Homily 11

1. This homily was addressed to the Jesuits of St. Aloysius Gonzaga, Washington, D.C., at their weekly community liturgy.
2. I have borrowed this parable from Megan McKenna, *Parables: The Arrows of God* (Maryknoll, N.Y.: Orbis, 1994) 53–54. I have presumed to alter the order of words in one of the sentences.

Homily 12

1. From the introduction to Tobit in *The Oxford Annotated Bible with the Apocrypha: Revised Standard Version* [63].
2. Ibid.
3. The occasion was the five-day retreat/workshop for the priests of the Diocese of Greensburg, Pennsylvania, within my project Preaching the Just Word, an effort to improve the preaching of justice issues across the country.
4. Decree on the Ministry and Life of Priests, no. 4.

Homily 13

1. This homily was delivered during my project Preaching the Just Word, with the participants mostly (but not exclusively) Jesuits of the New York Province.
2. John Courtney Murray, "The Danger of the Vows," *Woodstock Letters* 96 (1967) 421–27. The text of this conference (Feb. 21, 1947) was reconstructed after Fr. Murray's death (1967) from two of his personal copies, one with his own handwritten emendations, together with a number of slightly varying mimeographed copies. Years after its delivery, he was

reluctant to publish the conference without updating it in the spirit of Vatican II; death robbed him of the opportunity.

3. Infirmary of the New York Province.

4. Vatican II, Constitution on the Church in the Modern World, no. 35.

5. John Paul II, *Sollicitudo rei socialis,* no. 28 (tr. United States Catholic Conference 48–50).

6. Murray, "Danger" 427.

7. "Jesuits and the Situation of Women in Church and Civil Society," no. 9 (tr. *Origins* 24 [1995] 741).

8. John Paul II, *Mulieris dignitatem (On Woman's Dignity and Vocation)* IV, 9 (tr. *Origins* 18 [1988] 268).

9. Ibid. IV, 10 (*Origins* 269).

10. Murray, "Danger" 427.

11. Ibid.

12. John Courtney Murray, S.J., "Freedom, Authority, Community," *America* 115 (1966) 734–41, at 735.

13. Quotation from Vatican II, Declaration on Religious Freedom, no. 1.

14. William J. O'Malley, S.J., "The Goldilocks Method," *America* 165 (1991) 334–39, at 336.

Homily 14

1. The Gospel passage as proclaimed in Trinity Episcopal Church, Upperville, Va., for the Fourth Sunday after Pentecost (in the Roman liturgy, the 12th Sunday in Ordinary Time) comprised verses 16–33 of Mt 10 (in the Roman liturgy, verses 26–33). My homily is based on the longer text.

2. See Daniel J. Harrington, S.J., *The Gospel of Matthew* (Collegeville, Minn.: Liturgical, 1991) 140.

3. On this mission see Harrington, ibid. 135–44; John P. Meier, *Matthew* (Collegeville, Minn.: Liturgical, 1990) 100–109.

4. Bob Herbert, "Nike's Pyramid Scheme," *New York Times,* June 10, 1996, A17.

5. See *New York Times,* June 20, 1996, 1.

6. Quoted by Paul Giurlanda, "What about Our Church's Children?" *America* 168, no. 16 (May 8, 1991) 12–14, at 12.

7. "Jesuits and the Situation of Women in Church and Civil Society," *Origins* 24, no. 43 (April 13, 1995) 741.

Homily 15

1. The occasion for this homily was my retreat/workshop Preaching the Just Word, for priests of the Archdiocese of Melbourne, Australia, and adjoining dioceses.

2. Priest of the Archdiocese of Washington and co-ordinator of the project Preaching the Just Word.
3. Clare Richards, "The Clash in the Classroom," *Tablet* 248, no. 8076 (May 27, 1995) 668–69.
4. Ibid. 668.
5. Ibid.
6. Ibid.
7. Ibid. 669.
8. Ibid.
9. Ibid.
10. Ibid.
11. Ibid.
12. Quoted from Peter Hastings, "Education for Adults," *Tablet* 248, no. 8076 (May 27, 1995) 670.
13. See Richard A. McCormick, "The Gospel of Life," *America* 172, no. 15 (April 29, 1995) 10–17.
14. Vatican II, Pastoral Constitution on the Church in the Modern World, no. 62.

Homily 16

1. This homily was delivered during my retreat/workshop Preaching the Just Word, for priests and laity of the Archdiocese of Melbourne, Australia, and adjoining dioceses.
2. For this interpretation I am indebted to Richard J. Clifford, S.J., "Genesis," *The New Jerome Biblical Commentary*, ed. Raymond E. Brown, S.S., Joseph A. Fitzmyer, S.J., and Roland E. Murphy, O.Carm. (Englewood Cliffs, N.J.: Prentice-Hall, 1990) 2:29, p. 23.
3. Ibid.
4. Quoted from Clare Richards, "The Clash in the Classroom," *Tablet* 248, no. 8076 (May 27, 1995) 668–69, at 668.

Homily 17

1. Dietrich Bonhoeffer, *Creation and Fall: A Theological Interpretation of Genesis 1–3* (London: SCM, 1959) 38.
2. See ibid.
3. This homily was preached within my project Preaching the Just Word, sponsored by the Diocese of Buffalo, New York, for ordained priests, permanent deacons, and laity of that diocese and other dioceses.
4. John R. Donahue, S.J., *What Does the Lord Require? A Bibliographical Essay on the Bible and Social Justice* (Studies in the Spirituality of Jesuits 25/2; St. Louis, Mo.: Seminar on Jesuit Spirituality, 1993) 14.

5. See ibid. 18, quoting political theorist Michael Walzer, *Exodus and Revolution* (New York: Basic Books, 1985) 53.

6. Norbert Lohfink's term.

7. Donahue 19.

8. Paul D. Hanson, *The People Called: The Growth of Community in the Bible* (San Francisco: Harper and Row, 1986) 47.

9. Theodore Ross, "The Personal Synthesis of Liturgy and Justice," in *Living No Longer for Ourselves: Liturgy and Justice in the Nineties,* ed. Kathleen Hughes and Mark R. Francis (Collegeville, Minn.: Liturgical, 1991) 36–51, at 27–28.

10. Elizabeth Barrett Browning, "The Cry of the Children," in *Complete Poetical Works of Elizabeth Barrett Browning* 1 (New York: Thomas Nelson, n.d.) 356–61, at 356.

Homily 18

1. So Benedict T. Viviano, O.P., "The Gospel according to Matthew," *The New Jerome Biblical Commentary,* ed. Raymond E. Brown, S.S., Joseph A. Fitzmyer, S.J., and Roland E. Murphy, O.Carm. (Englewood Cliffs, N.J.: Prentice-Hall, 1990) 42:112, p. 661. He adds: "To humble oneself is to set a self-imposed limit; self-regulation checks the tendency to arrogance built into positions of authority" (ibid.).

2. See William F. Arndt and F. Wilbur Gingrich, *A Greek-English Lexicon of the New Testament and Other Early Christian Literature* (4th ed.; Chicago: University of Chicago, 1952) under *mikros* 1c.

3. See the examples from the Essene community at Qumran provided by Daniel J. Harrington, S.J., *The Gospel of Matthew* (Sacra pagina 1; Collegeville, Minn.: Liturgical, 1991) 266.

4. Ibid.

5. Léon-Joseph Suenens, *Coresponsibility in the Church* (New York: Herder and Herder, 1968) 31.

6. This homily was delivered during the retreat/workshop Preaching the Just Word, for priests and permanent deacons of the Diocese of Gaylord, Michigan.

7. For such insights and others, see Yves Congar, O.P., "Sacramental Worship and Preaching," in *The Renewal of Preaching: Theory and Practice* (Concilium 33; New York: Paulist, 1968) 51–63.

8. Ibid. 60.

Homily 19

1. For detailed data see Arloc Sherman, *Wasting America's Future: The Children's Defense Fund Report on the Costs of Child Poverty* (Boston: Beacon, 1994).

2. "Special Report: Welfare Reform," *CDF Reports* 16, no. 4 (March 1995) 5. The Personal Responsibility Act, already passed by the House, would eliminate existing federal welfare programs—in which the federal government funnels money to the states on an as-needed basis—and replace them with block grants. The amount of those block grants would be cut, with the full effect of those budget cuts felt beginning in 2000. States would have the authority to administer the block grants as they chose.

3. See Tracy Thompson, "Report Assails House Welfare Plan," *Washington Post,* March 29, 1995, D4.

4. *CDF Reports* 16, no. 4 (March 1995) 1.

5. I take this example from *CDF Reports* (n. 4 above) 1–2.

Homily 20

1. Quoted from *Mishna 'Abot* 3.2 by Benedict T. Viviano, O.P., "The Gospel according to Matthew," *The New Jerome Biblical Commentary,* ed. Raymond E. Brown, S.S., Joseph A. Fitzmyer, S.J., and Roland E. Murphy, O.Carm. (Englewood Cliffs, N.J.: Prentice-Hall, 1990) 42:131, p. 665.

2. Viviano, ibid., states that "This odd idiom [the last phrase] expresses a basic aspect of the biblical idea of justice, an impartiality that refuses to take a bribe and tilts in favor of the poorer litigant. This is the biblical basis for the preferential option for the poor." Viviano also refers to Lohse's article *euprosopeo* in the *Theological Dictionary of the New Testament,* ed. G. Kittel and G. Friedrich, 6.779–80, which I have also found useful. See the *NRSV* translation, "You do not regard people with partiality."

3. Published as "Say No to This Welfare 'Reform,'" *Washington Post,* Nov. 3, 1995, A23.

4. See *Wall Street Journal,* Feb. 1, 1996, 1.

Homily 21

1. This homily was preached during a Preaching the Just Word retreat/workshop for priests and some laity of the Diocese of Lafayette, Louisiana.

2. Quoted from Thomas B. Edsall, "GOP Battler Atwater Dies at 40," *Washington Post,* March 30, 1991, 1 and 7.

3. John Paul II, encyclical *Sollicitudo rei socialis (On Social Concern),* Dec. 30, 1987, no. 28 (tr. USCC, publication no. 205–5 [n.d.], p. 49).

4. *Washington Post,* Oct. 14, 1996, A26.

5. Vatican II, Decree on the Ministry and Life of Priests, no. 4. Since Latin does not have a definite or indefinite article, it is not clear whether the

council fathers intended proclamation of the gospel to be "the" or "a" primary duty; in either case, proclamation should hold a high priority in a priest's life. Also, proclamation of the gospel is indeed a broader concept than pulpit or liturgical preaching; but such preaching surely is a key element in gospel proclamation.

6. "Second Isaiah was announcing the Consolation of Zion to various groups in the Jerusalem community. Luke includes four of them in his quotation," actually a conflation of Isa 61:1a,b,d; 58:6d; 61:2a (Joseph A. Fitzmyer, S.J., *The Gospel according to Luke (I–IX)* [Garden City, N.Y.: Doubleday, 1981] 532).

Homily 22

1. For background and commentary on Malachi and his situation, see Aelred Cody, O.S.B., "Haggai, Zechariah, Malachi," *The New Jerome Biblical Commentary,* ed. Raymond E. Brown, S.S., Joseph A. Fitzmyer, S.J., and Roland E. Murphy, O.Carm. (Englewood Cliffs, N.J.: Prentice-Hall, 1990) 22:51–62, pp. 359–61.
2. *Coresponsibility in the Church* (New York: Herder and Herder, 1968) 31.
3. Janice G. Hutchinson, "Priority One for the District," *Washington Post,* October 20, 1996, C8. The author is working from a recent federal report, "Kids Count," an annual national survey of the social and economic conditions of children. The data and quotation in the following several paragraphs stem from the same article.
4. Data from Kentucky "Kids Count," graciously supplied by the Office of Catholic Charities of the Archdiocese of Louisville.
5. The latest year for which accurate county poverty data are available.

Homily 23

1. See verse 3 of this chapter.
2. Here I have profited from Joseph A. Fitzmyer, S.J., *The Gospel according to Luke (X–XXIV)* (Garden City, N.Y.: Doubleday, 1985) 1043–48, specifically 1045.
3. Ibid. 1045.
4. This homily was preached to priests, permanent deacons, and some religious sisters and laity of the Archdiocese of Louisville, Kentucky, on the first full day of a Preaching the Just Word retreat/workshop.
5. See in this collection my homily "Do I Hear the Children Crying?" for the 31st Sunday in Ordinary Time (A).
6. Data from Kentucky "Kids Count," graciously supplied by the Office of Catholic Charities of the Archdiocese of Louisville.

Homily 24

1. This homily was preached to priests of the Archdiocese of Chicago during the Woodstock Theological Center retreat/workshop Preaching the Just Word.
2. John L. McKenzie, S.J., "Faith," in McKenzie, *Dictionary of the Bible* (New York: Macmillan, 1965) 267–71, at 267.
3. Ibid. 268.
4. For an analysis of the "diverse descriptions" of faith in Luke's Gospel and Acts, see Joseph A. Fitzmyer, S.J., *The Gospel according to Luke (I–IX)* (Garden City, N.Y.: Doubleday, 1981) 235–37. A homily tends, of necessity, to simplify.

Homily 25

1. Here I am indebted to the succinct article by John L. McKenzie, "Widow," in his *Dictionary of the Bible* (New York: Macmillan, 1965) 927.
2. Ibid.
3. See Joseph A. Fitzmyer, S.J., *The Gospel according to Luke (X–XXIV)* (Garden City, N.Y.: Doubleday, 1985) 1322.
4. Ibid. 1321.
5. See ibid. 1318 for six possible interpretations of the phrase "devour the houses of widows."
6. A. G. Wright, "The Widow's Mites: Praise or Lament?—A Matter of Context," *Catholic Biblical Quarterly* 44 (1982) 256–65, at 262, as quoted by Fitzmyer (n. 3 above) 1321.
7. See the article, primarily concerned with Latin America, by John F. Talbot, S.J., "Who Evangelizes Whom? The Poor Evangelizers," *Review for Religious,* November-December 1993, 893–97.
8. From the Puebla conference's "Preferential Option for the Poor" (no. 11), quoted by Talbot (n. 7 above) 894.
9. Quoted by Talbot (ibid. 896) from Sobrino's *Resurrección de la verdadera Iglesia* 137–38.
10. Henri J. M. Nouwen and Walter J. Gaffney, *Aging* (Garden City, N.Y.: Doubleday Image Books, 1976) 101 and 102.
11. John Paul II, 1987 encyclical On *Social Concern,* no. 36 (tr. from United States Catholic Conference, Washington, D.C., Publication no. 205–5, p. 68).
12. John Paul II, 1984 apostolic exhortation *Reconciliation and Repentance* (this text tr. USCC Publication no. 205–5 [n. 11 above] footnote 65).
13. Ibid.; italics in text.
14. John Paul II, *On Social Concern,* no. 37 (tr. USCC 71).

Homily 26

1. I have profited from the treatment of Matthew's account of the baptism by Daniel J. Harrington, S.J., *The Gospel of Matthew* (Sacra pagina 1; Collegeville, Minn.: Liturgical, 1991) 61–65; John P. Meier, *Matthew* (New Testament Message 3; Collegeville, Minn.: Liturgical, 1990) 26–28; and Benedict T. Viviano, O.P., "The Gospel according to Matthew," *The New Jerome Biblical Commentary,* ed. Raymond E. Brown, S.S., Joseph A. Fitzmyer, S.J., and Roland E. Murphy, O.Carm. (Englewood Cliffs, N.J.: Prentice-Hall, 1990) 42:18, pp. 637–38.
2. Harrington, *The Gospel of Matthew* 63.
3. See Isa 42:1–4; 49:1–7; 50:4–11; 52:13–53:12.
4. This homily was delivered on the first full day of my project Preaching the Just Word, this time for priests and other preachers within the Diocese of Rochester, New York, including the Colgate Divinity School.
5. Joseph A. Fitzmyer, S.J., *The Gospel according to Luke (I–IX)* (Garden City, N.Y.: Doubleday, 1981) 834.

Homily 27

1. The Greek phrase *eis telos* can mean either (or perhaps both here) "utterly, completely, to perfection" or "to the end of life," i.e. to the death. See Raymond E. Brown, S.S., *The Gospel according to John (xiii–xxi)* (Garden City, N.Y.: Doubleday, 1970) 550.
2. On this verse see Joseph A. Fitzmyer, *The Gospel according to Luke (X–XXIV)* (Garden City, N.Y.: Doubleday, 1985) 1410.
3. I know this incident from "A Reprint from the 'Directors' Service' of the Apostleship of Prayer," Rome, January 1980, 13–14.
4. For a more complete treatment of the foot-washing, e.g., the interpretation that sees in it a prophetic action symbolic of Jesus' death, see Raymond E. Brown, S.S., *The Gospel according to John (xiii–xxi)* (Garden City, N.Y.: Doubleday, 1970) 563–72. "The simplest explanation of the foot-washing...remains that Jesus performed this servile work to prophesy symbolically that he was about to be humiliated in death" (568). This is not to deny plausibility to the interpretation that focuses on humility. But, "Even taken simply as an example of humility, the footwashing does not lose its association with the death of Jesus; the general context would indicate this" (569).
5. See ibid. 564–65.
6. Gerard Manley Hopkins, poem "Adoro te supplex, latens deitas," in *The Poems of Gerard Manley Hopkins,* ed. W. H. Gardner and N. H. MacKenzie (4th ed.; New York: Oxford University, 1970) 211.
7. Mary Rose McGeady, *God's Lost Children: Letters from Covenant House* (New York: Covenant House, 1991) Dedication.

8. See Arloc Sherman, *Wasting America's Future: The Children's Defense Fund Report on the Costs of Child Poverty* (Boston: Beacon, 1994) 86.

Homily 28

1. This homily was preached at the annual meeting of the Loyola Foundation, a charitable trust that supports Catholic projects, especially missionaries.
2. Gerard Manley Hopkins, "S. Thomae Aquinatis Rhythmus ad SS. Sacramentum," in W. H. Gardner and N. H. MacKenzie, eds., *The Poems of Gerard Manley Hopkins* (4th ed.; New York: Oxford University, 1970) 211.
3. This succinct sentence should not be interpreted as implying that the Church is not the (Mystical) Body of Christ. It is indeed, but the demands of this homily call for a simpler way of speaking.
4. See, e.g., Robert N. Bellah, "Religion & Power in America Today," *Commonweal* 109, no. 21 (Dec. 3, 1982) 650-55.
5. See *Time* 128, no. 10 (Sept. 8, 1986) 57; the institution was Harvard.
6. Joseph Nocera, "The Ga-Ga Years: Money Love, Market Lust, and the Seducing of America," *Esquire,* February 1988, 79-90, at 80.
7. The expression is taken from the title of Bonnie Angelo's interview with Pulitzer Prize winner Toni Morrison, *Time* 133, no. 21 (May 22, 1989) 120-22, at 120.
8. Frederick Buechner, *The Magnificent Defeat* (New York: Seabury, 1966) 23. I have used this material in a baccalaureate homily at Boston College, "Poet, Lunatic, Lover," published in my collection *Grace on Crutches: Homilies for Fellow Travelers* (New York/Mahwah: Paulist, 1986) 179-84, at 184.

Homily 29

1. I have not thought it advantageous, for the purposes of this homily, to discuss the disputed question of Jesus' "brothers" and "sisters" (vv. 55-56). The terms could refer to half brothers and half sisters, or to kin in general. See Benedict T. Viviano, "The Gospel according to Matthew," *The New Jerome Biblical Commentary,* ed. Raymond E. Brown, S.S., Joseph A. Fitzmyer, S.J., and Roland E. Murphy, O.Carm. (Englewood Cliffs, N.J.: Prentice-Hall, 1990) 42:94, p. 657, with references.
2. It is possible that here the Greek word *tekton* might mean mason rather than carpenter.
3. See Vatican II, Pastoral Constitution on the Church in the Modern World, nos. 33-35; also John Paul II, encyclical *Laborem exercens (On Human Work),* Sept. 14, 1981, nos. 24 ff.

4. See Viviano, "The Gospel according to Matthew" (n. 1 above) 42:11, p. 635.
5. A reference to the catastrophic bombing of a federal building that took 168 lives.
6. This homily was preached to priests of the Archdiocese of Hartford, Connecticut, within my retreat/workshop Preaching the Just Word.
7. See Robert J. Karris, O.F.M., "The Gospel according to Luke," *NJBC* (n. 1 above) 43:153, p. 709: "The point is not that disciples are not worth anything in themselves or in their work for the Lord. The fact that disciples have done their duty does not empower them to lay a claim upon God that they are worthy of God's graciousness. That graciousness is and remains sheer gift." For discussion of the possible senses of the adjective *achreios,* see Joseph A. Fitzmyer, S.J., *The Gospel according to Luke (X–XXIV)* (Garden City, N.Y.: Doubleday, 1985) 1147.
8. See Frederick Buechner, *The Hungering Dark* (New York: Seabury, 1969) 45–46.
9. I am citing data from the findings of the Advisory Board as reported in the *St. Louis Post-Dispatch,* April 27, 1995, 3A.

Homily 30

1. I ask this question because this homily was preached at the beginning of a Preaching the Just Word retreat/workshop for priests and permanent deacons of the Diocese of Crookston, Minn., June 2–7, 1996.
2. See J. F. Faupel, "Lwanga, Charles, St.," *New Catholic Encyclopedia* 8 (1967) 1106; id., "Uganda, Martyrs of," ibid. 14 (1967) 363.
3. See J. F. Faufel, "Uganda," *New Catholic Encyclopedia* 14 (1967) 362; Lawrence Njoroge, "Africa, Catholicism in," *The HarperCollins Encyclopedia of Catholicism,* ed. Richard P. McBrien (San Francisco: Harper, 1995) 19–22, at 22.
4. Quoted by Njoroge, ibid.
5. From an integral excerpt published in *Origins* 22, no. 36 (Feb. 18, 1993) 613–15 (in the margins). Besides the family, other pastoral concerns included the liturgy and the roles of catechists.
6. See John Paul II, "Africa's Second Birth of Freedom," ibid. 615–16.
7. All quotations from John Paul II, "Africa's AIDS Crisis," ibid. 613–14, at 614.

Homily 31

1. Desmond Reid, S.J., "St. Aloysius Gonzaga, Patron of Youth," in Robert Nash, S.J., ed., *Jesuits: Biographical Essays* (Westminster, Md.: Newman, 1956) 25–35, at 26.
2. This homily was delivered as part of a Preaching Day preceding but

intimately linked with the 1995 national conference of the National Council for Catholic Evangelization, held at the Marriott Hotel in Oklahoma City.

3. For details on this first point, see my essay "Aloysius Gonzaga: Role Model for Today's Young?" in Clifford Stevens and William Hart McNichols, eds., *Aloysius* (Huntington, Ind.: Our Sunday Visitor, 1993) 23–35, esp. 26 ff.

4. William Hart McNichols, S.J., "Saint Aloysius: Patron of Youth," in *Aloysius* (n. 3 above) 37–41, at 39.

5. See ibid. 39.

6. Translation as in C. C. Martindale, S.J., *The Vocation of Aloysius Gonzaga* (New York: Sheed and Ward, 1945) 128–29.

7. Ibid. 217.

8. On this see P. Molinari, S.J., "St. Aloysius Gonzaga," in *Companions of Jesus: Spiritual Profiles of the Jesuit Saints and Beati* (2nd ed.; Rome: Gregorian University, 1984) 73.

9. The remark stems from Scipio Gonzaga, one of the cardinals who frequented his bedside during his last days; quoted in Martindale, *Vocation* (n. 6 above) 222.

10. My translations in what follows are taken from *The Pope Speaks* 21, no. 1 (spring 1976) 1–51.

11. *Evangelization in the Modern World,* no. 27 (*The Pope Speaks* 16).

12. Ibid., nos. 29, 34, and 36 (*The Pope Speaks* 17, 19, and 20).

13. See Richard C. Hermes, S.J., "On Understanding the Saints," in *Aloysius* (n. 3 above) 67–83, at 77.

14. See ibid. 78.

Homily 32

1. This homily was delivered to priests of the Diocese of Fort Worth, Texas, during a Preaching the Just Word retreat/workshop.

2. James Brodrick, S.J., *Robert Bellarmine: Saint and Scholar* (London: Burns & Oates, 1961) 52–53. I am deeply indebted to this splendid biography, which "is a condensed and largely rewritten version of a biography of St Robert Bellarmine in two volumes, published in 1928, two years before his canonization" (ibid. ix).

3. The young Gonzaga always signed himself Aluigi or Luigi, never Aloisio or Aloysius; see ibid. 121 n. 1.

4. Ibid. 127.

5. Ibid. 226–28.

6. Ibid. 156.

7. Ibid. 366.

8. Ibid. 416.

9. Classicists will recall Cicero's practice of the rhetorical ploy called *praeteritio* ("passing over"): "I will not speak of the crimes of Catiline, such as...."

10. Here I draw largely from Brodrick, ibid. 163–69.

11. Ibid. 167.

Homily 33

1. One problem is the relationship between sanctity and passion. I preached on this several decades ago; see my sermon "St. Jerome: Sanctity and Passion" in my collection *Saints and Sanctity* (Englewood Cliffs, N.J.: Prentice-Hall, 1965) 49–59. The first part of the present homily reproduces in large measure the factual material on Jerome in that sermon.

2. This homily was preached during a Preaching the Just Word retreat/workshop for priests of the Archdiocese of St. Louis, Missouri.

3. Jerome, *Letter 22*, 30.

4. See ibid. 17.

5. *Letter 52*, 5.

6. *Letter 14*, 3.

7. *Letter 17*, 3.

8. *Letter 45*, 6.

9. Preface to *Commentary on Ezekiel.*

10. *Letter 52*, 11.

11. *Letter 22*, 27.

12. *Letter 22*, 25.

13. *Letter 22*, 7.

14. Quoted by William F. Buckley Jr. in a syndicated column I found in the *Stuart News* (Florida) of April 10, 1993, A17. The judge was Edwin Torres.

Homily 34

1. For a careful English translation of the letters, see James A. Kleist, S.J., *The Epistles of St. Clement of Rome and St. Ignatius of Antioch* (Ancient Christian Writers 1; Westminster, Md.: Newman, 1946; repr. New York/Ramsey, N.J.: Newman, 1978) 60–99.

2. *Letter to the Romans* 4–6 (tr. Kleist, ACW 1 [n. 1 above] 81–83).

3. Ibid. 7.2 (tr. Kleist 92). Kleist notes (136) that the Greek could be translated "My earthly passions have been crucified."

4. Pedro de Rivadeneira, *Vida del bienaventurado Padre Ignacio de Loyola* (2nd ed.; Barcelona: Subirana, 1885) 501–2.

5. Robert Payne, *The Fathers of the Western Church* (New York: Viking, 1951) 30.

6. How many years remained? Scholars disagree. For the problems in dating Paul's letter to the Philippians, see Brendan Byrne, S.J., "The Letter to the Philippians," *The New Jerome Biblical Commentary,* ed. Raymond E. Brown, S.S., Joseph A. Fitzmyer, S.J., and Roland E. Murphy, O.Carm. (Englewood Cliffs, N.J.: Prentice-Hall, 1990) 48:4–10, pp. 791–92.

7. *Letter to the Romans* 5.3 (tr. Kleist 82).

8. *Letter to the Philadelphians* 5.1 (tr. Kleist 86).

9. *Letter to the Romans* 9.1. My translation of *agape* as "community of love" instead of simply "love" has scholarly support.

10. Ibid. 8.2–3 (tr. Kleist 84).

11. This homily was preached at a convocation for priests of the Diocese of Madison, Wisconsin, within my project Preaching the Just Word.

12. *Letter to Polycarp* 1.2–3 (tr. Kleist 96).

Homily 35

1. This homily was delivered to priests of the Archdiocese of Los Angeles as part of my project Preaching the Just Word.

2. See A. M. Melville, "Cabrini, Frances Xavier, St.," *New Catholic Encyclopedia* 2 (1967) 1039; S. Le Dieu, "Missionary Sisters of the Sacred Heart," ibid. 9 (1967) 923. For detailed information see Mary Louise Sullivan, MSC, *Mother Cabrini: "Italian Immigrant of the Century"* (New York: Center for Migration Studies, 1992); also Pietro Di Donato, *Immigrant Saint: The Life of Mother Cabrini* (New York: McGraw-Hill, 1960).

3. The morning presentation that day, by John R. Donahue, S.J., had justice in Scripture for its topic.

4. The inscription is actually a poem, "The New Colossus," by Emma Lazarus.

5. See the statement issued by the California Catholic Conference on Aug. 25, 1994, published in *Origins* 24, no. 16 (Sept. 29, 1994) 279–81. See also the Nov. 24, 1994 statement of then Cardinal–designate William Keeler of Baltimore, president of the National Conference of Catholic Bishops and U.S. Catholic Conference, on behalf of the U.S. bishops during their Washington meeting, ibid. 24, no. 25 (Dec. 1, 1994) 430–31.

6. Ibid. 280.

7. Marian Wright Edelman, "Say No to This Welfare 'Reform,'" *Washington Post,* Nov. 3, 1995, A23.

8. Ibid. The preceding paragraph borrows largely the rhetoric of Ms. Edelman, without quotation marks.

Homily 36

1. For the homily on that occasion, see "This Day I Marry My Best Friend," in my collection *When Christ Meets Christ: Homilies on the Just Word* (New York/Mahwah: Paulist, 1993) 93–97.
2. See W. A. Wallace, "Friendship," *New Catholic Encyclopedia* 6 (1967) 203–5.
3. Kahlil [more accurately, Khalil] Gibran, *The Prophet* (New York: Knopf, 1961) 15.
4. Ibid. 15–16.
5. According to a report from the United Nations Children's Fund; I am using material cited in an article by Gayle Reaves in the *Kansas City Star* for Sept. 26, 1993, A-27 (itself taken from the *Dallas Morning News*).

Homily 37

1. Scholars differ on the meaning Godlikeness had for the human author(s): e.g., sovereignty over the nonhuman; the self-conscious, self-directing vitality that constitutes the sum of personal being; the fact that humanity is male and female. Some would claim that the writer(s) had no definite idea about the content or location of the image.
2. Clearly, Paul is speaking directly to *all* Christians, not expressly to the married. Still, his advice is splendidly pertinent to those Christians who have vowed to live together in a unique intimacy, those whose love is expected to reflect in a singular way the love that binds Christ and his Church.
3. Figures from the Children's Defense Fund, *The State of America's Children Yearbook 1995* (Washington, D.C.: Children's Defense Fund, 1995) 108.
4. Interview in *Parade Magazine,* July 9, 1995, 6.

Homily 38

1. From the introduction to Tobit in *The Oxford Annotated Bible with the Apocrypha: Revised Standard Version,* ed. Herbert G. May and Bruce M. Metzger (New York: Oxford University, 1965) [63].
2. Final Report of the National Commission on Children, *Beyond Rhetoric: A New American Agenda for Children and Families* (Washington, D.C.: National Commission on Children, 1991) 12.
3. In a message (September 1990) to the World Summit for Children, quoted in an editorial by Anthony J. Schulte, O.F.M., "Make Room in the Inn for the World's Children," *St. Anthony Messenger* 98, no. 7 (December 1990) 26.

Homily 39

1. See Evelyn Whitehead and James D. Whitehead, "Christian Marriage," *U.S. Catholic* 47, no. 6 (June 1982) 9.
2. Title of a powerful film.

Homily 40

1. Three renowned athletes in basketball, baseball, and gymnastics respectively.
2. See, e.g., W. Hill, "Isaia," *New Catholic Encyclopedia* 7 (1967) 665–66; and idem, "Isaia, Book of," ibid. 666–71. For the purposes of this homily, I see no reason for distinguishing Proto- , Deutero-, and Trito-Isaiah.
3. See Carroll Stuhlmueller, C.P., "Deutero-Isaiah and Trito-Isaiah," *The New Jerome Biblical Commentary,* ed. Raymond E, Brown, S.S., Joseph A. Fitzmyer, S.J., and Roland E. Murphy, O.Carm. (Englewood Cliffs, N.J.: Prentice-Hall, 1990) 21:11, p. 333.
4. References to the titles of two popular soap operas.
5. See Evelyn Whitehead and James D. Whitehead, "Christian Marriage," *U.S. Catholic* 47, no. 6 (June 1982) 9.

Homily 41

1. This homily was preached at the 45th Annual Assembly of the Greater Dallas (Texas) Community of Churches.
2. See Lawrence Boadt, C.S.P., "Ezekiel," *The New Jerome Biblical Commentary,* ed. Raymond E. Brown, S.S., Joseph A. Fitzmyer, S.J., and Roland E. Murphy, O.Carm. (Englewood Cliffs, N.Y.: Prentice-Hall, 1990) 20:5–6 and 20:35, pp. 306 and 314–15.
3. John Paul II, 1987 encyclical *On Social Concern (Sollicitudo rei socialis),* no. 28 (tr. United States Catholic Conference, Washington, D.C., publication no. 205–5 [n.d.] 48–49; italics in text).
4. Quoted from Thomas B. Edsall, "GOP Battler Atwater Dies at 40," *Washington Post,* March 30, 1991, 1 and 7, at 1.
5. Richard Corliss, "Elegy for Degeneration X," *Time* 146, no. 19 (Nov. 6, 1995) 78.
6. Marian Wright Edelman, "Say No to This Welfare 'Reform,'" *Washington Post,* Nov. 3, 1995, A23.
7. Rome's Congregation for the Doctrine of the Faith, 1986 letter *On the Pastoral Care of Homosexual Persons,* no. 10, par. 1.
8. Ibid.
9. "'I'm Here': An Interview with Andrew Sullivan," *America* 168, no. 16 (May 8, 1993) 5–11, at 10.

10. Ibid. 11.
11. I am following the translation favored by, e.g., Raymond E. Brown, S.S.:
The water flows from Jesus, not from the believer. See his *The Gospel
according to John (i–xii)* (Garden City, N.Y.: Doubleday, 1966) 320–23.

Homily 42

1. This homily was preached to the Jesuit community of St. Aloysius Gonzaga, Washington, D.C., during the Eucharistic liturgy celebrating the
65th anniversary of my entrance into the Society of Jesus, Feb. 11, 1931,
feast of Our Lady of Lourdes.
2. From notes of a lecture on biblical justice, during my project Preaching
the Just Word, by Father Raymond F. Collins, dean of the School of
Religious Studies at the Catholic University of America.

Homily 43

1. This homily was preached at the baptism of Katherine Stephanie
Christin Maria Beerkens, daughter of Frans and Cathleen Beerkens. I
decided, from practical experience, to address my homily to the child;
then it is that adults are more likely to listen with open ears and heart.
2. For details on Paul's "in Christ" and "body of Christ," see Joseph A.
Fitzmyer, S.J., *Paul and His Theology: A Brief Sketch* (2nd ed.; Englewood
Cliffs, N.J.: Prentice-Hall, 1989) 87–93, nos. 114–27.
3. John Paul II, encyclical *On Social Concern* (Dec. 30, 1987) no. 28.

Homily 44

1. John M. Buchanan, "Essentials of Preaching," privately produced for a
Living Pulpit conference on April 27, 1994, at the Chicago Temple—
First United Methodist Church, Chicago.
2. Such was the Residency Placement by States for the Georgetown University School of Medicine class of 1996. In double figures were DC
(32), California (24), Massachusetts (16), Illinois (13), New York (13),
Maryland (10), out of a class of 183.
3. Richard Selzer, *Mortal Lessons: Notes on the Art of Surgery* (New York:
Simon and Schuster. 1976) 94.
4. Bernie S. Siegel, M.D., *Love, Medicine & Miracles* (New York: Harper &
Row, 1988) 181.
5. Ibid. xii.

Homily 45

1. John R. Donahue, "Biblical Perspectives on Justice," in *The Faith That Does Justice: Examining the Christian Sources for Social Change* (Woodstock Studies 2; New York: Paulist, 1977) 68–112, at 69.
2. Quotations in William D. Miller, *Dorothy Day: A Biography* (San Francisco: Harper & Row, 1982) 341, 343–44; emphasis mine.
3. Mark Searle, "Serving the Lord with Justice," in Searle, ed., *Liturgy and Social Justice* (Collegeville, Minn.: Liturgical, 1980) 13–35, at 21–28.
4. Ibid. 23–24.

Homily 46

1. In *Gonzaga Memories* by Gonzaga Alumni 1917–1990 (Baltimore: Port City Press, 1990) 45. Buchanan's "memories" are reproduced from his *Right from the Beginning* (Boston: Little, Brown, 1988).
2. Quoted in Robert Coles, *The Spiritual Life of Children* (Boston: Houghton Mifflin, 1990) xiv.
3. Quoted by Sean McDonagh in a short "Viewpoint" article in the (London) *Tablet* 248, no. 8021 (April 30, 1994) 514.
4. See John Paul II, "Peace with God the Creator, Peace with All of Creation," message for the World Day of Peace, Jan. 1, 1990; English text in *Origins* 19, Dec. 14, 1989.
5. In the Contemplation for Learning to Love Like God, the last meditation in the Spiritual Exercises.
6. The title of a sobering film, a true story of the effect of a caring nun on a murderer on death row, with a fair look at capital punishment.

Comprehensive Index for Homily Books by Walter J. Burghardt, S.J.

Compiled by
Brian Cavanaugh, T.O.R.

Reference Key: TNG (Tell the Next Generation, 1980)
LSJ (Sir, We Would Like to See Jesus, 1982)
PYW (Still Proclaiming Your Wonders, 1984)
GOC (Grace on Crutches, 1986)
ENH (Lovely in Eyes Not His, 1988)
TCL (To Christ I Look, 1989)
DBC (Dare to Be Christ, 1991)
CMC (When Christ Meets Christ, 1993)
SWB (Speak the Word with Boldness, 1994)
LFL (Love Is a Flame of the Lord, 1995)
JRD (Let Justice Roll Down Like Waters, 1998)

LITURGICAL SEASONS:

Advent Season: TNG, pp. 25, 30
Advent: 1st Sun. (A)   LSJ, p. 17; DBC, p. 5
         1st Sun. (B)   GOC, p. 19; CMC, p. 15
Vespers: 1st Sun. (B)   JRD, p. 5
         1st Sun. (C)   CMC, p. 20
         2nd Sun. (A)   PYW, p. 19; ENH, p. 5; SWB, p. 3
         2nd Sun. (B)   LSJ, p. 23; TCL, p. 21
         2nd Sun. (C)   PYW, p. 25; TCL, p. 27
         3rd Sun. (A)   LSJ, p. 29; ENH, p. 11
         3rd Sun. (B)   LFL, p. 5
         3rd Sun. (C)   LSJ, p. 33
         4th Sun. (A)   SWB, p. 8
Christmas   TNG, p. 34

FEASTS:

THEMES:

Priests' Jubilees	CMC, p. 148
Red Mass	TNG, p. 121; TCL, p. 167; CMC, p. 192
Reformation Sunday	PYW, p. 226
Religious Profession	TNG, p. 85
Religious Anniversary	LSJ, p. 203; CMC, pp. 135, 141; JRD, p. 211
Retreat House Anniv.	PYW, p. 211
Sadat, Mohamed el	LSJ, p. 196
Search for God	TNG, p. 19
Seminar on Justice	CMC, p. 203
Seniors Clubs	SWB, p. 208
Social Justice	TNG, p. 167
Stewardship	TNG, p. 186
Teaching Anniversary	TNG, p. 93
University Opening Mass	PYW, pp. 183, 189; ENH, p. 157; JRD, p. 225
War/Peace	TNG, p. 181
Wedding	TNG, p. 83; LSJ, pp. 186, 189; GOC, pp. 155, 160, 165, 170, 175; PYW, pp. 201, 206; ENH, pp. 163, 168, 173, 177, 182; TCL, pp. 174, 180, 186, 191, 196; DBC, pp. 101, 106, 112, 117, 123, 129, 135, 141, 146, 152, 157; CMC, pp. 81, 87, 93, 98, 103, 109, 115, 121, 127; SWB, pp. 131, 141, 146, 151, 157; LFL, pp. 109, 114, 120, 125; JRD, pp. 175, 180, 186, 191, 196
Wedding: 50th Anniv.	CMC, p. 153

SCRIPTURE READINGS:

Genesis 1:26–28, 31	PYW, p. 206; TCL, p. 186; DBC, p. 152; CMC, p. 98; SWB, pp. 131, 151; LFL, p. 120, 125; JRD, p. 180
Genesis 1:26–2:3	JRD, p. 141
Genesis 2:4–9, 15	TCL, p. 161
Genesis 2:18–24	PYW, p. 201; GOC, p. 160; ENH, pp. 173, 177; TCL, p. 196; DBC,